MORPHENOMENAL

MORPHENOMENAL

How the
Power Rangers
Conquered the World

Joshua Moore

APPLAUSE
THEATRE & CINEMA BOOKS

APPLAUSE
THEATRE & CINEMA BOOKS

Applause Books
Bloomsbury Publishing Inc, 1385 Broadway, New York, NY 10018, USA
Bloomsbury Publishing Plc, 50 Bedford Square, London, WC1B 3DP, UK
Bloomsbury Publishing Ireland, 29 Earlsfort Terrace, Dublin 2, D02 AY28, Ireland
www.backbeatbooks.com

British Library Cataloguing in Publication Information available

Library of Congress Cataloging-in-Publication Data Available

ISBN 978-1-4930-8161-5 (pbk.: alk. paper)
ISBN 978-1-4930-8162-2 (electronic)

For product safety related questions contact productsafety@bloomsbury.com.

∞™ The paper used in this publication meets the minimum requirements of American National Standard for Information Sciences—Permanence of Paper for Printed Library Materials, ANSI/NISO Z39.48-1992.

For Jason Aldrich
When your mom and I are unable, may the power protect you.

Contents

Contents

A Note on Sourcing

This book includes recollections and re-creations of moments throughout the history of *Power Rangers*, informed by original interviews conducted by the author with participants and archival interviews, press clippings, and so on of participants. A complete list of author interviews is available at the back of the book, along with endnotes that include citations as well as additional context and author commentary.

Introduction
Legacy of Power

There were at least a thousand people in Panel Room A at the Anaheim Convention Center. Most were wearing morphers on their wrists.

Most convention panels center around Q&As with cast members or "first look" product demonstrations. Power Morphicon 2018's "Shattered Grid: Live" was unique: a table reading of an adapted story from the popular *Mighty Morphin Power Rangers* comic-book series. More than a dozen creatives involved with the books and TV series performed, including original series actors Barbara Goodson, David Fielding, Walter Jones, Jason Narvy, Paul Schrier, Michael Sorich, and Tom Wyner.

Fielding reprised his role as Zordon, the original Power Rangers' mentor, for the first time in more than 25 years. About 38 minutes[1] passed before he spoke. His first line—delivered through a device to achieve the same postproduction enhancement heard in the show—got the crowd roaring. A minute later, he closed with his signature five-word phrase: "May the power protect you." Deafening applause for 30 seconds.

I grew up in a small eastern Kentucky town filled with Free Will Baptists. But that fleeting moment, in a room accompanied by hundreds of people and morphers, is the closest I've felt to God.

Power Rangers has been there for me since it began in 1993, but I don't remember that. I was two years old. As my mom tells it, she couldn't leave our trailer for groceries until the show finished. My earliest recollections of the show are VHS tapes; my favorite was "Happy Birthday, Zack," in which Jones's character, Zack Taylor, mistakenly believes his friends have forgotten his birthday. Within a few years, I'd follow—and record—the show's reruns and newer seasons as they aired. Most of my bootlegs survived until a friend's house burned down in 2010 (ironically, while we were watching an episode of the re-versioned *Mighty Morphin Power Rangers*).

Power Rangers was there for me when my dad was in prison. I couldn't wait to get back home from visiting him because a historic episode, "Forever Red," aired the same day. I was 11 and far more worried about that recording than I was seeing my dad. With the benefit of hindsight, I feel even less guilty about that than I did then.

After helping develop *Kamen Rider*, manga artist Shotaro Ishinomori created *Himitsu Sentai Gorenger*. That creation eventually spawned a worldwide phenomenon. Photo by Sankei Archive via Getty Images

Before entering middle school, I allowed my mom to sell all my *Power Rangers* toys in a yard sale. I was 15 when I decided that was a grave error and frequently started purchasing new *Power Rangers* toys while perusing eastern Kentucky Walmart stores with my pals. What I lacked in girlfriends I made up for in rare *Power Rangers RPM* action figures.

Despite my rigorous recording schedule, I don't think I'd seen every episode of *Mighty Morphin Power Rangers* until college. Between beers and books, I plowed through all three seasons thanks to Netflix. I was 21. I can safely confirm that I've seen them all, many times over, and find new things to love about them—and every season of the show—each time I reexperience them.

The first time I boarded a plane was in 2016, to attend that year's Power Morphicon. The next time I flew was in 2018, to attend the next Power Morphicon. I was 28 and skipping the first week of Kentucky's high school football season—important to note because I was the lead high school sports reporter for one of the state's top news organizations. I missed touchdowns but got to touch the Command Center. Worth it.

I wore a *Power Rangers* sweatshirt while doing bourbon shots with friends on the morning of my wedding. I wore *Power Rangers* socks *in* the wedding. Instrumental music from *Power Rangers* played during the reception. I was barely 31.

Power Rangers was there for me when my son was born. I held him as I cried through the end of *Cosmic Fury*, the show's thirtieth season and, as of 2024, its last. I was almost 33 and about 30 months into writing *Morphenomenal*.

Power Morphicon in 2007 was founded as the first "comic con" dedicated to *Power Rangers* and other media adapted from or inspired by Japanese programs that combined lovingly crafted practical effects—like rubber suits, scale-model sets, and mini explosives—and cleverly placed cameras to create otherworldly scenes. This type of filmmaking—"tokusatsu," or special filming—was popularized throughout the 1950s and 1960s thanks to the international success of *Gojira*, produced by the Japanese film company Toho and Americanized as *Godzilla*. Eiji Tsuburaya, the film's special effects director and widely credited as the "father of tokusatsu," after *Gojira* founded a production company that launched another global tokusatsu franchise, *Ultraman*.

That series prompted rival studio Toei to develop a tokusatsu superhero of its own. *Kamen Rider*, the bug-themed, motorcycle-riding brainchild of renowned manga artist Shotaro Ishinomori and studio executive

Tohru Hirayama, hit big in Japan. But it was another Ishinomori project in 1975, *Himitsu Sentai Gorenger*, that would lead to global renown. It featured a team of five heroes, distinguished by their uniquely colored uniforms. Eighteen years later, the newest installment of the overarching series, *Super Sentai*, would get adapted for the United States and change the course of superhero history.

Superheroes have for so long dominated pop culture that the phrase "superhero fatigue"[2] has been in circulation since at least 2011—one year before *The Avengers* grossed a record $1.5 billion. As of 2024, *Spider-Man: No Way Home* was the fourth superhero film to since pass it. Still, by the 2020s, the Marvel Cinematic Universe (MCU) showed signs of wear and tear. Following *Avengers: Endgame*, the 2019 conclusion to a story that started in 2008, a string of big-budget titles failed to win over critics and audiences.

Was the MCU finished? No. But it was something else: old. For many who watched—and, importantly, grew up with it—the good ol' days were done. No matter how exciting the MCU's future stories are, it'll be hard to generate the same level of affection from millions who followed along as a multi-billion-dollar franchise sprung from comic-book pages. Hooking newcomers is even harder in an attention economy dominated by handheld screens, 15-second videos, and 13-year-olds who, like their parents, want their *own* corporate creations to love. Marvel's plight isn't new. It's the same one faced by any intellectual property (IP) fortunate enough to soar to great heights. It's the same one with which *Power Rangers* has struggled for most of its existence.

Power Rangers exploded in the mid-1990s. Its ratings immediately went through the roof and set the pace for half a decade. Parents ventured into Toys "R" Us stores, desperate to buy anything they could find with a *Mighty Morphin Power Rangers* logo on it. Parent-advocates blasted the show's "violent" content and the ease with which it programmed consumer behavior—but who was going to let $17.95[3] stand between them and becoming an official member of the Power Rangers Fan Club? If you opened a newspaper or turned on a TV and didn't see a Power Ranger, you were probably blind.

Beyond a two-year craze, *Power Rangers* stayed a staple among kids while stepping out of the spotlight. New seasons delivered good ratings into the 2010s and strong streaming numbers into the 2020s. It consistently churned out the top-selling action figure line for more than a decade. You're still bound to see *Power Rangers* costumes every Halloween, these days worn by kids whose parents wore their own in 1993—and still might be.

Power Rangers also remained a touchstone for adults who never turned it off. Many were kids, but others were in college or well into their careers when Zordon recruited "five teenagers with attitude" to save the world. Some fell in love with it while watching with their own kids, as was the case in 2011 for Mara, cohost of *Toku Ladies*, a *Power Rangers* podcast run by female fans. Two of the hosts, Margot and Danielle, are married and met thanks to *Power Rangers*. "The phrase, 'I have a Megazord on my desk,' has resulted in two marriages," said fellow host PockySquirrel, who met her husband in like fashion.

Millions of people follow official accounts, fan pages, and actors on social media. Thousands pour out every year to meet their heroes at shows like Power Morphicon. But one of the best examples of *Power Rangers'* staying power is, by internet standards, arcane. RangerBoard, a message board dedicated to the show, traces its roots to 1998. The site, which as of 2024 boasts more than 50,000 users, was essential to connecting the fans who in 2005 started laying the groundwork for Power Morphicon.

"It was a mom-and-pop convention at that point," said Christopher Hayden, one of Power Morphicon's cofounders. "It was a lot of faking it 'til you make it, 'cause none of us had ever put on a convention before, none of us had ever worked on a convention staff. We were all early twentysomethings. I was in film school at the time, and it was very much in the spirit of film school. You kind of learn as you go, and apply those things as you go, and hope for the best at the end of the day."

The story of *Power Rangers*—the show, toys, music, books, trading cards, movies, stationery, fishing bobbers, and so on—begins in Egypt and leads, most recently, to New Zealand, with stops all over the world in between. It's one of entrepreneurial spirit. Of a fledgling TV network seeking something the world (well, most of it) had never seen. Of women in power making decisions and receiving undersized credit for it. Of teamwork, on and off the screen. Of chaos and uncertainty. Of meteoric success. Of exploitation. Of marketing. Of backstabbing. Of futility. Of hope. Of resilience.

Mostly, though, it's one of colors. Black, blue, green, pink, red, white, and yellow: these are the seven colors featured in the trailblazing *Mighty Morphin Power Rangers* and the seven most used across the series. Ask anyone 40 or under which one is their favorite, and you'll probably get a hearty response.

These days, *Power Rangers* is more often cited as reference material than an object worthy of its own merit. Marvel Studios' *Eternals* drew unfavorable comparisons: *Rolling Stone*'s K. Austin Collins wondered why the titular heroes were "saddled with[4] refurbished Power Rangers costumes for eternity." When an episode of *The Book of Boba Fett* premiered in January 2021, the use of brightly colored scooters prompted *Power Rangers* to trend nationally on Twitter. If a collection of multicolored things is assembled, a mention of *Power Rangers* usually isn't far behind.

Most things in *Power Rangers* are coated with an over-the-top glaze—but especially its villains. Viewers suggested that Rita Repulsa sent Doja Cat to Earth when she showed up at the 2021 MTV Video Music Awards wearing a large, pastel, worm-like suit. Actress Jennifer Coolidge was the subject of an entire tokusatsu-themed photo shoot in 2023, wherein she channeled the exasperated spirit of Rita, the show's founding evildoer. Rita is casually evoked to bond the leads in the 2023 horror film *Unseen*. As embedded in people's minds as the Power Rangers are, so are the bad guys.

In his final hours as a bachelor, the author drank bourbon with friends while wearing a *Power Rangers* sweatshirt. Author's Collection

Power Rangers is as much an adjective as it is a television show. Whether deployed to praise or mock, its continued use as such requires a level of deference earned by few entities. Batman cornered the market on dark and brooding, but the Power Rangers have colorful and campy covered. In an increasingly fragmented media landscape, that kind of cachet is invaluable.

Mighty Morphin Power Rangers' progenitor, Haim Saban, felt like it would be a hit if a network would just give it a chance. Saban had vision, but even he couldn't have seen what unfolded in the months, years, and decades after the show premiered on August 28, 1993. That Saturday propelled him toward incredible wealth, turned the fledging Fox Kids Network into a television staple, and morphed a cheap Japanese program into one of the most iconic franchises in entertainment history.

Power Rangers spawned more than 900 episodes, thousands of action figures, and an unforgettable traffic jam. It led to three feature-length films, a best-selling comic book series, a live tour, McDonald's Happy Meal promotions, and thousands of counterfeit products. In its original form, it lasted for 30 years while changing hands among three unique owners airing across five networks and half a dozen streamers. It drew a thousand people to a room to listen to an hour-long reading.

To borrow a phrase coined by Kimberly Hart, the first Pink Ranger, it was morphenomenal. This is how *Power Rangers* conquered Earth.

CHAPTER 1

The Rockstar

If not for the kindness of an Egyptian police officer in 1957, *Power Rangers* might not exist.

In the 1950s, Egypt made a concerted effort to expel Jews from its country. "My father worked in a toy store,"[1] Haim Saban told *Variety* in 2017. "He used to give toys to the head of police when he would shop for his kids. One day the police head came in and told my father, 'You're on the list. Within two weeks, we're going to come and arrest you.' So within two weeks we got the heck out of there."

The Sabans—Haim, his parents, his brother, and a blind grandmother—fled first to Greece. Later, the Jewish Agency for Israel set them up in a one-room apartment in Tel Aviv. Decades later, Saban would rub elbows with presidents and prime ministers; when he was 12, he shared a communal bathroom with the prostitute and pimp who lived next door. He did some schoolwork between self-taught guitar sessions, usually in the apartment halls.

Throughout his impoverished youth, Saban honed a keen business sense. As a boy, he sold cactus fruit on the street and cleaned barn manure; eventually, he earned so much work that he paid other kids to hold the shovels. He wasn't the best student or musician, but his gut and wits were stout—and noted. When conscripted into the Israeli Defense Forces, he landed a noncombat role—organizing entertainment for troops.

While in the army, Saban visited a resort whose house band hadn't helped with its attendance problem. Ever the opportunist, Saban found the owner and convinced him that his band could play better; he promised big crowds befitting his swanky digs. Saban, the alleged bassist in this ensemble, didn't own an instrument. And while he had a good ear for music, his ability to play was just slightly more legitimate than the band he promised. So he contacted a music-store owner who gave him a lead.

During the group's first performance for the club owner, Saban faked an arm injury but "found" a replacement bassist. The show could go on.

The Lions of Judah, as they would be known, got the gig and several more despite hiring Saban as a "bassist" who faked his way through most shows. They toured around London, recorded a couple of singles that charted in the United Kingdom, and relieved Saban of his onstage duties to focus on managing them and others. By the early 1970s, Saban was managing legs in Israel for acts like Ray Charles and Blood, Sweat & Tears. Concert promotion became a lucrative grift[2] for Saban, who promised 10 percent advances up front to artists but seldom had that in hand; he'd turn around and offer ticket brokers exclusive rights in exchange for the advance he promised an act. It was an effective albeit shaky way of conducting business. Then the Yom Kippur War started.

The same night the two-week war began, Saban had scheduled an expensive and eclectic act to perform in Tel Aviv. He paid $350,000 to bring 45 Japanese harpists to Israel for a tour that died in a hotel lobby; they played a free show in the Tel Aviv Sheraton hotel before returning home. Overnight, Saban was $600,000 in debt. Following the war, his generous creditors allowed him to leave the country to recoup what he owed. He brought a nine-year-old Israeli boy, Noam Kaniel, with him; he had star potential, Saban thought, so he taught him French. They were off to Paris.

Television music boomed in the 1960s and 1970s. Twenty-nine TV theme songs charted on the Billboard Hot 100 over the course of the two decades, including two of the four to ever reach the top: "S.W.A.T.," an instrumental recorded by disco band Rhythm Heritage for the ABC drama *S.W.A.T*, and "Welcome Back," written and performed by John Sebastian for the same network's sitcom *Welcome Back, Kotter*.[3] TV on the radio wasn't a U.S.-only phenomenon: international audiences were even more eager to spin songs from their favorite shows.

On the back of his protégé, Saban settled his debt within a year. Kaniel sang, and Saban produced, and by the end of the 1970s, they sold more than 8 million records. Their catalog's biggest hit? A 12-song album that featured the theme song for *Goldorak*, the first Japanese anime series broadcast in France. Its success sprung from another Saban plot: he charged nothing to produce European themes for existing shows in exchange for exclusive record rights. Saban Records forged a relationship with Paris animation company D.I.C. Audiovisual and through it produced a number of top sellers. Saban, Kaniel, and a new partner, Israeli musician Shuki Levy, found so much success that their move to Hollywood in 1983 felt less like a calculated risk and more like an inevitability.

Kaniel, in exchange for a steady salary, signed away his rights to substantial royalties. This would become standard operating procedure for Saban employees, leaving most of the pie to the publisher (Saban) and writers (in most cases, Levy and Saban). If there's a cartoon theme from the 1980s that's impossible to get out of your head, they're probably the team who put it there. *He-Man and the Masters of the Universe*? Them. *Heathcliff*? Mm-hmm. *Inspector Gadget*? Yup, Gadget, yup.

Saban and Levy were on their way to becoming multimillionaires when they sought a new challenge: making TV. *Kidd Video*, cocreated by Saban Productions and D.I.C., premiered in 1984. It follows a live-action teenage band that gets transported into an animated world; for 26 episodes, they fought evil with the power of popular songs and music videos. *Kidd Video*, a consistent rater among the top 10 kids shows, was a successful first try for Saban Productions. The show reflected Saban: cheesy, colorful, musical, resourceful, and, importantly, profitable. Each episode cost $200,000 to make but netted $120,000.

Haim Saban (right) is worth billions and wields significant influence in geopolitical affairs. In 1993, he was trying to get *Mighty Morphin Power Rangers* on TV with the help of his wife Cheryl, who wrote 18 episodes. Photo by Frank Micelotta/ImageDirect/ Getty Images

Saban Productions—renamed Saban Entertainment in 1988—partnered with D.I.C. on a few short-lived cartoons, most based on existing IP, through the 1980s. Saban also tapped preexisting relationships with Japanese companies to dub and distribute shows in America. None of those imports became hits, but they were cheap to license, helping Saban build a catalog. Any content was better than no content. "I realized that to be considered a significant player you need a significant library,"[4] he told *Forbes* in 1991.

Saban Entertainment in the late 1980s also secured foreign distribution rights to D.I.C. shows when D.I.C. ownership changed and needed cash; Saban quickly flipped those rights. The relationship between Saban and the new D.I.C., led by former Hanna-Barbera creative Andy Heyward, was severed when the latter filed a lawsuit in 1990; the parties settled in 1991, but Saban and Heyward didn't speak for a decade. "He's loyal and generous to his friends, but in business he is deadly,"[5] Heyward said. "If you took all Haim's money away and took him to a Casbah, gave him some rugs and said, 'Stay here'—a year later he'd have a billion dollars."

The dissolution was inconsequential to Saban. Soon, his company would be at the forefront of a project, one that would boost his clout. That show kicked off with an all-time banger of a theme song and starred a team of superheroes.

It wasn't *Mighty Morphin Power Rangers*.

On the heels of her first breakout hit, Margaret Loesch craved something special. *X-Men* delivered in a big way for the nascent Fox Children's Network (FCN), and other Marvel adaptations already were in the works. She was certain they too would capture the hearts of children. But *Spider-Man* wouldn't swing into her schedule for a couple years at least, and Loesch wanted something special *now*. It was the fall of 1992.

X-Men, a coproduction between Marvel and Saban Entertainment, excelled just like Loesch knew it would when she was president and CEO of Marvel Productions. There, she helped bring to life several kids shows that spawned dynastic franchises, *Transformers* and *My Little Pony* chief among them. Despite a clear knack for creating strong kids TV, Loesch in her six years at Marvel couldn't sell a single show based on its well-known comic properties. The best she managed was a half-hour pilot special, *Pryde of the X-Men*, developed using funds earmarked for a floundering *RoboCop*[6] animated series. It didn't impress enough to prompt a series order.

Loesch, who became the first president of FCN in 1990, believed in the mutants. Now on the other side of the pitch table, she could make good on a promise made to her longtime friend and colleague, *Spider-Man* creator and future cameo maestro Stan Lee. They wanted to bring quality comic-book storytelling to TV screens.

X-Men premiered in 1992 and took FCN from No. 4 to No. 1 among children's programming blocks aired by the four major broadcast networks (ABC, CBS, and NBC in addition to Fox). Teenagers and adults watched. Girls were paying attention too. "[The networks] felt that girls would not watch action-adventure at all, and they felt that Marvel properties were too verbose, too dark, too philosophical, too talky. They didn't think the characters resonated with kids," Loesch said. "I specifically was told by one network executive, and I've never forgotten this, 'The only people who liked Marvel comics were 18-year-old nerdy boys.' When the executive told me that, I was aghast."

Loesch was never a boy of any age, but she loved comics as much as any other child growing up in Pass Christian, Mississippi, during the 1950s. *The Amazing Spider-Man*, *Wonder Woman*, and *Superman* were among her favorite reads, and it was stories like those that convinced Loesch to abandon her pursuit of a master's degree and tag along with some friends when they moved to California. She bought a one-way plane ticket and brought $40, all spent by the time ABC hired her as a typist a month later. Within three years, she headed ABC's creative services. Then she took a stint guiding kids programming at NBC before parlaying that into a vice presidentship at Hanna-Barbera Productions. There, she helped shepherd the longest-running Saturday morning cartoon in the history of broadcast television: *The Smurfs*. Loesch's eye for hits was finely tuned when Marvel Productions called in 1984.

However, the "meh" launch of FCN strained whatever grace period Loesch earned through past performance. A 65-episode original animated series, *Fox's Peter Pan & the Pirates*, anchored FCN (which later rebranded to Fox Kids Network). The show went overtly out of its way to avoid stirring Disney's lawyers; after the theme song's title card, the first frame isn't of Peter Pan, Tinker Bell, or Captain Hook but a still image with words effectively serving as a disclaimer: "A new and independent series inspired by J. M. Barrie's original novel 'Peter and Wendy.'" It may as well read, "Dear Mickey, please don't sue!"

Fox's Peter Pan & the Pirates didn't lack talent. It featured voice work from Jason Marsden, Debi Derryberry, Cree Summer, and Tim Curry as—who else?—Captain Hook. Executive producer Buzz Potamkin later earned five Emmy Award nominations. The animation holds up well too: Japanese studio Tokyo Movie Shinsha,[7] which Fox Kids would later use for *Animaniacs*, *Batman: The Animated Series*, and *Spider-Man*, created it. But *Fox's Peter Pan & the Pirates* struggled to hook viewers, perhaps because the 1953 classic had taken the wind out of its sails: Disney's *Peter*

Pan returned to theaters the year before and made its debut on home video 11 days after the Fox version premiered. Death, taxes, and Disney.

It didn't matter, but Loesch thought it was doomed due to all the creative headwinds it faced. She came aboard in March 1990, six months out from FCN's launch, and begged Fox network executive Jamie Kellner to delay the programming block. He was unmoved. "The long and short of it is, the show was a failure," said Loesch, saddled with a literal anchor whose deployment she lobbied to delay. Immediately, she was on thin ice with Fox affiliates across the country. If not for the mild success of *Bobby's World*, an acquisition created by comedian Howie Mandel and produced by Film Roman, calls for her head might've come quickly.

Two years later, *X-Men* rescued Loesch and FCN. From the jump, it's the antithesis of *Fox's Peter Pan & the Pirates*: the guitar-stuffed theme—credited to Levy—plays over a minute of animation that excitedly introduces the main players and promises lots of action. It was based on characters you might know, but if you didn't, you'd want to. The only thing airing elsewhere that even sort of resembled it was *Teenage Mutant Ninja Turtles*, by then in its sixth season. *X-Men* delivered to the tune of audience shares in the upper 30s and low 40s.

With her first smash hit in the bank, Loesch for the first time had leverage. She wanted to take a big swing, and a man who helped get *X-Men* off the ground had a viable pitch, though not one he was necessarily eager to throw. Saban had watched it die on the way to the mound too many times already.

As Saban and Levy carved their path throughout the 1970s and 1980s, Stan Lee, for the first time in his career, enjoyed celebrity status, though not in his home country. An adaptation of his most popular comic book, *The Amazing Spider-Man*, was a big hit in Japan.

The series, produced by Toei, was a tokusatsu take on the famous web crawler. And it took liberties. Simply titled *Spider-Man*, it featured motorcyclist Takuya Yamashiro, not Peter Parker, as the titular hero. A dying warrior from Planet Spider gives him his powers, not a radioactive spider. And this Spider-Man fought oversized monsters using a spaceship that transforms into a giant robot, Leopardon. The 41-episode series could not have deviated further from the source, but it resonated so much that merchandise is still produced. Its contemporary success and lasting impact starkly contrasted with 1977's *The Amazing Spider-Man*, a live-action peer that lasted only 13 episodes on CBS.[8]

Israeli musician Shuki Levy (left) partnered with Haim Saban to create TV theme music not long after he was part of a successful pop duo with Aviva Paz. Photo by Gilbert TOURTE/Gamma-Rapho via Getty Images

The Marvel–Toei pairing extended to the creation of the third, fourth, and fifth seasons of *Super Sentai*. Spurred by Leopardon's popularity, *Battle Fever J*[9] became the first season in *Super Sentai* history to include a giant robot. Although Marvel was hands-off in their production, the company also retained copyright on the next two seasons, *Denshi Sentai Denziman* and *Taiyo Sentai Sun Vulcan*. Both embrace the dominant *Super Sentai* aesthetic—brightly colored fabrics and helmets with unifying elements rather than the disparate, exaggerated, and abstract elements seen in non-*Gorenger* precursors. *Sun Vulcan* especially piqued the interest of Marvel's Gene Pelc, the company's head of overseas licensing. Pelc sold Lee on the notion of an American adaptation, musings about which he described in an editorial for *Comics Interview* in 1983.

"[Stan] said that in all his experience of writing for people, if they could see this show in America on Saturday morning, it would wipe out anything because it's full of action and very entertaining," Pelc wrote.[10] "He can sell it as is with a new voice track, or take the prints and cut out the parts where Japanese actors appear, which is about one-third of the film, re-shoot that with American actors, and cut back to the show with the special effects and opticals [*sic*] and visuals, thus creating a series that looks American."

Lee took a tape of *Sun Vulcan* to Loesch's office and proclaimed, "Maggie, I think I found a hit for us!" She couldn't believe what she had just watched. The action and humor came through despite a vast language barrier. It didn't resemble anything airing on American kids television at the time—or almost anytime, really. *Ultraman* shows were dubbed and aired sparingly in syndication but couldn't get consistent traction in the United States; that and the *Godzilla* films were the only exposure most Americans had to tokusatsu. Loesch wanted to change that. Marvel Productions put up $25,000 to cut a presentation tape with American dubbing and presented it to the three existing broadcast networks—ABC, CBS, and NBC—as well as HBO. They were in disbelief. How could the same woman who'd delivered *Muppet Babies*—the winner of four straight Emmy Awards for "Outstanding Animated Program"—show up at their doorsteps peddling, in a word, "crap"? Their vision firmly nixed by suits with none, Loesch and Lee relinquished the U.S. licensing rights to *Super Sentai*.

Eight years later, Saban sat across a table from Loesch, pitching show after show for her 1993 programming slate. They were all fine. She could have taken a number of them, placed them into the fall schedule, and maintained the network's position as a plucky disruptor in the kids broadcasting space. Most were animated, and several hailed from Japan, but America's warm embrace of anime was still a few years away. They were funny, which certainly wasn't a negative but wasn't explicitly what Loesch was after. She wanted something different. Something with humor, sure, but also with action that she could put on the weekday morning schedule to counterprogram against more comedic and classic syndication fare. Loesch needed something special, and nothing Saban brought with him was special. There was a tape in his car, though, that might be. He rushed out to retrieve it.

"He said, 'Don't get mad at me but take a look, you might like this,'" Loesch said. "'It might be what you're looking for.'" It wasn't just the show she wanted; it was almost exactly the same show she'd pitched with Lee more than a decade earlier.

Saban's first pilot for the show that would become *Mighty Morphin Power Rangers* didn't utter any of those four words. He called it *Bio-Man*, named from the *Super Sentai* series *Choudenshi Bioman*, from which it was to be adapted. He'd acquired the rights to the 1984 series through happenstance; he became infatuated with it while channel surfing in his hotel room while on business in Japan. That pilot failed to impress the same networks that Loesch had failed to impress a couple years prior and has never publicly emerged in its entirety. Clips of it were repurposed for a refreshed sizzle reel, *Galaxy Rangers*.

Galaxy Rangers, created in 1992 and set to Judas Priest's "Electric Eye," includes footage of *Bio-Man* actors who could have been the original Power Rangers. Among them were future TV and movie stars Mark Dacascos (2010's *Hawaii Five-0, John Wick: Chapter 3—Parabellum*) and Miguel A. Núñez Jr. (*Return of the Living Dead, Juwanna Mann*). They played Victor Lee, "an expert in martial arts," and Zack Taylor, "a detective with an unusual style," respectively. Four first names of the original five Power Rangers were determined by 1986, when filming for the *Bio-Man* pilot completed: Zack, Kimberly, Billy, and Trini. Except for Trini, they all kept their last names from the original pilot too. (This disputes the long-held belief that Billy, whose last name was Cranston, was surnamed after Bryan Cranston, who voiced monsters on the show decades before becoming one in *Breaking Bad*.)

Another fun "fact": It is believed that an unidentified actor to whom Núñez Jr. speaks in the pilot is Chris Farley; no one has ever gone on the record to confirm it's him, but it sure looks and sounds like the late *Saturday Night Live* star. Spliced around the near-decade-old footage was fresh material from the current Japanese series, *Kyōryū Sentai Zyuranger*. That show revolves around a team of warriors who'd spent the last 170 million years in suspended animation after sealing away their archnemesis, Witch Bandora, who killed all the dinosaurs after her son was executed for breaking some Tyrannosaurus eggs.

Of course, none of the Jurassic-period backstory needed to travel to the United States. All Saban needed people to see was the action, the sitcom-like footage, the colorful spandex suits with diamond patterns and helmets with dinosaur imagery, and the creatures against whom the "Americans" in the suits would fight to save the planet. At the forefront was Witch Bandora, a heavily made-up sorceress in a brown dress with a magical staff that towered over her own frame. Among her minions were a gold, winged gorilla holding a sword; a pair of blue guys distinguished by their portly and scrawny figures; and an elderly leprechaun with a passion for pottery.

Before she ran the Fox Kids Network, Margaret Loesch (right) was an executive for Marvel Entertainment producing shows like *Muppet Babies,* created by her friend Jim Henson (left). That show won three consecutive Daytime Emmy Awards for Outstanding Animated Program from 1986 to 1988. Courtesy Margaret Loesch

Since the 1980s, Saban thought he had a hit. But one can get laughed at only so many times before they finally start leaving the tape in their car.

"I don't want to say Haim had given up," Loesch said. "But I think he was shocked when I looked at the material and said, 'I know this material, I'll buy it.' That's what I said right there. 'I'll buy it.' I thought, 'This is it.' He was shocked, but of course happy, because he'd been talking to the Japanese for a number of years, and he liked the property." Saban finally had a network executive on board, and Loesch finally had a show she believed could solidify Fox Kids as the No. 1 destination for two- to 11-year-olds—as long as Kellner was on board.

This adaptation, ideally, would make kids laugh, excite them, and even teach a lesson or two between brightly colored images. It could be made cheaply: more than half the footage for each episode was already shot, and the nonunion production would be filled with eager upstarts. The entire operation could be buoyed by merchandise sales, thought Saban, especially from the toy aisle. He reckoned that Bandai, the Japanese toy manufacturer that cofinanced *Super Sentai*, could port over many of its same products. It was foolproof, but if it flopped? The up-front investment would be so low that Fox Kids' coffers would be fine.

Loesch's boss didn't see it that way. Kellner battled her on *X-Men* because he felt the comic's stories were too "dark" to adapt for an animated children's series. Now he had trouble visualizing how a "cheesy" show that had delighted Japanese kids since 1975 could work in America. "I showed him a clip, and he says, 'Oh no, oh no,'" Loesch said. He relented, as he eventually did with *X-Men*, in part because of that show's success but also because of the intensity with which Loesch went to bat for this . . . *crap*.

Super Sentai transported Loesch to a time when she and her friends spent Saturdays watching triple features at their local theater. They'd scream and laugh at the likes of *The Werewolf* and *Abbott and Costello Meet Frankenstein*. They knew what they were watching was cheap—she distinctly remembers pointing out costume stitches in *The Creature from the Black Lagoon* to her brother—but that didn't take away from the experience. Often, it enhanced it.

"When I saw *Power Rangers*, it reminded me of those movies that I saw as a kid in the theater," Loesch said. "I remembered what I felt like. I remembered how much I got a kick out of them. I didn't care if the production values were lousy. I didn't care if they looked cheap, because they were entertaining and they were fun. And you could cheer and you could clap. You could yell in the theater. I remembered all that. That's what gave me confidence."

Even if she hadn't tried to bring it over herself, adapting *Super Sentai* made sense to Loesch because it had proved itself for almost two decades in Japan. Dismissals of the show called to mind her time working on *The Smurfs*, another Emmy winner. The tiny, blue characters debuted in a 1958 French-language comic strip by Pierre "Peyo" Culliford but didn't gain global attention until the Hanna-Barbera series arrived 23 years later. They had made U.S. merchandising inroads prior to their small-screen success, though. One day, a development associate brought Loesch and Joe Barbera key chains they picked up from a local car wash.

"Joe picks up one of the key chains and he looks at it and says, 'All these little blue bastards look alike,'" Loesch said with a laugh. "And I picked up the key chains and said, 'Oh, they're so cute.' And so he points to me and says, 'It's your show.'"

When she spoke with Freddy Monnickendam, Peyo's licensing representative, Margaret wondered why a property she found so adorable wasn't already on TV. Monnickendam's words stuck with her.

"'Because Margaret, in America you don't buy things that look too foreign,'" she said. "And he was right. They'd already pitched it to all three networks when Fred brought it to us, and all the networks had turned it down because it was quote 'too foreign.'" A decade later—and enough Emmy trophies in hand that she could have melted them into armor— Loesch again heard "too foreign" lobbed in her direction. Regardless of xenophobia, the *Super Sentai* adaptation would have at least a few things going for it from a marketability standpoint—stuff that would help it play better with local advertisers and affiliates afraid to bite.

It was determined from the get-go that the cast would be ethnically and gender diverse; that the latter demanded a swap from the source footage—*Zyuranger* had just one female hero, the Pink Ranger—was a "problem" only if one cared that the Yellow Ranger didn't have a skirt (and sometimes had a noticeable bulge in the pelvic region). The American footage would center around high school kids, potentially helping it leech an audience of fans from the soon-to-be-finished NBC sitcom *Saved by the Bell*. The giant robots piloted by *Zyuranger*'s heroes were modeled after dinosaurs and other prehistoric creatures—a tyrannosaurus, triceratops, mastodon, pterodactyl, and saber-tooth tiger—that never go out of style with the elementary-age set. It also didn't hurt that Steven Spielberg's *Jurassic Park* was set to debut in the summer of 1993, preceding the adaptation's target launch date.

What their pet project had in its favor, more than anything, was that it didn't look like anything else on television. Sure, the American shots might take a few cues from *Saved by the Bell*, but the overall aesthetic, plotting, and language would be less sitcom and more live-action cartoon. This show would have more in common with *Teenage Mutant Ninja Turtles* and *X-Men* than anything that had ever been filmed with living, moving human beings.

Now it just needed to find some living, moving human beings.

CHAPTER 2

Day of the Dumpster

Jamie Kellner didn't believe in *Power Rangers*. He believed in Margaret Loesch enough, though, to okay the use of $100,000 to film a new pilot. If that tested well, he'd begrudgingly approve the 40-episode order she and Haim Saban sought.

One problem: that wasn't nearly enough money. Saban was willing to match anything Fox put up, so they had $200,000—just enough to shoot a decent amount of original footage to supplement the source footage from *Zyuranger*. They began assembling a development team that could whip the concept into shape; Saban's worn-out tape didn't jibe with 1990s sensibilities.

Tony Oliver wrote the script for "Day of the Dumpster." Oliver, also a trailblazing voice actor in the anime space, had worked for Saban Entertainment since 1988. Among other things, he helped produce an adaptation of Rudyard Kipling's *The Jungle Book* and was story editor on an English-language import of *Noozles*, a Japanese cartoon about a pair of koalas named Blinky and Pinky; it lasted only 26 episodes, but Nickelodeon aired it for five years.

When Saban first showed him the *Super Sentai* footage and explained his vision, Oliver feigned excitement. Truthfully? "I thought he was out of his mind," Oliver said. "But I went to work on it because I worked for the man."[1]

Beyond not-so-veiled xenophobia, why did Saban's earlier pilot fail to connect with network suits? Incoming director Strathford Hamilton, turned on to the project while directing Helen Slater and Billy Zane in the thriller *Betrayal of the Dove*, pinpointed a key ingredient that had been missing: kids couldn't easily relate to the heroes.

Tony Oliver, pictured here with part of the Mega Tigerzord costume in the mid-1990s, wrote and produced more than 200 episodes of *Power Rangers* from its onset. He's since had a prolific voice-acting career. Courtesy The Morphin Museum/© Saban Entertainment

Hamilton knew a thing or two about making media work across borders. Before moving to Los Angeles, he was a music executive for U.K. label Decca Records, which worked closely with The Moody Blues, and was instrumental in creating the first music videos released by Queen and The Clash. He came over to the United States with Queen and decided to stick around to pursue a career in film, studying under screenwriting aficionado Robert McKee, then a professor at Southern Cal.

Dino Rangers, the new working title, was unlike anything Hamilton had worked on. But at its core were themes he and other creatives believed were universally important, especially to children: teamwork, friendship, and helping others. The most transformative changes from Saban's first crack were the protagonists' ages and circumstances. They'd be high schoolers and friends, not young adults disconnected from one another until they teamed up as superheroes. The former was far more aspirational for the target audience, and Hamilton believes it's the single element that made the show pop. The Power Rangers, he believes, would have been far less impressionable to kids if they were desk jockeys, aerobics instructors, or police detectives—or even college students.

"The kids could see themselves, like they were looking into a mirror," Hamilton said. "That's what made it sink into their subconscious. They loved these characters because it was them. This is who they could be. It was within their grasp to be these people. They weren't grown-ups. They weren't kissing and hugging and doing all that stupid stuff, and they also weren't killing and shooting a bunch of people. They were just jumping around and having fun."

Hamilton, Oliver, producer Ellen Levy-Sarnoff, and casting director Katy Wallin found the would-be teenagers. Among their priorities, legitimate acting skills were no higher than third behind impressive physical abilities and natural charms. Their ideal targets were described as follows in an open casting call sheet from 1992:[2]

Victor: Sexy teen heart-throb. A Luke Perry, Brian Bloom, Jason Priestly or Marky Mark type preferred. Must have excellent Martial Arts/Kickboxing skills.

Zack: Streetwise, cocky, fast-talking, black teen. Cool dance moves required.

Billy: Quintessential Nerd. A young Rick Moranis type.

Kimberly: Blonde, beautiful teen gymnast with an attitude. We're looking for the next "Buffy."

Trini: Attractive, athletic female teen. An eternal pessimist.

The first round of auditions took place from 9 a.m. to 5 p.m. on September 11 and September 12, 1992.

Audri Dubois, a 25-year-old from Arizona, had never given much thought to acting before a boyfriend encouraged her to send headshots to an agent. She attended an open casting call for *Dino Rangers* mere weeks after signing a Screen Actors Guild (SAG) contract.

"Trini was supposed to be afraid of her own shadow, be very insecure and know zero karate,"[3] said Dubois, who embodied Trini nicely because she was, in fact, terrified throughout the audition process. She sensed skepticism from the producers, who confirmed her suspicion as she left the room, asking why she exaggerated about being a third-degree black belt on her résumé. But she hadn't. Dubois couldn't act, but she knew a thing or two about martial arts; she'd just kept it hidden because Trini was supposed to be a peacemaker. "I did this performance that was off the charts, just tried to scare the hell[4] out of them." She kicked across a banquet table and stopped inches from a producer's head; it left enough of an impression to get her through several rounds of callbacks over the course of a month and finally the gig.

David Yost brought legitimate acting chops to the table. A transplant from Iowa who moved to Los Angeles after graduating from Graceland University in 1991, Yost grew up in the theater. He wanted to work in the entertainment industry since an onstage epiphany at seven years old while portraying Dopey in *Snow White and the Seven Dwarves*.

David Yost was the oldest member of the original *Mighty Morphin Power Rangers* cast, clocking in at 24 years old by the time the show premiered in August 1993. Courtesy PR Media Info/© Saban Entertainment

"I got left on stage singing, "Hi ho, hi ho, it's off to work we go,' by myself, and I did it in such a way that everybody was laughing,"[5] Yost said. "And in that moment . . . this peace came over me and [an inner voice] said, 'This is what I'm gonna do.'"

Yost went through eight rounds of callbacks, the first three for "Victor." By the third audition, he determined he wasn't enough of a "leader type" or a skilled enough athlete to fully realize what producers wanted from the character. He asked to give Billy a go, and it fit him like a glove.

"It's not uncommon in the casting process for somebody to come in for one role and then end up getting cast in another,"[6] Wallin said. "David ended up coming in for the Red Ranger and was perfectly suited for the Blue Ranger. He was the Blue Ranger."

Amy Jo Johnson, cast as Kimberly the Pink Ranger, spent her youth on balance beams and uneven bars. She got kicked out of a private school in her teens but showed a knack for performing both on the mat and stage. But it wasn't until she attended the American Musical and Dramatic Academy in New York City that Johnson figured out she suffered from a career-threatening condition: stage fright.[7] AMDA didn't want her to return for a second year—in part because of that but also because she skipped too many classes—so for about six months, she studied method acting at the Lee Strasberg Theatre & Film Institute until her then boyfriend decided to move to Los Angeles. Johnson followed.

Wallin and Johnson met at an acting class, and the former encouraged Johnson to audition for *Dino Rangers* about a week after she'd returned to Los Angeles following a brief move back home; she and her boyfriend had broken up, and she was ready to call it quits. But her drama coach, Walter Raney, convinced her to return. "He believed in me when I didn't," Johnson said. "He pumped me up until I could fly."[8] During her first audition for Kimberly, Johnson performed a back handspring—a move where a gymnast takes off from their feet, jumps backward onto their hands, and lands back on their feet. Her athleticism set her apart from the get-go, but she also had an "it" factor that made her irresistible.

Walter Emanuel Jones grew up in the west side of Detroit, where he'd become the vice president of his high school's acting club before attending the United States International University School of the Performing and Visual Arts on a partial scholarship.[9] He earned a degree in musical theater and threw himself into the profession, breaking in as a dancer and actor for Princess Cruises, a job he enjoyed so much that he, at the time, considered becoming a cruise director.

Jones was in Florida for an appearance on *Star Search* when his agent called him about *Dino Rangers*. He initially declined but opted in after further urging when he returned to Los Angeles. Jones's audition for Zack was no different from the others—he went through numerous callbacks—but it did feature one quirk: Hip Hop Kido. During his first audition, Jones, at the producers' request, invented a one-of-a-kind fighting style—a blend of martial arts, hip-hop dancing, and gymnastics.

"I started it like I started a kata,"[10] Jones said. "Did some kicks and punches, threw in a break-dancing move, it's a swipe where my legs kick in the air. Made that into a kick, though, 'Yea that looks very kick-like.' Did some stuff on the floor, maybe a sweep, did a spinning back kick. Then [I] came up, did a back flip, landed it and bowed out. They went, 'That was great. Can you come again tomorrow?'"

During callbacks for Victor, Jason Lawrence Geiger adopted a stage name:[11] Austin St. John. Of the five who would play high schoolers, St. John was the only one *in* high school. He was a week away from turning 18 when he attended the cattle call on a lark; a buddy bet him that it wouldn't be a waste of his time. "I lost 20 bucks,"[12] St. John said.

Participants with no martial arts experience were quickly shown the door, but, fortunately for St. John, those without acting experience were welcome. He didn't realize that the cheesy monologue given to him after a successful first audition had to be memorized for the next one.

Amy Jo Johnson eventually grew unsettled by the fame *Power Rangers* brought and until the late 2010s shied away from the convention circuit. Following a steady acting career, she worked mostly as a director and writer. Courtesy PR Media Info/© Saban Entertainment

"I had to work with them a lot on the acting," said Hamilton, the director. "They were all great in the martial arts, but part of directing a pilot is to make sure—a little bit like a conductor in an orchestra—that you have everybody on the same page, that they're all acting at the same level, tempo, and pacing."

St. John was unqualified as a thespian, but he made up for it with his martial arts mastery. He wasn't an actor, but he oozed charisma and confidence that suggested he could be the kind of leader the show needed.

Tadashi Yamashita, a skilled martial artist with ample experience translating punches and kicks to film, sparred with St. John and others in the penultimate round of solo auditions. Hamilton wanted Yamashita to assess whether the high school senior had what it took to be the Red Ranger. St. John received Yamashita's blessing after that session, but it was just a prelude. At the final solo audition, Yamashita reconvened with St. John and informed him they'd need to choreograph a fight to perform in front of the executives from Fox and Saban Entertainment. The product of their collaboration lasted only a few minutes but contained hundreds of rapid movements. A segment near the end concerned St. John: Yamashita wanted him to perform a reverse crescent kick—a swinging kick used to hit targets from their sides—at full power and full speed toward his head. St. John worried that, if he did as asked, Yamashita's body would be without a brain. He held back while rehearsing, and Yamashita knew it.

Hamilton stressed to St. John that, if the staged fight went well, the role was his. "My pulse is 5,000 just standing and I haven't even thrown a punch yet with a guy who could kill me with his pinky,"[13] St. John said.

In a room full of suits, Yamashita and St. John performed without a hiccup until the crescent-kick segment. Yamashita loudly whispered, "Do it!" as the time came for his rival to deliver the kick. This time, St. John set personal discipline aside and followed orders. Yamashita gracefully launched into the air—"I don't know how he made it look so pretty,"[14] St. John said—and rolled back into a standing position on his return to the mat, conveniently in front of Haim Saban. The fighters reengaged in their routine, now more improvisational than rehearsed. Yamashita came at St. John faster than they'd ever practiced, but he continued to hold court with the master through the final flurry.

The executives stood, fawning over what they'd just witnessed. They'd seen all they needed. A green high schooler would be the first Red Power Ranger, and his name wouldn't be Victor. Their leader deserved something stronger: Jason.

The last round of auditions consisted of three groups of five: chemistry was the final test for all.

During the inaugural Power Morphicon[15] in 2007, Oliver showed final-callback tapes from the winning group and the runners-up. Based on three minutes of selected footage from each, the callback seems more like a formality. Although the "almost" Power Rangers don't seem dispassionate toward one another, they've got nothing on the five who would become superheroes. These clips also offer insight into what the producers did and didn't want from their principals.

Both Zacks, Jones, and a runner-up best identified by his Stanford University cutoff, are Black men with a cool, easygoing attitude. Stanford's demo-reel performance is more over-the-top than Jones's, whose general vibe feels more authentic. But the spirit of Zack is there with both actors.

Among the original cast members, Walter Jones—21 when filming of the pilot began—had the most experience in showbiz. In this production still, he's holding a Power Morpher to the sky as part of a morph sequence that ultimately didn't materialize in the show long term. Courtesy PR Media Info/© Saban Entertainment

Runner-up Jason had bouncy, shoulder-length hair befitting a quarterback who moonlights as a model. He's got the leading-man look down better than St. John, but his on-screen punches and kicks are noticeably stiffer than his rival's, as is his one-on-one conversation with Stanford Zack. He too, like St. John, is white.

Both second-place Kimberly and Trini appear to be white women. "Almost" Kimberly plays a harsher version of the Valley girl archetype that Johnson brought to life in the show. Her response to a mousy Trini, who approaches her for confidence-building tips is closer to "mean girl" than friendly; this Kimberly's charity seems contingent on an unspoken agreement that Trini will have to do her homework later. "Almost" Trini is the hardest of the runners-up to imagine as a Power Ranger in any season—the personality exhibited seems severely disconnected from the show's overarching vision of togetherness.

And then there's Billy. David Yost was the right choice—his performance in the demo reel is, of all the actors, the most endearing. But it might have been possible to pluck Aaron Atinsky from the runner-up group and have him work alongside the other winners. The Billy we see Atinsky play much more resembles that of the show than the one in Yost's audition, who is nearly manic. Yost reeled in the expressiveness with which he played Billy by the time *MMPR* went to air—and over the course of four seasons, the character's most exaggerated quirks disappeared altogether—but his enthusiasm was instantly infectious.

Mighty Morphin Power Rangers was named in 1992. Beyond that fact, the title's origin is lost to three decades of collective memory erosion.

According to interviews given in a 2019 episode of *The Toys That Made Us*, a Netflix documentary series, the name originated with toy manufacturer Bandai America. In that telling, the name "Power Rangers" seemingly sprung to life quickly, which makes sense, as it's not that far removed from two of the three working titles, *Galaxy Rangers* and *Dino Rangers* (a third, *Phantoms*, was also used during the audition process).

The name needed to evoke strength and be "bigger than life," according to Shien Ueno,[16] Bandai America's former vice president of marketing. Trish Stewart, former director of marketing for the company, says in *The Toys That Made Us* that "Morphin" was a play on metamorphosis and used to indicate that the kids in the show would transform—sort of like some popular robots from a decade earlier. Peter Dang, another Bandai executive who shortly would become president of Saban Children's Entertainment Group, is credited with coining "Mighty Morphin." It marked the strength checkbox, evoked *Transformers*, and acted as a multisyllabic sparring partner with another recent toy-aisle leader, *Teenage Mutant Ninja Turtles*.

In a 2022 interview, Oliver disputed the origin as told by *The Toys That Made Us*. "The show was named in the back of a bowling alley while we were shooting the pilot, quite literally,"[17] Oliver said with a laugh.

Levy-Sarnoff was among the people in Corbin Bowl with Oliver on October 10, 1992, the pilot's second day of shooting. She attributes "Rangers" to the show from which it was sourced, *Zyuranger*. "Power" and "Mighty" sprung elsewhere from the discussion, but "Morphin"? "The Michael Jackson video for 'Black or White' was really popular at the time, and he had all those morphing faces," Levy-Sarnoff said. "Someone came up with 'Mighty,' so we had 'Mighty Morphin Power Rangers.'"

On the pilot's second day of shooting, as Oliver told it in 2022, Saban approached the creative team with a mandate: create a name by the end of the day and—at Bandai's behest—make it sound like it could go toe-to-toe with *Teenage Mutant Ninja Turtles*, on which Saban had passed in 1987. Whatever the origin, it's just about certain that the Power Rangers' half-shelled predecessors influenced their branding. Its logo and that of *Teenage Mutant Ninja Turtles* could easily be mistaken for one another if not for the lightning bolt splitting "Mighty Power" and "Morphin Rangers." "Mighty Morphin Power Rangers" can be swapped in for "Teenage Mutant Ninja Turtles" in the clever theme song for the original 1980s cartoon, right down to the cadence, and not lose any timing or rhythm. It wouldn't be jaw-dropping to learn that the "power" in "Power Rangers" originated from a line in that theme song: "Turtle Power!"

"He passed on the [Teenage] Mutant Ninja Turtles and never forgave himself for that," Hamilton said. "This was his chance. He really believed in it."

The breakneck pace at which the pilot came together was a glimpse into how the series' production would unfold. Original footage was captured over four days using two locations—the Vasquez Rocks Natural Area and Nature Center and Corbin Bowl—in addition to the Command Center set, then called the Control Room. Eleven days of postproduction stood between the shoot and its delivery date.

Later, as its popularity grew, *Mighty Morphin Power Rangers* would increasingly become a target of anti-violence groups. Those who rushed to its defense would consistently note that none of the heroes ever directed violent acts toward another human.

Three minutes into the 16-minute pilot, however, every soon-to-be Power Ranger delivers at least one punch or kick into the body of another teenager. A misogynistic greaser spurs the lengthy fight after a rogue bowling ball flattens his hot dog; he retaliates by strongly coming on to Kimberly and Trini. Kimberly shoves him away, prompting the bully's gang to gather 'round. They picked the wrong fight: the would-be sexual assaulter meets Trini's fists and a fate similar to his wiener. Jason, Kimberly, and Zack dispatch of the other goons through a series of signature maneuvers—Jones's Hip Hop Kiddo is on full display—while Billy's lone, well-timed strike is delivered accidentally to the gut of an assailant as the scene transitions to a news brief about a startling development on the moon. Even by today's more liberal standards for TV violence, this sequence tiptoes the line for two- to 11-year-olds. That it was played for intended comedic effect—and that the bullies earned their comeuppance—wouldn't have mattered to the slew of angry mothers who champed at the bit when a much tamer version of *MMPR* hit the air. "It all comes back to tone," Hamilton said. "How can something work for kids but also work for parents?"

Jason Lawrence Geiger, better known by his stage name Austin St. John, was the show's first Red Ranger—the de facto leader of the Power Rangers in almost every season. Courtesy PR Media Info/© Saban Entertainment

On the moon, we get our first use of *Zyuranger* footage: a couple of astronauts have stumbled on a "big trash dumpster" emitting an intense odor. Because they're men who can't fathom the notion of leaving well enough alone, they decide to open it, unleashing four aliens of various shapes and sizes: Goldar, Finster, Squatt, and Baboo.

Squatt, as plump and blue as he is short, speaks first.

"Hey Rita, wake up," he shouts into the cannister. "Come on, come on, we're free."

Squatt's addressee, Rita Repulsa, emerges. Her arms stretched to the sky, Rita lets out a long, delighted yawn. Apparently, the foul scent is her breath because Squatt starts scavenging for a mint in his fanny pack.

Finster—an elderly leprechaun—shakes his head dismissively while rejoicing that their 10,000-year-long captivity is over. Baboo, as blue as Squatt but much ganglier and monocled, offers to assist Rita as she exits the trash can but causes her to step in a puddle (which clearly doesn't exist).

After berating her subordinate, Rita blows the trash can to smithereens with her gaudy wand, which would tower over her if her hair wasn't wrapped into two 45-degree . . . horns? On closer examination, they seem more like tattered witch's hats, her feather-adorned neckpiece acting as something of an extended brim for both. While her hairdress is weathered, the pair of witchy cones aggressively protruding from her breastplate—tastefully adorned in gold—still look sharp after 10 millennia. A brown dress with a gold-trim pattern completes the bombastic ensemble.

Machiko Soga portrays Bandora, the Japanese equivalent of Rita Repulsa in *Zyuranger*. The character's entire look was conceptualized with Soga in mind; she was a veteran tokusatsu actress who'd previously starred as Queen Hedrian, one of the few major villains in *Super Sentai* history to have a recurring role in two seasons, *Denziman* and *Sun Vulcan*. For Toei artist and designer Tamotsu Shinohara, who conceptualized Bandora and the other members of her dumpster-dwelling gang, the opportunity to build a character around Soga was years in the making. In 1987, he started the concept for Soga's spider-themed villainess in *Sekai Ninja Sen Jiraiya*—part of another Toei superhero series, *Metal Hero*—but couldn't finish due to school obligations. "From the beginning, we knew Machiko Soga would play Bandora, so we put our heart and soul into making this character," said Shinohara, by way of a fan translation[18] of a Japanese book celebrating the first 20 years of *Super Sentai* monster designs.

While Soga and her delightfully animated physical performance made it to American televisions, her voice was dubbed over by American actress Barbara Goodson. Rita Repulsa is her defining role, but Goodson could have stopped voice acting before 1993 and she'd still be regarded as an industry legend. Among her credits are *Akira* and the original dub of *Kiki's Delivery Service*, two of the most important anime films ever produced. She also worked alongside Oliver on *Robotech*, which adapted footage from three distinct Japanese anime shows to create an 85-episode "robots versus aliens" show for U.S. audiences. Goodson, a five-foot powerhouse with more than 20 years of experience, at the time was a Saban Entertainment employee and a no-brainer to cast in the role.

In the pilot, her performance is much more subdued than the villain she'd play for more than 200 episodes. Saban Entertainment originally asked for a "Wicked Witch of the West" take, so she delivered accordingly.

"They did a study of what people thought of it, and they said, 'Oh it's not so scary,' and so they fired me," said Goodson,[19] who sought a second stab at the character. Auditions were already in progress, but she was encouraged to try out for a part she had briefly been gifted. "I was pretty pissed off that I was fired. So, I said, 'You want it scarier? *I'll give it to you scarier.*' That's how she was born."

It's irreplicable. High-pitched but gravely. A controlled yet unrelenting shrill. The Wicked Witch of the West is still there but doused in Roger Daltry. That she was still able to speak, let alone continue working as a voice actor into her seventies after producing *that* voice for five years, is a remarkable achievement.

The American team concocted their own batch of strange characters to referee between Rita Repulsa and the Power Rangers rather than outright duplicate *Zyuranger* mentor Barza, a wizard who goes back millions of years with Bandora.

Zoltar (a floating head in a tube) and his trusted assistant Alpha 5 (a robot slightly more articulated than the one from *Lost in Space*) are monitoring the moon developments from their base in the mountains of Angel Grove. They call it the Command Center, but in real life, it's the House of the Book on the Brandeis-Bardin Campus of American Jewish University. The building might be the most recognizable piece of American architecture in the non-landmark category; in addition to being featured prominently across *Power Rangers'* first five seasons, it's been used in dozens of other films and TV shows, including multiple *Star Trek* titles, as well as music videos from Marilyn Manson ("The Dope Show"), Chris Brown ("Wall to Wall"), and Kelly Price ("As We Lay"). Most recently, its facade was used in the 2023 Emmy-winning Netflix series *Beef*.

The facility's prominent cylindrical exterior inspired the design of Zoltar, an interdimensional being trapped in a time warp. His face originates from David Fielding, the character's voice actor for the pilot and through the series' first 31 episodes. Fielding, one of only two actors in contention for the role, was cast swiftly. His face soon after was motion captured for about four hours.[20]

In the pilot, Zoltar's animation is much greener and blockier; Fielding's face is indistinguishable compared to the series, throughout which it would appear in more than 200 episodes. Of course, zero of those episodes yielded residuals: Fielding says that he was paid $150 for the day he filmed and that he made less than $1,000 in his short time recording dialogue.[21] He also had to lose his hair.

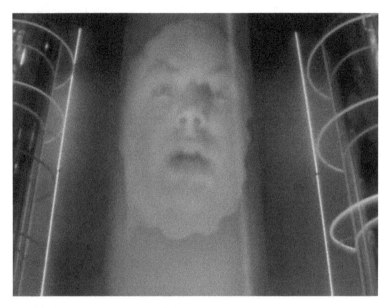

David Fielding's face provided the basis for the original Power Rangers' mentor, Zordon. He also voiced the character for the show's first 31 episodes. Screenshot, Author's Collection

"I went into the makeup area and they shaved me bald, applied a base foundation to my face and darkened my eyebrows," Fielding said.[22] "They glued my ears back so they would lie flatter to my skull and then painted the upper have [sic] of my chest and shoulders with green latex paint, so when the film was processed the only thing that would show through was my head."

Beyond a visual shift more kind to Fielding's facial performance—production designer Yuda Acco opted for white backlighting and nixed a fishbowl effect used in the pilot—Zoltar's name changed. Conventional wisdom suggests it was done to avoid a potential trademark or copyright claim brought on by the owners of "Zoltar Speaks," a fortune-telling machine featured in the 1988 Tom Hanks flick *Big*; funnily, that machine was a fictional prop based on an existing character, Zoltan, and "Zoltar Speaks" went untrademarked and copyrighted until 2006.

If overt concern about potential litigation is to blame, then fortune in this case favored the cautious: the new name, Zordon, came with zero baggage and a greater level of gravitas. It also lent itself favorably to being repurposed for another crucial aspect of the show. In the pilot, giant machines piloted by the Power Rangers to battle giant monsters are called "Dinodroids." That more likely was a play on the familiar Droids of *Star Wars* rather than Marvel villains who made a lone comic-book appearance in 1988, but either way, it too would have been catnip for entertainment lawyers. And thus, "Dinodroids" became "Dinozords." Zordon, it seems, was compensating for something.

In the original pilot, Zoltar makes a request of Alpha 5 after his sensors pick up on Rita's "evil vibrations." (Hey, the two *do* go back at least 10,000 years.)

"Teleport to us the most dangerous group of ruthless, underhanded, overbearing, self-absorbed, and overly emotional humans in the area," the disembodied head suggests. His ally shrieks in disgust. "Not teenagers!"

Of note, this is Zoltar's Plan B, in lieu of an undisclosed Plan A. The disparaging descriptions get softened in the aired version—"overbearing and overemotional"—but still drip with self-awareness as to the silliness of this recruitment. Many superheroes undergo a journey—often starting from childhood—that leads them to a cowl. Others are exposed to something radioactive and must rediscover themselves as they harness new abilities. The Power Rangers? Plucked off the street by an interdimensional being who, from the jump, sends mixed signals about their viability as superheroes.

The five teens get transported to the Command Center. Immediately, Billy is enamored by the "fully sentient, multifunctional automaton" who greets them.

Alpha 5 underwent his own metamorphosis from pilot to production. Pilot Alpha—Alpha Beta? Alpha 1.0?—sports an elaborate, LED-fitted circuit board on his chest and a fin curving down toward the "face" of his gold dome, essentially two cymbals whose clashing is stalled by a thin glass-like ring. He is bulkier and much more susceptible to wear and tear than his sleeker evolution; exposed wiring slips in and out of view from under his arms, which display an incredible range of motion despite enough padding to safely suit up for the Los Angeles Kings.

"Yuda Acco was the one who designed the original Alpha," said Mark Richardson, prop master for the show's first 10 seasons. "He looked like one of the dancing mushrooms from *Fantasia*."

By the time production went full throttle, the dancing mushroom's exposed knobs and bobs were cased in a red chest shield with underwear to match. His cymbals became slightly more circular and the interruptive ring was refined to give his "face" more room to emote. Proto-Alpha's blinking interface was more machine than man; the production version's "eyes" were still just blinking red lights but displayed a deeper humanity.

Alpha 5 suit actress Romy J. Sharf probably had the most demanding on-screen job throughout the pilot and first two seasons given the frequency of the robot's appearances. Sharf recalls getting a call from her casting agent for a kids show and impressing in her audition with some robotic moves. Two days later, she got the part—and future physical therapy bills.

"On a scale from one to ouch, mega ouch,"[23] Sharf said. "Not comfortable at all. Very heavy, very cumbersome, hot. And visibility was kind of limited. I could only see through the visor where the red lights were."

Sharf spoke all of Alpha 5's lines while scenes were filmed, but her voice never made it to air. Richard Steven Horvitz, fresh off recurring sitcom roles in *Safe at Home* and *The Munsters Today*, took the reins in the studio. "I had a friend who was editing the offline version of the show, and it was about 7 o'clock at night one night,"[24] Horvitz said. "He called me up and said, 'Look, I'm editing this show and it's not gonna go anywhere, it's a dumb show, it's silly, but they need a temporary voice track of a robot. Can you come in and do it?'"

Horvitz cashed his $50 check for the pilot and forgot about it until his phone rang again when the "dumb show" got picked up. He went on to voice Alpha 5 in 208 episodes, a live tour, three direct-to-video offerings, and two feature films—longer than any other character in a career that spanned more than 40 years and encompassed multiple animated hits, including the lead role in a short-lived cult classic, *Invader Zim*. And he did it under a partial pseudonym: Richard Wood.

Despite Billy's nerdgasm over Alpha 5 and Zoltar, skepticism runs rampant among the teens. Surrounded by cheap computer terminals and a few tubes that evoke *Tron*, they're brought up to speed on Rita Repulsa's evil plot. Zoltar presents to them "Transmorphers," silver devices powered by gold coins that he says will infuse them with the power of dinosaurs. The kids decide it's not a battle worth waging. They leave, collectively choosing not to become superheroes.

Rita Repulsa, portrayed on-screen by Machiko Soga via footage from *Zyuranger*, is voiced by Barbara Goodson—including future appearances when other actors portray Rita Repulsa in U.S.-produced footage. Screenshot, Author's Collection

The dialogue, staging, and set dressing from pilot to production improves but the overall vibe of this sequence stays intact. It's the part of the episode that, more than 30 years after it premiered, resonates strongest. *Power Rangers* didn't pioneer reluctant heroes, but it unashamedly embraced the idea that "the good guys" in a kids TV show might not actually want to sacrifice their lives to save the world. They would rather be *bowling* than using superpowers to protect the planet. One could interpret that as selfish or shortsighted, but it's also relatable. Sure, the notion of jumping into a giant robot to fight a monster sounds fun, but if the opportunity were in front of you, it would be much more difficult to accept. Just ask anyone who's ever been asked—or forced—to serve in an army.

The tens of millions who've seen either version of "Day of the Dumpster" know what happens next: Rita's foot soldiers—Putty Patrollers, or Putties for short—ambush and eventually corner the teens. The fight is so much better in the production version than the pilot—the choreography is much stronger in the former, and the scene is played with more tension rather than for comedy—but in both, the teens realize they need to do something to tip the fight in their favor. They have no choice but to use the Transmorphers, later renamed "Power Morphers."

"Mastodon!"
"Pterodactyl!"
"Triceratops!"
"Saber-Tooth Tiger!"
"Tyrannosaurus!"

Of all the things that changed from pilot to broadcast, most pressing was this: the production team needed to recast Trini, the Yellow Ranger.

Dubois halfheartedly went to an audition and ended up in the right group of attractive, physically gifted young adults. She had cold feet, and the terms of her proposed contract did little to warm her to the notion of uprooting her life. "We didn't know the show was gonna be big, and even if it was big, the contract was the contract,"[25] Dubois said. "That's a different thing than being famous. If it says in your contract that for any reason whatsoever, at any time, we can just say goodbye to you? They could."

Hamilton got to know the cast well—they'd stayed at his home while filming the pilot because Saban didn't provide budget for hotel expenses. "She just wanted $1,500 a week," Hamilton said. "I think he was offering $1,200 or something. She wanted a couple hundred dollars more and he fired her. I thought that was really wrong. We'd spent months casting these people!"

That Saban was committed to *Power Rangers* being a nonunion production might have roots in 1986,[26] when the possibility of an actors' strike nearly derailed filming of the *Bio-Man* pilot. His TV dealings up to that point also largely dealt in kids animation, which historically lagged the rest of Hollywood in terms of wages and other working conditions. (As of 2025, many creatives involved with animated television shows still don't receive residuals for their work.) Charming, funny, loyal, sharp, fast—these are some of the words most often used to describe the man who fathered *Power Rangers*. Cheap is another.

Low wages prevented Hamilton's further participation. He enjoyed working with Saban, whom he'd known for years. He thought that the team bringing *Power Rangers* to life had enough spunk to make it work, even if he didn't outright believe in the program the way that Saban did. But away from the *Power Rangers* pilot, he'd averaged $50,000 shooting others; Saban wanted to pay Hamilton $2,000 per episode to stick around on *Power Rangers*. Even if he directed every second of the proposed 40-episode order over 10 or so weeks—filming footage for three to four episodes a week, which would become standard operating procedure—the opportunity cost was too high to stomach.

"It was a terrible amount of money," Hamilton said. "So, I jumped ship. It was amicable."

After morphing, the teens don't even have time to observe how good their spandex looks before they're teleported again. They land in downtown Angel Grove to continue the battle, which now includes Rita's top general, Goldar (voiced by Kerrigan Mahan). Most of the remaining run time in both versions of "Day of the Dumpster" leans on *Zyuranger* fight footage, but even there, the differences are notable—the more violent bits (Black Ranger heaving a Putty Patroller off a building, Yellow Ranger shooting at a group of them with a blaster) are confined to the unaired version. So is King Sphinx, a "Monster of the Day" whose footage is quickly exhausted but whose presence in this trial run led to a slew of early merchandise that overinflated his import in the actual series. He and Goldar are engorged by Rita's magic wand. That's a sentence that sounds only slightly more sexual than her actual catchphrase: "Make my monster grow!"

Instinctively, the Power Rangers call on their Dinozords, modeled after dinosaurs and prehistoric beasts and painted in their respective colors. The machines combine into an even larger one—the Dino Megazord—and enable the heroes to thwart the oversized evildoers. There's not a single hint that these machines are physical manifestations of a sentient, all-knowing god, as is the case in *Zyuranger*; suspension of disbelief is critical to one's enjoyment of any superhero media, but *Super Sentai* often requires even more than its anglicized offspring.

Back at the Command Center, the teenagers bask in victory. Riding a high, Zoltar has them in a disadvantaged position but nonetheless offers them a clear opportunity, again, to get out of this war. Faced with another choice, only Kimberly feigns disdain—"Even though the outfits are cool and everything, my hair gets tangled up inside the helmet"—before deploying a bit of 1990s slang to leave no doubt about her true position. "PSYCH!" (The broadcast version replaces this with another era-defining retort: "Not!")

The aired version of this scene is, like most of the pilot, more robust. Zordon's sale job is a bit stronger in the canonical edition. Amid the teens' celebration, he slyly transitions into offering up his equivalent of a terms of service agreement—which, based on their use of the Power Morphers, they've already signed. Ignore the fine print, and the "protection of the power" will be lost for good.

What Zordon describes as "three basic rules" are, from a TV storytelling standpoint, ingenious:

Never use your power for personal gain: A kid-friendly version of "don't be an asshole."

Never escalate a battle unless Rita forces you: It's just not Ranger-like to make a scene. Fancy weapons and 60-foot robots are reserved for the right occasions; deployment outside of them could cause unnecessary collateral damage.

Keep your identity secret; no one may know you are a Power Ranger: Just quintessential superhero stuff, this one.

These were rigid tenets that helped create narrative tension throughout the show's first six seasons while also providing protection against mockery. ("Why don't the Power Rangers just call their Zords to squash monsters while they're small?" Zordon's second rule, duh.) Over the course of three decades, those rules to varying degrees were bent, challenged, and outright ignored—especially the last one—but their spirit carried through 30 years of interconnected stories. Oliver never could have dreamed that, after more than a dozen rewrites of the script, some of its final additions would provide a lasting framework for multiple generations.

The episode culminates in an "all-in" huddle. As they break, the teens jump into the air and shout "Power Rangers!" before freeze-framing into the credits.

Zordon's blessing says it all: "The five of you have come together to form as fine a group of superheroes as there has ever been."

CHAPTER 3

Teamwork

Standing behind a two-way mirror, staring into a room flush with bean-bag chairs, Maureen Smith was confident that those flanking her would leave wearing smiles. Two of them—Margaret Loesch and Haim Saban—were eager to see how kids responded to their makeshift pilot. Others watched the clock, wondering why they were party to a charade.

Smith was barely out of the University of Southern California's film school when she got hired by Fox Broadcasting ahead of its launch on October 9, 1986. Her first job: identify target markets for her colleagues in affiliate relations to bring into the Fox family. When Smith caught wind that the Fox Kids Network was imminent, she wanted in. That Loesch—already a legend at that time in Smith's eyes—would be in charge made her want in even more. She worked out a unique arrangement: she'd still be employed by Fox proper but get to spend the bulk of her time performing data and research work in the children's space.

By 1992, she oversaw focus-group tests. For *Mighty Morphin Power Rangers*, all the stops were pulled out to give it a shot. The beanbags were planted to better simulate how a kid might watch TV at home as opposed to the de facto conference-table arrangement provided by ASI Entertainment, the research firm contracted for most Fox Kids shows. A total of 22 kids—14 boys and eight girls—participated and were split into four groups by gender: six- to eight-year-olds and nine- to 11-year-olds. As was the case on-screen, diversity was prioritized.

The six- to eight-year-old boys walked in first.

"Within 10 minutes, they were flying around the room, karate-chopping in midair—not hitting each other, but just overwhelmed with

33

energy by what they were seeing," Smith said. "They were laughing at all the parts that we hoped they'd laugh at and bouncing up and down in the beanbag chairs. By the end of that session, we had to keep the 9- to 11-year-old boy group waiting because the beanbags were popped, and those little tiny, white Styrofoam beans were everywhere in the room."

That was probably the only vote of confidence Saban, Loesch, and Smith needed to confirm their own. But then the older boys came in. They didn't get up and move around as much, but they were visibly engaged—with the show but also with one another. They talked about what they watched. In a room of kids who've never met each other, that's gold.

But the girls were the real ringers. While not as amped as their male counterparts, their body language was positive throughout—and especially so once they saw the Pink and Yellow Rangers morph into action.

"They lit up," Smith said. "It was almost like they were taking on the persona. And when the moderator would meet with the kids after and ask, 'What did you think?,' overwhelmingly the girls said it was so cool to see girls, in their words, 'kick butt.'"

Those sessions sealed the deal. *MMPR* got its 40-episode order, and its parents could breathe a sigh of relief before embarking on another round of casting.

The producers found their new Trini in Thuy Trang, a Vietnamese American. More than any of its original cast members, Trang embodied the guiding philosophy of the TV show that would make them famous: anyone can be a Power Ranger.

Trang's father fled to the United States following the fall of Saigon in 1975. She, her mother, and two brothers boarded a refugee ship five years later. There were about 3,000 people on the boat. Some died, and she was almost among them. After not eating for several days, Trang's health deteriorated to the point that other refugees wanted to throw her overboard to create more favorable conditions for healthier passengers. Her mom forced food down her throat to keep Trang alive enough to justify her continued occupancy. "It's strange to witness how ugly our human race can become in desperate situations,"[1] Trang said.

Perhaps no actor in *Power Rangers* history personified the show's commitment to inclusivity and perseverance more than Thuy Trang, a Vietnamese immigrant whose mother defended her from bad actors while on a boat coming to the United States. Courtesy PR Media Info/© Saban Entertainment

The family eventually made it to the United States, reunited with their patriarch, and settled in Orange County, California. Trang learned English as she attended elementary school and found an early role model in Lynda Carter.[2] *Wonder Woman* encouraged Trang to study martial arts and showed her that a woman could be just as or more powerful than a man.

When she enrolled at UC Irvine in 1992, Trang sought a degree in civil engineering, following her father and two older siblings into the field. But Trang, like so many teenagers growing up near Tinseltown, daydreamed about working in front of a camera. She never could have dreamed that a 100-level acting class would be the launchpad for her career.

A talent scout approached her one day after class. He told Trang that she looked "very exotic" and that his agent could find her work. The racist observation led to an ironic first gig: the agent placed Trang in a local public service announcement denouncing racism. Not long afterward, she was among 20 individuals cast in a commercial for the Church of Scientology. The actors—who span a wide array of ethnicities, ages, and other religious backgrounds—appear on-screen for a second and speak just one word, "trust," in different languages. They converge for a group bonding session as Scientology founder L. Ron Hubbard delivers a voice-over. "On the day when we can fully trust each other, there will be peace on Earth."[3]

Not too long thereafter, the college student found herself in the running for a show keen on addressing the same themes—and full of martial arts.

"We brought probably 20 people back for the screen test,"[4] Wallin said. "And it was Haim Saban and everybody in one room. Thuy was sitting outside of the room and she said, 'I don't know if I can do this, Katy. I don't know if I can walk into that room and audition. I am terrified.' And I said, 'Here's what we're gonna do. You're not only gonna walk into that audition, you are gonna walk in and jump on the table where all the executives are sitting. And you are going to own that audition.' So I walk in, the videos are rolling and Thuy runs in and she jumps on the table and proceeded to do her audition and went crazy.

"And she became a Power Ranger."

In tandem with its search for Dubois's replacement, production sought two additional male actors. One needed to complement an existing comedic character, the other to fill spandex for about 10 episodes before getting written off the show.

A diamond was unearthed during the quarrel between the heroes and greasy teens in the original pilot. Paul Schrier, last seen sliding down a bowling lane, became half of a comedic duo, Farkas "Bulk" Bulkmeier and Eugene "Skull" Skullovitch, with whom the civilian Rangers sparred—verbally rather than physically—for more than 200 episodes. Early on, they'd receive lighthearted comeuppance after altercations, usually by way of food to the face. By the end of their tenure, they were the original show's most well-developed characters.

Schrier—a large, classically trained 22-year-old actor—was Bulk the moment he showed up early for his first audition. He accidentally walked into the middle of a fight rehearsal between Walter Jones and Tony Oliver.

"Tony doesn't like to fight,"[5] Schrier said. "Tony was standing in because he was somewhat portly those days—rotund, if you will—so when I walked in, he was like, 'Finally, I don't have to stand here for Punk No. 5.' So I got to stand in and, basically, it was all about fight reactions, and I had a lot of theatrical fighting experience. I was lucky to be perfect for that, I could take a punch."

Schrier's timing and improvisational skills were quickly appreciated by all parties on set, particularly by Saban himself. "He was sitting on an apple box, and [Saban's wife] Cheryl came to visit, and I was just standing nearby quietly,"[6] Schrier said. "And he said, 'Cheryl, you have to meet this guy. He's an idiot.' . . . That is a crystalline memory because, really? I am an idiot."

Schrier needed a partner in comedic crime. Producers first looked to Bobby Valva, a stuntman who played the lead bully in the pilot, but he wasn't sidekick material—too handsome and intimidating to be a believable minion to Schrier. None of the other punks in the pilot fit what they had in mind, so they scoured their reject piles. In them: Jason Narvy, who'd originally auditioned for Billy. Narvy, like the character he'd soon portray, was something of a delinquent—not a bad kid, but one who often found trouble if it didn't find him first. Throughout his youth, the only thing that kept him engaged with academia was theater.

"By the time I graduated high school, it was really my only chance to not go to jail almost," Narvy said. "I was really good at it, and I had a passion for it."

He attended the Lee Strasberg Theatre & Film Institute campus in Los Angeles and through a family friend connected with an agent who'd worked with Jodie Foster before she ascended. Between auditions, he worked as a parts driver at a Ford dealership with his stepfather, a mechanic. Six months into auditions that led nowhere, the impatient 18-year-old was ready to give up.

"When I would make parts deliveries," said Narvy, "I'd have to call the shop and be like, 'Do you all need anything else while I'm down here,' and my boss is like, 'Yeah, come back, you've got an audition.'"

It was the producers of *Power Rangers*. They wanted him to audition again, but for another part. They faxed the sides to the dealership but told him he didn't really need to pay attention to them. This time, they were more interested in what he could bring to the table as an improviser.

He didn't even rush home to take a shower. Narvy showed up covered in motor oil and wore a leather jacket in a room of rejects—he most looked the part.

"I'm like, 'Fuck these guys, they're not gonna give me the role,' so I'm gonna do what I want and I'm gonna make them remember me—and not in a kind way," Narvy said. When asked to flirt with producer Ellen Levy-Sarnoff during the read, Narvy laid it on thick. That interaction left a big impression, but his final act sealed the deal.

"They're like, 'So, can you do slapstick?'" Narvy said. "I'm like, 'Slapstick comedy? Dude I'm a fucking actor, I don't do slapstick comedy, this is bullshit.'" Narvy stormed off toward the door and grabbed it, planting his foot against it as it swung back. He flipped backward into a table where the producers sat. Their stack of résumés and headshots still midflight, he told them, "Yea, I could do slapstick."

Producer Jonathan Tzachor told Narvy the exact opposite of what he was told at his previous audition—*If we don't call you, you call us*—and was fitted for wardrobe the following day. Across the way, he saw Schrier, already in costume on a juice bar set where they'd spend most of the next several years receiving pies to their faces and bruises on their asses. "I didn't realize it was a costume. He just looked like a dick," said Narvy.

Schrier approached and whipped out a hand as big as Narvy's head.

"'Hi, I'm Paulie,'" Narvy said. "'Let's get to work.'"

Jason Narvy was among the last members of the cast hired but remained on *Power Rangers*, alongside Paul Schrier, longer than any of the original cast members. He holds a PhD in theater studies and is now, among other things, a college professor. Courtesy The Morphin Museum/© Saban Entertainment

When Paul Schrier and Jason Narvy weren't portraying comedic foils to the Power Rangers, they could frequently be found around Los Angeles directing and participating in Shakespeare productions. Courtesy The Morphin Museum/© Saban Entertainment

Burai, the DragonRanger, debuts in episode 17 of *Zyuranger*. His green costume is patterned similarly to the other suits but accented by the gold rims of his boots and gloves, gold arm cuffs, and a gold triangular shield covering his shoulders and chest.

The addition of a sixth hero (and more) became common practice in *Super Sentai*, but *Zyuranger* blazed the trail. *Power Rangers'* producers didn't realize they'd need to cast an additional member of their team until after shooting the pilot and on discovery hurried to identify another American to stand in. As far as rush casting goes, it might be the best in children's television history.

Jason David Frank, the son of truckers Ray and Janice, happened onto a location shoot of *Knight Rider* when he was a child. Watching how his favorite TV show got made left a big impression on him.

"I was always attracted to the camera,"[7] said Frank, who landed his first gig at 12 years old. It was short-lived, but for a moment, Frank was a preteen heartthrob named "Jason Barnes" who peddled skateboarding and martial arts equipment in teen magazines across the country.

His parents often joked that his "acting up" should make him perfect for acting. He learned to harness and channel an overabundance of energy through martial arts. From age four, he studied under Grandmaster Louis D. Casamassa of Red Dragon Karate, earning his first black belt the same year he started modeling. Not too long after, he became an instructor, sometimes demonstrating katas for people twice his age. By the time he was 18, Frank—by then a fourth-degree black belt—had saved enough funds to buy the martial arts school that helped instill in him the discipline needed to manage his bank account so well. And then he bought another.

But the sensei/entrepreneur couldn't get the camera off his mind. A talent agent told Frank he couldn't represent him unless he cut his long, luscious hair. The 19-year-old loved his locks, but he played the good soldier, only for the agent to still dismiss him. As a minor concession on his way out the door, the agent handed Frank an open casting call flyer for *Phantoms*—a kids show seeking a martial artist. He went and received a callback. Then another.

Entering its search for a Green Ranger—at that time unnamed and working with the same casting sides written for Victor the Red Ranger—production hoped to cast an actor of Asian descent.[8] If they'd gone with a more natural actor, that's how it would have panned out. "I was so nervous,"[9] Frank said. "I was cotton mouth, couldn't get my lines out.'"

Whether they wanted to be him or be with him, producers believed every kid watching would want to have a poster of Frank on their wall. And his martial arts skills were better than anyone they'd seen through all the auditions. "He was perfect for this role,"[10] Wallin said. "Jason had confidence, charisma, a solid sense of himself. He was an outstanding martial artist. . . . Everything flowed with him, and he was so dynamic. He's also very attractive, which I think people loved. And so kind."

At his second callback, Frank was the only male actor among a dozen could-be Power Rangers. His concern that production had turned Victor into Victoria was quickly extinguished: he learned the part was his, and these women were vying to replace a previously cast role. Wallin waited to tell him he got the part at this callback because she wanted him to work with one of the actresses in contention, a soft-spoken Vietnamese American. "And then Thuy[11] ended up getting the part, so me and her kind of bonded because of that," Frank said.

Frank signed a contract for 10 episodes. His character's name became Tommy Oliver, the surname originating from story editor Tony Oliver. It might not be for long, but the kid who just a decade earlier couldn't get enough of *Knight Rider* was going to get to play a hero on TV.

The first words uttered in the TV cut of the first *Mighty Morphin Power Rangers* theme song aren't "Go Go Power Rangers." The iconic lyric—a rallying cry for multiple generations—isn't sung until 21 other words have passed. In every first-season episode, it's preceded by a voice-over and instrumental, set to a flurry of images that condense the events of "Day of the Dumpster" into about 20 seconds. "Ahhhhh, after 10,000 years I'm free," Rita exclaims. "It's time to conquer Earth."

Half a beat later, Zordon issues a declaration.

"Alpha, Rita's escaped," the tubed wizard says before asking his comrade to "recruit a team of teenagers with attitude."

An intense guitar riff grows louder before unleashing into a theme song for the ages. Well, it sounds like a guitar track.

"I love guitar[12] but I can't play it," said Ron Wasserman.

Jason David Frank was cast for a short-term role as Tommy Oliver, the Green Ranger who starts off as an adversary to the team. Courtesy The Morphin Museum/© Saban Entertainment

The lightning-quick chords and riffs of "Go Go Power Rangers" were produced on a keyboard system, the E-mu Proteus 1. It contained thousands of sound samples from E-mu's popular sound library, housed on a 4 MB drive (expandable to 8 MB), and featured 125 instruments, 32 voice options, and 16 MIDI channels. The line of products remained popular throughout the 1990s and was used in the development of several memorable arrangements from the decade, including the soundtrack for the Nintendo 64 shooter *GoldenEye 007* and the theme song of *The X-Files.*

Wasserman, an in-house musician for Saban Entertainment, and Ron Kenan, the company's head of music, used the Proteus 1 to create another unforgettable superhero theme song a year prior: that of the 1992 *X-Men* animated series. It's a much different track than "Go Go Power Rangers." It's purely instrumental, no vocal accompaniment. It opens with a steady, pulsing bass line before piercing strings barge in. That gives way to the heart of the track: an adrenaline-fueled guitar riff supplemented by hi-hat tracks. "There's so many fucking hi-hats[13] on this thing," Wasserman said. More than 100 tracks were melded together to make the *X-Men* theme; Wasserman estimates that at least 20 of them were hi-hats. Its development proved all-consuming, taking weeks to go from the first demo to TV-ready.

Kenan—who *could* play guitar and was a metal fan—wanted *X-Men* to have a rock-centric score and had Wasserman develop several rock instrumentals with that aim. That sound, however, got pushback from Sidney Iwanter, a Fox Kids executive in charge of the show. The Wasserman rock track that made the cut for *X-Men* was its end-credits song; following the first of that show's five seasons, it too was eliminated in favor of a repeat of the iconic opening title theme written by Kenan and series producer Winston Richard.

Their efforts weren't for naught, though. A year later, they were tasked with developing the title theme for *Mighty Morphin Power Rangers*—another superhero show, but in live action. It also had a more accepting executive, Ann Austen (née Knapp), on the network side. "I said, 'Oh yea, this is finally going to be a rock show,'" Kenan said. Before commissioning new work or laying tracks himself, Kenan often revisited unused tracks in the Saban Entertainment archives. There were three unused demos for *X-Men* that he really liked, so he took them to Haim Saban's home for a face-to-face listening session.

"He didn't get involved in the music decisions on 95 percent of the shows, but the high-profile ones he wanted to," Kenan said. "*Power Rangers* was going to be a high-profile one, and definitely something that was close to his heart, so he was eager to see what I had in mind. So, I play him these three tracks, and he says, 'This one. This one. This one.'"

In addition to giving the track his blessing, Saban made one request.

"He says to me, 'Do something like, go, go, go, go Power Rangers,'" Kenan said. "That was his shtick from back with *Inspector Gadget*, which had 'Go, Gadget, Go.' Haim and Shuki were always great with gimmicky hook ideas."

One more request: the song had to be ready by the next day. Saban Entertainment was scheduled to meet with executives from Fox Broadcasting, and Saban wanted a finished theme song to present to them. The demo track was great but had no vocal track or melodic hook.

Kenan rushed to his car and, on a cell phone the size of a brick, dialed Wasserman, who already was in the studio awaiting orders.

"I said, 'OK, we picked *X-Men* song number 7 or 11,' whatever number we'd given the track," Kenan said. "And I literally sang to him the melody, it just came to my mind. 'Go, Go Power Rangers. Go, Go Power Rangers. Mighty Morphin Power Rangers.' Just like that."

By the time Kenan made it to the studio, Wasserman had recorded the vocals and squared it away. All told, the process to create the final vocal tracks for the *Mighty Morphin Power Rangers* theme took under three hours. "I didn't even bother laying down a real guitar track," Kenan said. "It was still a demo."

Despite sucking down Diet Pepsi to tighten his vocal cords, Wasserman still wasn't impressed by his effort—"My high harmony on that original, I'm crazy flat"[14]—but figured it would be a solid guide track for the eventual singer. "The next day they called and said 'Fox loves it,' and I said, 'Great, who should we get to sing it?' And they said, 'You're the singer, they love it.'"

A few months out from its premiere, *Mighty Morphin Power Rangers* had a theme song perfectly suited to its content—distinct from anything else in kids TV—and a music team at the reins that was eager to unleash even more rock music on the youth of America and beyond.

"It was the first time there was a children's series that had rock music—and really, hard rock music," Kenan said. "Wasserman and I wrote many more rock songs for all the fight scenes. I played the live guitars, and he of course was the singer." In 1994, their music was compiled for *Mighty Morphin Power Rangers the Album: Rock Adventure*, interspliced with voice-over clips from the TV cast to create a 40-minute audio drama.

"Sometimes I look on YouTube and read some of the comments, and it's amazing what kind of impression it left on kids and how it changed their perception of music, and their lives," Kenan said. "A lot of change was going on in music, and rock was changing colors. Grunge music was sort of replacing traditional rock music, so maybe rock seemed a little dated at that time but to young kids it was fresh. It was quite an adventure. I often wonder whether any successful artists that followed were actually inspired by our work."

Saban Entertainment previously had made its fortunes in creating quirky and orchestral themes, mostly for animated fare or existing shows to which it owned overseas music rights. Talent responsible for the company's earworms received either a flat fee or, for staffers, a salary—often a lucrative one. For the most part, however, they received nothing in the way of royalty payments. Those went to two men: Saban and Levy. (Wasserman and Kenan were co-credited for other *Power Rangers* songs, if not the theme.)

"As far as the theme, all Haim did was give it his approval," Wasserman said. "What Shuki did, I have no idea."[15] Kenan credits Saban for the "Go Go Power Rangers" chorus lyric. While Levy was not directly involved in every note of every score in hundreds of series and thousands of episodes, particularly in later years, Kenan said he was highly inspirational and a godfather figure. He often wrote key themes on which additional underscore music was based too.

A 1998 *Hollywood Reporter* investigation surfaced how Saban and Levy greatly expanded their wealth on the backs of other musicians. Saban contended that he, Levy, and Saban Entertainment had committed no wrongdoing—and by the letter of the law, they probably hadn't. At the time, between music entities ASCAP and BMI, the duo was credited for having "written" more than 1,600 pieces of TV music and cues. By 2008—just 10 years later—Saban was listed as a "writer" on nearly 4,000 pieces of music. In a 2008 *Portfolio* profile, Saban said that 10 of his former composers once threatened to sue him for $1 million apiece but that each ultimately received only $10,000 as part of a settlement.

"The company was a pioneer in a lot of their business practices, which have been commonplace for years now," said Jim Cushinery, a vocalist and former head of technical services at Saban Entertainment. "Which is, sadly to say, underpaying people. Musicians, songwriters, composers, script writers, everybody. Ron [Wasserman] and I have this conversation all the time—we blame ourselves because we and everyone else were willing to do the work on the cheap. Just so we could do the work, because it beat doing anything else." Cushinery, the would-be singer of the *Mighty Morphin Power Rangers* theme if Wasserman's take hadn't been so well received, brought vocals to dozens of *Power Rangers* tracks as it continued over the next decade. He was tailor-made for—and accidentally cast into—a technical services role at Saban Entertainment following a long stint with Cannon Films, a similarly loose environment ripe with opportunity.

"I was supposed to work for six days cleaning out a closet, and I ended up staying there for six years," Cushinery said. "This place was so crazy that I ended up doing everything you can possibly do on a film over the course of six years, from writing to directing, a little bit of editing all the way to foreign distribution. It was like getting paid to go to film school."

At Saban Entertainment, Cushinery became a go-to guy when it came to sorting out whether film and TV acquisitions were technically sound, sometimes traveling to the point of origin to help filmmakers the next time to avoid constant reworks. During the day, he'd watch movies, frame by frame, to make sure everything was broadcast ready. At night, he'd kick it with Wasserman in the studio. The two remain close friends three decades later.

Barron Abramovitch, a music engineer and editor for Saban Entertainment who was among the company's first hires, says those on the ground thought of their day-to-day jobs as creating "music by the pound." Working in Saban's music department might not have been incredibly financially rewarding, but it could have been worse. There was ample vacation allotted plus a generous December holiday package (10 to 14 days, depending on the calendar) and plenty of invites to parties held at the Saban residence.

"Those were good times," Abramovitch said. "We had a lot of fun. When you're working on cartoons your whole life, or live action like *Power Rangers*, what better job can you have? And we had a great boss. I know other people have bad things to say about Haim, I'm assuming the composers and stuff, but as far as regular employees like me, he treated us great."

"In the creative world you eat what you kill," Kenan said. "The sad reality is that most starve. . . . At Saban, composers would arrive in the morning to a cushy studio and were provided an assignment on a proverbial silver platter. They didn't have to beat dozens of other talented composers for the privilege. Most came to me fresh from music school with little to no credits and got much of their training on the job. All were talented, but let's face it, how many would have actually gotten these scoring opportunities in the cruel world outside? In the many years that I ran the music division, no one ever wanted to leave. It was a great job for an aspiring young composer. There were many benefits like free use of our state-of-the-art studios for their personal projects and a very respectable, steady income, some at six figures. When it came to eating what you kill, it was Haim who developed, invested in, and sold the shows to the networks and earned that coveted real estate on the cue sheets. I don't begrudge him for a moment.

"Would I like to have credit and royalties for the *Power Rangers*, *X-Men* and other themes I wrote? Sure, but like the rest, I was fairly compensated. We all knew the deal and happily accepted it. Creatively, it was amazing. And good people. We always had really great people. I won't say everybody was happy, you know people always complain, especially after the fact. But now everybody looks back at those days like, 'That was so great.'"

Saban's sizable reputation as a dealmaker is well earned. Loesch's is far less heralded but no less impressive.

The original agreement between Fox Kids and Saban Entertainment called for Fox to pay Saban a licensing fee of just $15,000 an episode. That was the tier allotted for syndicated programs in the only time slot where Loesch could put *Power Rangers*: 7:30 a.m., Monday through Friday. Fox Kids affiliates would also get a small percentage of the show's merchandise sales.

"I bought *Power Rangers* because I thought it was excellent counterprogramming to everything else on TV," Loesch said. "It was unique. It was different. That's what I said to Haim when I first described to him what I was looking for; I wasn't thinking of *Power Rangers*, I was just using adjectives that I felt were important."

Focus-group testing confirmed Loesch's hunch that *Power Rangers* could connect with girls as much as boys, the difference between having a hit and a *hit*. Skeptics still roamed the hallways at Fox, but they quieted into 1993. With production going full throttle, Loesch's next challenge was to convince Fox affiliates that this amalgamation was something they should be comfortable airing.

Smith, with her background in station relations, equipped Loesch with valuable data for affiliates who either didn't quite understand what she was selling or didn't care to try. Going back a couple years, some major affiliates had not wanted to bother with kids TV at all. Now they were being asked to throw their support behind a show that, on the surface, broke with conventional wisdom.

"Margaret really did all the heavy lifting with it," Smith said. "She knew how to talk to these people and present it all. She was such a pro."

Usually, affiliates' complaints were tied to advertising dollars. Before kids programming blocks existed on weekday mornings and afternoons, Fox stations typically aired syndicated classics or news broadcasts. It was easy to get local lawyers and used-car dealers to pony up money to chase adults. The affiliates had a harder time selling national breakfast cereal ads.

"'Now you're bringing us this piece of trash that's not even made here in America,'" Smith said. "Margaret would say, 'Trust me. Channel your inner kid. This is the kind of show they want.'"

The Command Center exterior—actually the House of the Book on the Brandeis-Bardin Campus of American Jewish University—does sit on a hill in real life but not the one seen in the show. Screenshot, Author's Collection

The focus-group data were helpful, as was the revelation that *Super Sentai* had been successful in Japan since the 1970s. There was an entire country—roughly 5,520 miles from Los Angeles—whose children had endorsed the source program for 16 years. What could it hurt to see how American kids would respond?

Lucie Salhany,[16] who came up through the affiliate ranks and was as respected as any woman in the TV business, was immediately appointed chairman of Fox Broadcasting by Rupert Murdoch when Jamie Kellner resigned in early January 1993. Salhany, a key figure behind Oprah Winfrey and her rise to stardom, became the first woman in U.S. history to lead a broadcast network. One of her earliest trials: Loesch, a close ally, wouldn't shut up about a goofy action show that most of her colleagues felt would flop.

"Whenever I showed clips, they'd cringe and say, 'Oh my gosh, it's horrible, cheap and violent.' And I kept saying, 'You're taking this too seriously,'" Loesch said. "It's fun and it's funny. Are kids going to get scared about a pig who eats everything on Earth?"

CHAPTER 4

A Pressing Engagement

It had gotten an order. Now Saban Entertainment had to reinvent how to make a television show—and on a budget that was modest, to put it mildly.

In an interview with *Broadcasting & Cable* published a couple weeks before the show premiered, Haim Saban said *Mighty Morphin Power Rangers* would cost "upwards of $600,000[1] per episode" to produce. He noted that his estimate included Toei's cost to produce the footage it supplied to the American production, which on average accounted for more than seven minutes of each episode's run time (typically about 20 minutes and often less than that, including credits). With that in mind, it's reasonable to assume that the cost to produce the original pilot for *Mighty Morphin Power Rangers*—$200,000—was close to the per-episode amount spent by Saban Entertainment throughout the first season. If one is generous and assumes that Saban Entertainment's up-front investment was more than half the budget estimated by its founder—let's say $400,000 per episode, or $16 million for the 40-episode order—it would still have cost his company little compared to other kids shows. Ahead of its 1992 debut, Loesch said the Fox Kids hit *Batman: The Animated Series* was "the single most expensive[2] 65-episode order of an animation series ever." It cost more than $30 million. Of all the criticisms about to come *MMPR*'s way, "cheap" was the most earned.

But the pilot, as a proof of concept, showed that cheap could lift kids out of their chairs and send them running, shouting, and kicking. The guiding plan, dating back to the early 1980s, seemed simple enough: dub action-packed Japanese footage and marry it with local shots to create an illusion that the people wearing spandex were the same as those sipping smoothies minutes earlier. The concept wasn't uninspired: the Americanization of *Gojira* features made-for-America inserts starring Raymond Burr as a reporter commenting on Godzilla's destruction, and *Robotech* managed to manufacture 85 episodes from parts of three unrelated anime series. But *Power Rangers* would require a greater suspension of disbelief about who was behind the visor. The pilot showed that kids wouldn't call into question what they were seeing—the illusion worked—but how might it play out over the course of several weeks? Months? Years? Decades?

When the first five Power Rangers posed for this press-release photo, they had no idea that within a few months, their characters and show would be the No. 1 topic among children across the world. Courtesy The Morphin Museum/© Saban Entertainment

"On the surface it looks like a dream," Loesch said. "'Oh, we've got this live action show. We only have to recreate the outer edges of it. Everything else, the Japanese footage, we can keep.' Well, it didn't quite work out that way. It became a complicated process. I think Haim's team did a very good job, especially under the circumstances—the circumstances being no time and no money."

Burbank, California, on average gets about 15 inches of rain in a weather season, most of it falling in the winter. After five months with nary a sprinkle in the 1992–1993 season,[3] December brought about six inches. January delivered double that.

Tony Oliver knew that the pilot needed work but also had 39 other scripts to worry about. He took the lead on getting "Day of the Dumpster" ready for broadcast along with Shuki Levy; Saban's longtime partner had been "semi-retired"[4] but reemerged to help bring *MMPR* across the finish line. Oliver could supervise and get additional scripts into the shape as needed for shooting, but *MMPR* needed more writers—ones who could afford to work for a small sum while also learning how to write for a new kind of television show.

On one of the year's rainiest days—nearly three inches fell—Oliver and Co. held an open call for writers. Among dozens who piled into a conference room that day, Stewart St. John stood out for two reasons: he wore a long, black trench coat to shield himself from the unusual precipitation, and he was the last person to sidle in. He was late and couldn't find a seat, so tried his best to blend into the back wall.

St. John had written some episodes of *Tom and Jerry Kids* and *Droopy: Master Detective*, two Hanna-Barbera shows that aired on Fox Kids. He'd earned that work through a spec script for the *Beetlejuice* animated series; St. John slipped it under the door of Neal Barbera, son of studio cofounder Joe Barbera. It was the first animation script St. John—who in high school wrote his own soap-opera series, inspired by his love for *Dallas*—ever wrote.

"The next Monday, I got a call from my agents, and they were really mad that I did this," St. John said. "But also, really happy because they'd given me a two-year contract and Joe wanted to meet me. I got to sit with him once a week. He must've been 80-something at the time. We'd go to his office and sit there, with all of his Oscars and Emmys and everything for all the shows that he'd done, and [I got to] really learn the craft of writing animation."

As much as he grew to love working in cartoons, St. John had come to Los Angeles to do live action. His agents were quick to let him know about the open call for *MMPR*. He leapt at it without hesitation—it didn't matter that it was for a kids show. He was eager to tackle the medium head-on.

Oliver played footage from the pilot for the writers turned sardines.

"I just saw superheroes, live action, actors, and real sets," St. John said. "Sign me the hell up. I'd been dreaming of this since I was 18. There were writers there that didn't have any idea what they were seeing. There were guys there who were like, 'I don't care what I'm seeing, I need a job.' For myself, I was excited because it seemed like the natural next step for what I really wanted to do and have fun with."

After the presentation, producer Ellen Levy-Sarnoff addressed the room and gave them a simple task: write a five-minute scene for the show they'd just watched. St. John, always a fast worker, scurried to his condominium in Woodland Hills and wrote five pages of soapy dialogue tied to a minor crisis involving the Power Rangers. A decade earlier, role models George Perez and Marv Wolfman captivated comic-book readers with their own teenage heroes in *The New Teen Titans*. St. John saw this as "a comic book come to life," one that could captivate kids the same way he'd fallen in love with their stories.

That same soggy Friday, St. John faxed his sample to Saban Entertainment and anxiously awaited through the weekend. Another fortuitous Monday call came from his agents, this time all smiles. One meeting with Levy-Sarnoff later, St. John was hired—not just as a writer but also as a story editor, along with Mark Hoffmeier. They'd help guide the entire first season of script development and the creative course for a first-of-its-kind program. Not many who worked on *Mighty Morphin Power Rangers* ahead of its launch fully understood what the show could be. Even fewer thought it would succeed. But St. John was wide-eyed.

"Comic books, they're like soap operas for kids almost in the fact that they continue on and there's a lot of depth to them that people at the time didn't realize," St. John said. "We're seeing it in the Marvel movies now. But that's what I gravitated toward, and I saw *Power Rangers* as a canvas for me to be able to do that. A little bit of camp, a little bit of drama, a little bit of action."

And a whole lot of glue.

Before any episode of *MMPR* could be written, available footage from *Zyuranger* had to be parsed through and dissected for its usability. Some cuts were easy. Anything that showed the civilian cast of *Zyuranger* was clearly off the table. The same held for any footage involving other visible Japanese faces in the foreground, with the necessary exceptions of Witch Bandora (turned Rita Repulsa) and Lami, a female character who appears about one-third of the way through *Zyuranger* and was adapted as Scorpina. In fact, the villain carve-outs were so important that, as part of its agreement with Toei, Saban Entertainment commissioned additional footage of "the players who perform the role of the Sorceress character and her disciples"[5] to be shot in Tokyo over two eight-hour days (with a one-hour lunch break). This shoot resulted in 70 unique scenes used in *MMPR*, as cataloged extensively by *Power Rangers* historian John Green.

While the effect- and stunt-laden battle footage from *Super Sentai* fueled *MMPR*, it couldn't be copied one to one into the adaptation. Broadcast standards and practices had already run Fox Kids through the ringer with *X-Men*; their new "live-action cartoon" presented a whole new window to jump through for would-be-angry parents. A sword visibly connecting with the face of a rubber-suited monster was perfectly acceptable in Japan; the only chance that could make it Stateside would be if a barrage of sparks covered up the strike. And even that wasn't guaranteed to pass the censors.

Sifting through the footage to assess its fitness required producers to be able to watch *Zyuranger*, which proved complicated. Saban Entertainment received 16-millimeter prints—not negatives—that then had to be converted to videotape and later hacked away at because of how the original print had been spliced. Hot glue was rampant and resulted in highly visible jumps throughout the video.

"It was crazy," said Paul Rosenthal. "So, we went through and pulled out those hot splices as much as we could, but without taking too much, because otherwise you'd still have these weird jumps. 'Oh shit, we're missing two frames there, it's gonna look funky.' Sometimes you could blow up the image to lose the splice, but sometimes you'd get to a jump and just be like, 'Oh well, I guess we have to take it out.'"

Rosenthal, *MMPR*'s postproduction supervisor, was the postproduction coordinator for the Emmy-winning CBS crime drama *Jake and the Fatman* before landing at Saban Entertainment. As far as live-action credentials were concerned, the 27-year-old was the belle of the ball when he walked into Saban's office, where he interviewed with Saban and another producer, Ronnie Hadar.

"They showed me the pilot and I'm like, 'What the hell is this? This is insane,'" Rosenthal said. "I thought, what the hell, if they offer me the job, I'll take it and it'll be a few weeks' work."

A few weeks of work, for Rosenthal, entailed much more front-end involvement than was typical for people in his role. After he converted the prints to video, those tapes were handed over to another editor responsible for removing the indisputably unusable footage. From that point, the tapes were delivered to writers, who took the first crack at deciding how to build a story within the confines of whatever footage remained—while, preferably to Saban Entertainment, choosing to use as much of that remaining footage as possible.

One frequently used plot device from *Zyuranger* that became an early crutch for *MMPR*: kidnapped children. Bandora on the surface appears to loathe children; they're often at the center of her bad deeds. By show's end, we learn that she lost her own son in his youth, and it's implied that her actions were driven, at least in part, by grief and envy. Child-driven plots of the day carried over to quite a few episodes of *MMPR*—though they'd never appear to be in as much mortal danger as their Eastern counterparts.

Take, for example, the episode "No Clowning Around," one of the first eight episodes produced and the tenth to air, but officially recognized as the show's eleventh episode. In it, the Monster of the Day—Pineoctopus—transforms Trini's cousin Sylvia into a cardboard cutout. That's a scary predicament, especially for a young child in a pre-Fathead world. But in *Zyuranger*, Bandora used Pineoctopus equivalent Dora Endos to distribute a powder that subjected people to fatal sneezing fits. Suddenly, getting turned into a human standee doesn't sound so bad.

Sylvia suffers her fate because she ran off with Pineapple the Clown, outright ignoring advice Trini gave her minutes earlier. If you boil down "No Clowning Around" to a single word or phrase, it's "stranger danger." Most early *MMPR* scripts were constructed around general themes or ideas rather than specifically tailored narratives. Anything resembling character development was largely dependent on a Power Ranger's place in the footage pecking order.

"You'd give the writers a VHS tape and say to them, 'Here's your footage, go write an episode about the Yellow Ranger that has to do with courage,'" said Judd "Chip" Lynn, a unit production manager on the first season who started writing for the show in the second season. "That was all the instruction the writers got. You had to be somewhat familiar with what had happened in the show before that point, but it wasn't very serialized. To some degree that was on purpose, because they knew the episodes would often be aired out of order or kids might watch them out of order. They didn't want anybody to be confounded by having missed an episode."

Case in point: the first episode of *MMPR* broadcast after the premiere was "Food Fight," written by Cheryl Saban and officially the sixth episode. In it, the Rangers face off against Pudgy Pig, an endearingly grotesque bipedal pig sporting a Spartan helmet. After he dives through a dumpster and interrupts a couple's picnic, our heroes combat Pudgy Pig with their iconic Power Weapons—Jason's Power Sword, Zack's Power Axe, Kimberly's Power Bow, Trini's Power Daggers, and Billy's Power Lance. Leaning hard into his modus operandi, this Monster of the Day wolves down every weapon without a hint of indigestion. The Rangers remain without their own meal-prep tools until making a keen observation:

Pudgy Pig, while bingeing on leftovers from an international food festival at the Angel Grove Youth Center, left the spicy radishes untouched. They trick him into eating the heartburn inducers during their next tussle and use their regurgitated weapons to end his suffering.

It's a delightful episode that touches on so many of the aspects that helped make *Mighty Morphin Power Rangers* stand apart in its time and persist 30 years later: nothing says "live-action cartoon" more than a guy in a pig costume running around a juice bar, throwing popcorn into his mouth. But in the context of a season-long narrative—no matter how episodic—it's weird to watch it prior to "Teamwork," the third episode and wherein the Power Weapons are first introduced. It aired four days after "Food Fight."

As far as stakes go, the threat posed by Pudgy Pig is more existential than concrete—he's hurting humanity by way of his mouth, not his fists. He's also the most slapstick villain among the early Monsters of the Day, if not the entire first season—so Fox Kids thought it might go over more smoothly with critical parents and special interest groups. "Fun and funny," right?

Folks like postproduction supervisor Paul Rosenthal (right) and editor Adi Ell-Ad (left) were essential to bringing episodes of *Mighty Morphin Power Rangers* to their final form. Rosenthal was part of the crew from the start, while Ell-Ad joined during production of season 1. Courtesy The Morphin Museum/© Saban Entertainment

The key words in Margaret Loesch's defense of *Power Rangers* colored every aspect of its production, but fun and funny are, of course, subjective. Take fart sounds, for example. Fox Kids' president wasn't amused when she saw the penultimate cut of "Food Fight," which had a couple of fart sound effects mixed in during the portion where Pudgy Pig devours the Rangers' weapons.

"Haim and I showed it to her and she's like, 'Now guys, we can't do any farts in this,'" said Rosenthal. "And I was like, 'Come on, this is for 5-year-old, 6-year-old boys. Farts are funny.' She goes, 'No, farts are not funny.' And then Haim's like, 'Ah, Margaret come on, farts are funny.' She says, 'No farts, Haim.'"

In the elevator as they left the meeting, the future billionaire continued to lobby for potty humor.

"Haim looks at me and says, 'Put farts in it if you want,'" Rosenthal said. "We went back and basically covered every movement of this monster with a fart, so everything was just pfft, pfft, pfft, and then sent her the episode. Margaret said, 'Fine, do what you want.'"

Adrian Carr directed only four episodes of *Mighty Morphin Power Rangers*. Three of them, assuredly, have been seen more than most in the series' vast canon.

They include the first two official episodes—the final broadcast cut of "Day of the Dumpster" and "High Five," an episode centered around Trini's fear of heights—as well as "A Pressing Engagement" and "No Clowning Around." The first two, as well as the one featuring a clown who turns little kids into cardboard, were among the first five episodes simultaneously released on VHS tapes when that medium was the be-all and end-all.

Carr met with Saban and Levy, who showed him the original pilot and said they wanted to alter its vibe. They wanted the teenagers to be more appealing and the violence tempered. They knew they didn't have the greatest actors in Hollywood, but they loved their chemistry and physical gifts and sought (affordable) directors who could bring out the most from them. Carr, who'd directed martial artist and fellow Australian Richard Norton in 1989's *The Sword of Bushido*, was a recent transplant to the United States. For two decades, he'd worked mostly as an editor for popular TV dramas in his home country—*MMPR* was an opportunity he felt he couldn't pass up.

His first day on set was purely observational. Carr was set to direct the show's second block of episodes and wanted to get a sense of the actors as well as a feel for the unique manner in which the show was shot.

The first director to shoot a scene of *Mighty Morphin Power Rangers* after the original pilot? Jeffrey Reiner, whose career since has included stints on more than 40 TV shows, among them *Friday Night Lights*, of which he was also an executive producer. At that time, though, Reiner's biggest claim to fame was either *Blood and Concrete*, an R-rated film starring Billy Zane, or a segment for the Playboy soft-core porn anthology *Inside Out*.

Each shooting "block," in the early going, was made up of four episodes. Over the course of seven to nine days, crews collected daily footage for those four episodes, working under one guiding principle: efficiency. Any scenes that took place on the Command Center set, for example, were shot on the same day, the only distinguishing element most of the time being characters' wardrobes. In an effort to maximize the small budget of a nonunion kids show, Saban Entertainment unwittingly blazed a trail for production managers across the industry. This practice, now often called "cross-boarding," has become more prevalent in TV production, though rarely for more than coverage used across two episodes.

Collective burnout of actors' memories is an unfortunate long-term outcome of the way *MMPR* was shot. Often asked about their favorite scenes or episodes at conventions, cast members seldom recall what was even happening in any given episode. And why would they? Each day's shoot, militaristic in its design, was structured less toward maximizing their talent than it was their time. If you're shooting parts of four different episodes over the course of little more than a week, eventually it all just starts to mush together—especially when those days started at 5 a.m. and often lasted past dinnertime.

"You'd see them huddled up in a corner on the floor asleep," Carr said. "They were exhausted. People forgot they were teenagers. They weren't seasoned actors who knew how to take their time and pace themselves."

To Carr, it was clear that if sleeplessness didn't eventually derail production, the cast's lack of experience might. Keeping five rookie actors on the same page would have been difficult even if *Power Rangers* were made under typical circumstances. Trying to do it while reinventing TV production on the fly was a whole ordeal.

At a minimum, regardless of skill level, an actor must know what their motivation is in any given scene. Ignorance is easier to see on film than mastery and is especially noticeable in trivial moments—like, say, when you're standing in the middle of a computer-console–filled room for an hour with no lines to read while watching your castmates fumble over theirs. Austin St. John once asked Carr why he was in a scene and expressed concern over what he should be doing. It was an astute question: creatively, why *did* Jason need to be in the shot? Carr couldn't answer that for the writers, but he could provide guidance: sometimes acting is just listening.

"It's a very simple lesson," Carr said. "Just listen, so you don't feel blank or lost. Listen to what the other characters are saying, and that way you'll look interesting and not out of place. He took that and ran with it."

As requested, Carr's version of "Day of the Dumpster" plays it much safer than Strathford Hamilton's, who still managed to have two brief sequences featuring Audri Dubois sneak into the final episode: a distant wide shot of the teenagers exiting the Command Center on foot and a medium shot of an explosion as they're hoofing it. The wide shot was an oversight, but the explosion was intentionally left; Saban didn't want to foot the bill to re-create the boom with Thuy Trang. It's a blink-and-you'll-miss-it frame, but its preservation was paramount to Saban—not so much because he cared about the explosion but because it had already been paid for. "So, I had to try and make it less obvious," Carr said with a laugh.

Directing with an editor's eye helped Carr push through the long, unconventional days. Most feature films during an average shoot day manage to complete about 20 setups, each of which entails the gathering and moving of cameras, lighting equipment, props, set fixtures, and players needed to shoot a scene. An average scripted TV shoot will knock out 25 to 30 setups in a day. *Mighty Morphin Power Rangers*—for which one-third of most episodes were already shot in another country—on a slow day would knock out 40 unique setups. Most days finished closer to 60.

"We would shoot all four episodes in one direction, and then we would do the reverses of all four episodes in that same location," said David Blyth, a New Zealand director whose only four-episode block included scenes for "I, Eye Guy," one of the first scripts penned by Stewart St. John and whose grotesque, titular monster became, ahem, eye-conic. "It was real factory work in a way. It was unbelievable. Of course, it's logical to do it that way, because it's all about time and money."

The four main sets, all designed by Yuda Acco and initially housed in a Culver City soundstage, were built with haste.

The Command Center interior, since most of its fixings had been rented for the pilot, underwent further development. Black curtains arranged around the walls were fitted with Christmas tree lights to improve the lighting and give off a more galactic vibe. The pilot's set featured two columns with six static neon-light rings; a third was added, and the lights changed to flash on and off—sometimes blinking, other times in a descending pattern. To varying degrees of success, these columns also were moved around to create the illusion that there actually were four present in any given scene. The knobs, dials, and screens of its computer podiums were retooled to seem much more futuristic than the pilot's circuit-board patchwork with flickering analog monitors; they also were arranged in a more open circle and painted a bright blue—a calm, orderly color befitting its head occupant, Zordon, digitally housed in a large glass tube adjacent to the podiums. About 20 feet across from the tube, through the computer-console area, was a completely new addition: a yellow-lit cylindrical table with a cloudy, glass fixture atop—the Viewing Globe. Effectively a basketball-sized version of Sphere arena in Las Vegas, 30 years before U2 performed the first show there, it became an essential tool for Zordon to deliver an exposition ("Behold the Viewing Globe!") and showcase additional *Zyuranger* footage.

Angel Grove High School's classroom and hallway were simple but standard for the time—traditional classroom chairs, metal lockers, standard-issue chalkboard. The latter offered a long runway for slapstick gags and the occasional skirmish between characters. The fourth set, though, was the show's MVP.

As timeless as the Command Center feels three decades later, the Angel Grove Youth Center seems of a time that never actually existed but would have been wonderful to experience. Formed from the need for a hangout location that wasn't an expensive-to-rent bowling alley, Acco and his team, on a single two-level set, managed to squeeze a gym fitted with mats, a balance beam, weightlifting equipment, exercise bikes, punching bags, climbing ropes, *and* a full-service juice and food bar, complete with a small arcade.

"[Yuda] really doesn't get props for what he did," said Mark Richardson, the show's prop master. "It was his vision, that low-budget, '80s style juice bar and the Command Center. That was all Yuda."

The Angel Grove Youth Center is the most lived-in set across all of *Power Rangers*—episodes across six seasons featured scenes on this set or a slight variation of it—but it was especially critical in *MMPR*. It could morph as quickly as the Power Rangers themselves.

"Stewart and I, we got paid to rewrite most of the second half of the first season so that they could fit the format," said Hoffmeier, credited with 27 total episodes of *Power Rangers* across eight seasons. "Is there a scene that calls for them to be on a mountaintop with snow? That's gone. There was all this stuff we were trying to figure out. You ended up in a place where the Juice Bar became an everything space, which is frankly what we needed. And I think it was OK to show a place where it was safe for teens to hang out and that they're not going to some alleyway and shooting craps, learning how to gamble or something."

Alpha 5 and the Command Center interior as they appeared in the first pilot for *Mighty Morphin Power Rangers* directed by Strathford Hamilton. Courtesy Yuda Acco

Richardson cut his teeth at Troma Entertainment, a shoestring-budget stalwart, and was the armorer for PM Entertainment prior to working on *Mighty Morphin Power Rangers*. He'd been highly recommended to the production team, but the parties initially failed to connect because they wanted Richardson to come and interview early in the morning; at that time, Richardson was working until 5 a.m. It was Acco who finally made first contact.

"I'd never met the man," Richardson said. "He calls me and says, 'Mark, if you want the job, you can have it. But you have to come in today.'"

He relented and was shown footage to get a feel for what the show was and what they hoped it could become. Unlike most folks confronted with *Zyuranger*, Richardson got it. As a child, he'd developed a fondness for *Godzilla*, *Astro Boy*, and "all these other weird Japanese films" that were much less accessible in his youth than international media are today.

It also seemed to him like a far more earnest attempt to adapt *Super Sentai* for a U.S. audience than the only other previous domestic effort. Five years before *MMPR* recontextualized *Zyuranger* footage with America-slice-of-life inserts, a short-lived parody of *Kagaku Sentai Dynaman*, the seventh *Super Sentai* series, aired as part of *Night Flight*, an adult-targeted variety program on USA Network. To call it poorly dubbed would be an understatement but also dismissive of the clear intent at hand: the source footage is used only as a vehicle through which to tell off-color jokes, in the spirit of Woody Allen's *What's Up, Tiger Lily?* As of December 2024, all six episodes were available via Night Flight Plus, if you'd like to spend time with "five good-looking Japanese friends from all walks of life."[6] If nothing else, it's a curious cultural artifact. Richardson was certain *Mighty Morphin Power Rangers* would leave a more lasting impression.

"I remember being at Bronson Caves with the entire cast and telling them, 'You guys don't understand. This time next year, on Halloween, every one of you are going to be a mask. All the kids are going to want to be you.'"

Bronson Cave, also called Bronson Canyon, is part of Griffith Park, a 4,355-acre behemoth described as an "urban wilderness"[7] by the Los Angeles Department of Recreation and Parks. In 1896, the park's benefactor and namesake, Colonel Griffith J. Griffith, envisioned his donated land as a "safety valve" from urban sprawl. There's no way he could have imagined that a century later, its landscapes would be rife with stuntpeople in multicolored spandex and rubber suits.

Cast and crew frequented Griffith Park and Vasquez Rocks, whose signature formation was composited with the iconic Brandeis-Bardin building to create the illusion that the Command Center sat atop a high mountain. Vasquez features prominently in "Day of the Dumpster" as well as the second episode, "High Five."

The day of the "High Five" location shoot, a giant boulder was moved from another area of the park to further dress a scene in which Trini and Billy are chased by Putty Patrollers. Carr had assumed that all Hollywood rocks were fake until the slab was dropped off at the foot of a narrow foothill with a dolly and a few grips. Fearing for their safety, Carr insisted they stay put and consulted with director of photography Ilan Rosenberg on how to reblock the shot without the boulder, which was to be used to conceal Trini from a bad guy in hot pursuit.

"Twenty minutes later, I turn around and this rock is halfway up the hill," Carr said. "I look at Ilan and go, 'I told them to not do it.' He says, 'That's why they're doing it. They don't want to let you down.' I think that's reflective of what happens when you treat people as human beings and not just commodities on a set. They're not workers, they're colleagues, and that's something you can't buy. Producers don't always understand that."

Despite both parties' interest in his continued participation, Carr left *MMPR* after his four-episode block was completed. Jeff Roberts, a first assistant director, was soon to be dismissed, and Carr didn't want to work without him. "He made sure I got what I needed, and it may have ruffled a few feathers in another department," Carr said. "Haim and Shuki were fine, but there was another area that didn't coalesce with him. . . . I knew I couldn't do what I was doing without Jeff."

Some of the earliest "Monsters of the Day" vanquished by the Power Rangers. From top left, moving clockwise: Bones, Madame Woe, Pineoctopus, Knasty Knight, Pudgy Pig, and Eye Guy. Screenshots, Author's Collection

"No Clowning Around" lit the fuse.

"I had written this thing to be a fair," Hoffmeier said. "I envisioned something where they could just set up static booths, and you could do the milk jugs, throw darts at some balloons, something very easy to set up, with little pop-up tents and stuff in the parking lot. Instead, they got a whole carnival with rides and all this stuff. I was really shocked. I thought, 'they're never going to be able to finish this.' I mean, they did a whole fight with Putties on a Ferris wheel!" The shoot went a day over schedule. "I never felt the pressure as a writer that I think some of those directors felt, because they were actually having to get this on film and do it in 10 days. That's nuts. It was like guerilla filming at its best."

Carr's influence extended well beyond his four episodes. In *Zyuranger*, the heroes wear their "henshin" devices on their belts, for all the world to see. This happens briefly in "Day of the Dumpster" but was nixed further. So from where do the teens retrieve their Power Morpher when needed? Their back pockets, apparently. A brief but memorable retrieval motion, signaling that "It's Morphin' Time," was improvised while filming "High Five." It was used as recently as 2023's *Mighty Morphin Power Rangers:*

Once & Always. Fittingly, Norton, the martial artist with whom Carr had worked years before, inspired it.

"I used to watch his classes sometimes and he did a part of a kata where they would do this breathing exercise and he would end up pushing his energy out," Carr said. "So I go, 'Hey guys, I've got an idea, here's what we're gonna do. We'll bring your hands from behind your back with the Morphers in them and you're going to bring them up and push them out.'"

The phrase "fix it in post" refers to the practice of using digital effects and editing to address an error or mistake not accounted for during principal photography. Typically, it's more cost-efficient than conducting reshoots, even if the results don't always come out stellar.

Mighty Morphin Power Rangers wasn't fixed in post. It was made in it.

"It's an editor's show," said Adi Ell-Ad. "This show is created in the editing room. And that intrigued me."

Ell-Ad had been working for a small trailer house that handled independent and "leftover" work; two of the last movies he helped promote were *Dazed and Confused* and *Reservoir Dogs*. Saban Entertainment brought him aboard midway through *MMPR*'s first season, after he made a foolhardy call to the office of Shuki Levy. Levy's assistant, Nancy Kennedy, picked up the phone.

"I don't know what came out of my brain, but my mouth was saying, 'Hi Nance, this is Adi, is Shuki in?'" said Ell-Ad. "It just came out like that, out of nowhere. And she goes, 'Oh my God Adi, of course, one second,' and suddenly I have Shuki on the phone."

Ell-Ad didn't even know what Levy looked like. The two had never talked before this phone call. After realizing that the Adi to which he was speaking wasn't the one he anticipated, Levy gave the cold caller two minutes to explain himself.

In 1992, AVID Film Composer came to market and slowly consumed the marketplace. Ell-Ad already knew the fledgling software like the back of his hand and confidently told Levy that he wasn't just the right guy for the vacant job but the *only* one for it. After 20 seconds of silence, Ell-Ad second-guessed his swagger. Finally, Levy cut the tension.

"'Tomorrow night, I'll leave you footage for a show,'" Ell-Ad said. "'If I like what you cut, you're hired.'"

He'd never auditioned for a job before, but the prospect excited Ell-Ad. He went to Saban Entertainment headquarters the next night and left with a job into which he could sink his teeth.

MMPR's core reason for existence—mixing Japanese footage with a made-in-America story—was a small part of what made the job inviting. Its scripts were often nonsensical, leaving room for interpretation on the page but also well after filming. The actors were physically gifted, but their on-screen performances wildly varied among one another and from episode to episode. Much of the footage was evergreen, making it either reusable in a pinch or transplantable into an otherwise unrelated episode. An example: for his version of "Day of the Dumpster," Carr shot a scene in which a pot of chili is accidentally poured onto Bulk. It wasn't used in that episode but was deployed as the final scene for the episode "Big Sisters," shot as part of the first cluster helmed by Reiner.

"It was such a fun job because I wasn't just following the script and clipping things together," said Ell-Ad, who relished the creative input he had from his seat. The overall look of the show, managed due to the decision to shoot on 35-millimeter film versus video, made the footage a hoot to work with in the edit bay. So many colors!

"Salute to Ilan for achieving that look, because people thought we were a cartoon," Ell-Ad said. "And that means we did our job, because we wanted it to feel like a cartoon even though it was live-action. When video was invented, nobody shot film anymore on TV, it was almost all recorded on tape. They needed to shoot on film to get the colors they wanted."

Directors, especially those in charge of second-unit action like Isaac Florentine, often worked alongside Ell-Ad to develop the first cut—unheard of at that time in live-action TV.

"I used to have a heavy jacket in my car, because outside it was hot but in the editing room it was like Siberia, it was so cold," Florentine said, laughing. The collaborative spirit at Saban Entertainment showed on-screen. "Everybody is important. The actor, the director, the electrician, the wardrobe department. Everybody is important. And when you have a good crew, you have a great atmosphere, and people are willing, because of that, to walk the extra mile for you."

That it was shot on 35-millimeter film isn't the only thing *MMPR* has in common with the acclaimed drama *Breaking Bad*. Both also feature Bryan

Cranston in vile roles that challenge our notion of what humanity can accept and overcome.

Walter White has nothing on Snizzard, the bipedal snake-lizard with an archery hobby whom the Rangers take down in "Foul Play in the Sky," or Twin Man, a deceptive shape-shifter at the heart of a doppelgänger plot in "A Bad Reflection on You." Cranston voiced both Monsters of the Day about 15 years prior to the start of his spiral from lovable schoolteacher to crystal meth kingpin and nearly a decade before his breakout role in the Fox sitcom *Malcom in the Middle*. Before his midlife career explosion, Cranston was a jobber who booked bit roles across several TV dramas and sitcoms. Often under the pseudonym "Lee Stone"—likely to avoid union wrist slapping—he also voiced anime dubs.

Snizzard and Twin Man essentially were anime villains, just formed out of foam rubber rather than ink. In recollections[8] over the years, Cranston—born on March 7, 1956—says he was in his twenties when he was paid $50 an hour for those voices, but the calendar math doesn't add up. When he tried twice to destroy the Power Rangers, Cranston would have been approaching 40 and fatherhood; his only daughter, actress Taylor Dearden, was born in February 1993.

Cranston is, unquestionably, the most famous actor to lend a voice to the show as part of a process called automated dialogue replacement (ADR), often shorthanded to "dubbing" or "looping." ADR does exactly what it says: replaces dialogue that was recorded or provided as part of filming. It's a much-underdiscussed element of film and TV production— Marvel couldn't have taken over Hollywood without nailing it—and getting it right was essential to making *MMPR* work.

In most episodes, for at minimum one-third of the run time and often much longer, the heroes wear helmets and fight monsters whose mouths are either comically large or immovable. That's been true from the very beginning, when *Zyuranger* footage was milked as much as possible, to the most recent season, *Cosmic Fury*, wherein all of the ground-fight footage was filmed by the *Power Rangers* production team. Every face actor must learn their way around a mic and lean into their performance as much as they would if a camera were pointed at them. And they do all of it while watching their character—portrayed by a stuntperson, not them—fight outrageous monsters, pilot a gigantic robot, or do any number of zany things that might happen within a given 20 minutes. Often too, they had to redub lines for scenes where they had been mic'd up.

Scott Page-Pagter, a keyboardist who dabbled in audio engineering, landed a job in his mid-twenties doing sound effects and ADR work at Saban Entertainment. "Back then you could lie your way[9] into postproduction," said Page-Pagter. For 10 years, he was the guy who guided the show's stars through ADR, shepherded and reworked ADR scripts, and managed the voice-only actors who worked on *Power Rangers*.

"The studio, with us, was always a sanctuary for people cause you got to get away from the madness on set and come in and just play around and be silly,"[10] Page-Pagter said. "That's one of the things that was consistent with every season, whether it was me or someone like me, [we] had to teach all these guys to go, 'Hyuh, ha, yuh.'"

Michael Forest, who appeared on *The Dick Van Dyke Show* and *Star Trek* before a lengthy voice-acting career, told Page-Pagter in 2000—while he was providing the voice for Prince Olympius, a recurring villain in *Power Rangers Lightspeed Rescue*—that the show's actors would eventually have lucrative careers on the convention circuit and that he was part of something that would stand the test of time.

"I said, 'You're out of your mind,'" said Page-Pagter, recounting the exchange 18 years later in front of hundreds who packed a hotel convention hall to hear him and others share memories from the show. (Page-Pagter died from cancer in 2021. "Scott was so special," said Anne Britt Makebakken, who worked with him for *Power Rangers*' first nine seasons. "He really was the glue that held everything together.")

A trio of sound mixers—Tim Harsh, Bob Manahan, and Andrew Somers—brought together the sound effects, dialogue recorded across a multitude of venues, and exhilarating rock music to form a coherent, ear-pleasing package. A single episode required at least 16 hours of audio editorial, followed by about four hours to create the mix. They did it using a Fairlight MFX2, which released in 1991 and had become the industry standard thanks to the breadth and depth of its audio layering and time-tracking abilities. "That was at the very birth of doing digital audio on TV shows," Somers said. "We still had very tight time constraints, and it was a very-low budget show, but I think we were able to make a show that had a lot more layered sound than a lot of shows had up to that point."

If Saban's pet project had landed with network executives any earlier, it's unlikely that it could have looked or sounded as good as it did on a shoestring budget. All the happenstance that helped get *Mighty Morphin Power Rangers* to air mattered, but its inability to get there for so long might have been its greatest stroke of good fortune, if for no other reason than it gave it time to find all the right people to get it off the ground.

"The most professional crew I've ever worked with is the crew in Los Angeles that made *Power Rangers*," said Florentine, who's since directed more than 20 action films, many of them starring widely acclaimed martial artist Scott Adkins. "It was the most dedicated group."

CHAPTER 5

High Five

Mere weeks before it finally aired, *Mighty Morphin Power Rangers* remained on thin ice.

Former Fox Broadcasting chief Jamie Kellner hadn't been a fan, and now neither was his successor, Lucie Salhany. And affiliates were chirping.

Advertisers weren't sold on what they'd seen. Salhany asked Margaret Loesch to satellite a full episode to the affiliates so they could get a better sense of the show. After that, several large affiliates refused to broadcast *MMPR*. Salhany's sentiments to Margaret Loesch, shared via telex, echoed theirs.

"'Please, please, please don't put the show on the air,'" Loesch recalled Salhany saying. "'Maybe I'm too old, but I think this will be a disaster.'"[1]

Loesch and Salhany had a playful running gag—Salhany was ahead in the chain of command, but Loesch was a couple months older. Loesch, midway through packing for a family weekend getaway to Santa Barbara when she received Salhany's plea, capitalized on the chance to snipe back at her superior. She circled "Maybe I'm too old" and again went to bat for the show she'd tried to broadcast for two decades.

"I wrote back, 'You are,'" Loesch said with a laugh. "'It's going to work, you have to trust me. If it doesn't work, don't worry, I have a backup.'"

Loesch didn't have a backup, but if all the naysayers were right, she reckoned she could pick up another cartoon in syndication or fill the time slot with another episode of *X-Men*. As far as Loesch was concerned, the things affiliates and advertisers most feared about *MMPR*—its campiness, cartoon-like violence in a real-world setting, and being "too foreign"— were its biggest strengths. Adults just had to get out of the way and let kids figure it out. Children's imaginations, not Rita Repulsa, were the Power Rangers' greatest challenge.

Salhany's respect for her friend exceeded her own lack of faith. It was Loesch's career to lose, Salhany warned, but she would have her back as much as she could in the lead-up to the premiere. To buoy the show's chances of finding a captive audience, Loesch circled a "sneak peek" premiere date of August 28, 1993, two weeks before the traditional start of TV's broadcast season. Kids who didn't normally watch Fox Kids might be bored enough to check out the show simply because it was new or because it called to mind a recent blockbuster their parents might have taken them to see. *Jurassic Park* premiered two months earlier, and dinosaurs were *in*. If *MMPR* failed to find a captive audience, it would not have been for poor timing.

A production scan from *Mighty Morphin Power Rangers* season 1, episode 12, "Power Ranger Punks." Courtesy Yuda Acco

Loesch began to wonder if ordering a show informed by her own love of kitschy monsters was misguided.

"I had to call Haim and tell him that five of our biggest stations weren't going to air it," Loesch said. "We were nervous. You can only champion something for so long until, when everybody tells you you're wrong, you start to believe it. I never thought we were wrong, but I thought I'd made a mistake because we were getting so much pushback.

"I remember my husband saying, 'Are you sure you want to fight for this?'"

Unsurprisingly, there's very little press coverage of *MMPR* to be found prior to its debut. Not only was it projected to fall flat on its face, but it was a TV show made for *children*. The notion of writing about or critically reacting to media made for kids isn't a common practice among most traditional institutions today; for the *New York Times* or *Washington Post* to pay a reporter in 1993 to write thoughtfully about kiddie fare, Bugs Bunny would have had to leap off the screen and start twerking—in full drag, of course.

In those days, sections dedicated to the fall TV season sometimes carved out a short block dedicated for (typically syndicated) coverage of kids TV, often spotlighting new shows with slightly edited snippets from press releases. The *Chicago Tribune*,[2] as part of a dedicated kids section published on May 4, 1993, offered the rare look-ahead to *MMPR* that was longer than a sentence. The Zoltar name was still in circulation, as was this piece of goofy lore: Rita Repulsa was imprisoned in a cylinder made of a made-up element, zithium, because she lost a coin toss to Zoltar, against whom she retaliated by trapping him in his tube. This background is never canonized in the show, though it was reshared and expanded on as part of an officially licensed story featured prominently in a press-out-and-play package published in September 1994, a full year after the show debuted. In that telling, the life-altering galactic coin toss was a best three out of five, but Zordon rigged the outcome by using magic coins—the Power Coins. One wonders if the wise sage also counts cards.

Broadcasting & Cable, an industry trade magazine, published the show's most substantial prerelease coverage a couple weeks before its "special premiere" date. Author Mike Freeman[3] wrote in his lede, "Take the cult classic *Ultraman*, throw in some Sid and Marty Krofft and a smidgen of *Captain Planet* and you get some idea of Fox's new kids offering, *Mighty Morphin Power Rangers*." It's a description that holds up well and sets the table for the first public comment from Loesch regarding affiliate concerns: "Quite frankly,[4] some of them think I may have gone off the edge on this one."

That article points out that the individual monster and robot costumes from *Zyuranger*—reminder, paid for by Toei—cost upward of $50,000 apiece to produce, which would mean they accounted for about 10 percent of the $600,000-per-episode budget. It mentions that Saban Entertainment had extensive international distribution rights—as defined in the company's original contract with Toei:[5] the entire universe outside of Brazil, Japan, and a few other Asian countries, including China, Indonesia, Thailand, and Vietnam. What it fails to note is the bridge that connected Saban and Toei, without which *Super Sentai* likely would have died prematurely, and *Power Rangers* would not have come to life at all: Bandai.

Spun off from a textile business in 1950 by founder Naoharu Yamashina,[6] Bandai forged its way to the top of the Japanese toy industry but couldn't gain a strong foothold in the U.S. market despite a long track record of toys generally regarded as more durable than domestic equivalents. A rival, Takara, made significant gains in the 1980s with its transforming robots licensed to U.S. toymaker Hasbro, which through a collaboration with Marvel launched a TV show and comic series to sell the reimagined brand: *Transformers*. In the United States, Bandai was recognizable only in markets with significant Asian populations like Hawaii, where dubs of *Kamen Rider* had been a consistent presence through the 1970s, driving steady toy sales.[7]

Frank Ward long admired Bandai. Ward had worked in the American toy industry throughout the 1960s and 1970s but became unenthusiastic about the domestic approach to product—licensing for lunch boxes, pencils, and stationery was hip, but there was little integration between TV producers and products in the toy aisle. The model worked in Japan—why couldn't it work in the United States?

Bandai got on Ward's radar while he was vice president of international sales for Tonka, a producer of toy trucks at that time based out of Minnesota. In 1970, Bandai became Tonka's distributor in Japan, and Ward formed a close friendship with Makoto Yamashina, Naoharu's son, over the decade. In 1980, Makoto Yamashina succeeded his father as president, and he had his heart set on making a bigger impact in the United States. A few years later, Yamashina asked Ward to come aboard and spearhead the company's fledging business in the States. Bandai America, launched in 1978, initially was just two Japanese men importing toys from the homeland.

"I said, 'Well not in New Jersey I won't,'" Ward said, laughing. "I hate New Jersey. He says, 'OK, go wherever you want.'"

Ward lived in California and wanted to stay put. The job was his last as a toyman; just a few years later, he didn't believe there was a robust enough market for the company's products to warrant the existence of his job. But he had an idea to stay employed: Ward wanted to set up an independent TV production company that, essentially, was a surrogate for Bandai. It would facilitate deals to bring to the United States shows in which Bandai had a stake as well as scout out and develop potential entertainment properties for which the company could produce new products. On a whim, he named it Renaissance Atlantic Entertainment. If there was any significance behind it, "I don't even remember," said Ward.

The one-man company's first production to make it to screen, 1991's *Little Dracula*, was an adaptation of a popular U.K. children's book series. It briefly aired during Fox Kids' second season on the air and yielded a colorful, accessory-packed toy line that could be ripe for nostalgic exploitation in a culture that's more warmly embraced all things spoopy.[8] But for all intents and purposes, Ward was "trying to pretend" he was a TV producer when Saban walked into his one-room office, eager to show him *MMPR*'s pilot.

The two had crossed paths a time or two at MIPTV, an annual TV trade show that takes place at the same site as the Cannes Film Festival, while schlepping cartoons. Saban was much better at it "and made a lot more money," Ward said. Based on Ward's recollection, Bandai wasn't even aware that Saban was developing an American TV show based off a Japanese TV show it helped produce—monetarily and materially, as all of *Super Sentai*'s most toyetic elements (suits, Zords, monsters, and so on) were designed by Bandai's in-house studio, PLEX. That Toei had licensed out the footage for international use without Bandai's direct knowledge wasn't a surprise to Ward.

"In Japan, they don't tell each other things," Ward said. "Bandai had a working deal with Toei, but that doesn't mean they knew what Toei was doing at all. They didn't own each other, but they had a shared purpose. With Japanese companies, you always have to remember there are very strange things that you don't know about. You don't ever know who actually is calling the shots. You just don't, even when you're inside."

What both Saban and Ward knew was that if *MMPR* were to succeed on any level, the toy rights holder would need to be a key partner. It made logistical sense for that partner to be Bandai, so it became Ward's job to encourage the company to support development of a new toy line for a reimagined version of a show for which it had already made toys. It sounds easy but wasn't exactly a given since the company's reputation with American kids was essentially nonexistent. While this could enable Bandai to get more mileage out of the costly injection molds used to produce *Zyuranger* toys, it would also mean more expenditures on storage, labor, and transportation on top of its ongoing support for in-production Japanese shows, like the forthcoming *Gosei Sentai Dairanger*. If *MMPR* flopped, it would be another stain on Bandai's Stateside reputation.

Character mattered too, and Toei's faith in Saban to take its product and make something successful wasn't enough of an endorsement. Without Ward, a confidant of Bandai's president, *Power Rangers*' toy rights easily could have ended up with the likes of Kenner, Mattel, or a less adept player in the action-figure game like Tiger.[9]

In Ward, Bandai would have a boots-on-the-ground operative through which it could observe, influence, and—critically—help pay for the show's production. Renaissance Atlantic Entertainment was a coproducer in name, and the checks Saban cashed said as much, but it effectively was a three-word way of writing "Bandai."

"They were putting big amounts of money in my bank account hoping I won't steal it and that I'll use it well," Ward said. "Haim was happy to get the money, but he always worried about me—because look at the number of ways I could have screwed up the whole thing. It was an ideal situation for crooks, and there were a lot of crooks in Hollywood. I wasn't a crook."

After wondering for so long why producers of American kiddie fare were reluctant to meld minds with toy manufacturers, Ward found himself at the center of a budding experiment that embraced it to an unprecedented degree. *Power Rangers'* father was an Egyptian immigrant with a fixation on adapting a Japanese TV show for American kids, and its mother was a Mississippian who refused to let a fun, campy idea escape her grasp a second time without giving it a legit shot. In Ward, the show now had a generous uncle—the kind who'd show up at your birthday party with lots of gifts and maybe an unsolicited opinion about your baggy jeans.

"Power Rangers, on a lot of levels, was personal," Ward said. "The president of Bandai Japan was kind of making decisions based on what I said to him. I can't put it any more simply than that. It's a personal thing. All of these things are, whether you're talking about movies, TV, it's such an ephemeral thing. It often relies on just this coincidental relationship between two people. I don't know how to say it without seeming self-important, but a lot of this depended on people trusting me. I was just in the right place at the right time."

Mighty Morphin Power Rangers' fate was decided over the two Saturdays before its broadcast season officially began on Monday, September 6, 1993.

"Day of the Dumpster," after a flurry of revisions, finally debuted as a "special premiere" on August 28. "Food Fight" aired the following Saturday, September 4.

Two promotional spots were in heavy rotation.[10] The first opens on a close-up of a teenage girl screaming before a rapid cut to a flashing WARNING graphic paired with an alarm bell. Over it, a voice-over starts:
Lock your doors and run to safety.
Now visible: a series of monsters, including Goldar and Pudgy Pig.

Monsters are at large and they're closing in. Our only hope . . .

Cut to more *Zyuranger* footage, this of the heroes' weapons, then them standing in a team pose.

The Mighty Morphin Power Rangers!

The other ad focuses far less on the "scary" monsters and puts at the forefront the Dinozords and the Power Rangers' iconic morphing sequence, tying it all together with the forward tagline, "You thought they were extinct." This one got the most airtime, probably because it was more affiliate friendly. But regardless of which ad, kids were sure to see them if they tuned in to Fox at any point during the week: unlike its competitors, Fox often promoted kids shows during programming windows aimed at older viewers. If *MMPR* flopped, it would be because kids didn't want to see it, not because they didn't know it was on.

On August 26, two days before "Day of the Dumpster" aired, Haim Saban sat in an edit bay picking through footage with some Israeli compatriots: Ilan Rosenberg, the director of photography who'd pinned down the cinematography that made a live-action sci-fi sitcom feel like a cartoon; Ronnie Hadar, the former vice president of Cannon Films and, especially by Saban Entertainment standards, a well-seasoned Hollywood producer; Jonathan Tzachor, a line producer who right away embraced the constraints of the shoestring budget and managed his time (and that of others) with precision; and Isaac Florentine, a director with an incredible eye for action.

As they all finally exited together at 3 a.m., just a bit more than a day until the show's fate would be decided, Saban remained confident.

"'If this does not succeed, it means I know nothing about kids TV and I'm going to close my kiosk,'" said Florentine. "Well, a little bit more than 24 hours later, it became a hit."

That's an understatement. "Day of the Dumpster" pulled an 8.2 rating[11] and a 33 share among kids ages two to 11 nationally, per Nielsen. How does that translate? A rating reflects a percentage of a group that watched a show based on the entire population of the country (so here, 8.2 percent of kids ages two to 11 in America watched "Day of the Dumpster"). A share is also a percentage, but of all the estimated members of an audience that were actually watching TV at that time. Thirty-three percent of kids in front of the tube saw Zordon recruit the Power Rangers.

These numbers weren't just good. They were among the best to date by any Fox Kids broadcast and edged the highest averages put up by any kids show in the preceding 1992–1993 season. This was just a singular taste, and construing that over the course of weeks and months would be foolish, but from the get-go, *MMPR* posted affirmative numbers. Maybe, just maybe, this *crap* was gold.

The second preview was an even bigger indicator. "Food Fight" got dropped at the end of a four-hour morning block that also featured promotional segments wherein the five *MMPR* actors, in character, introduced themselves to viewers while promoting other Fox Kids shows. It delivered bigger numbers than "Day of the Dumpster." The fart-filled affair smelled like a rose by the time overnight reports arrived.

"It was unbelievable," said Loesch. "It was so big that I had to go back to research over and over to say, 'Are you sure this is right?'"

It got crazier.[12] By the end of September, a show that in most markets aired before the start of a typical school day averaged a weekday-leading 6.6 rating and 44 share among kids ages six to 11 and challenged afternoon stalwarts like Fox's own, much pricier *Batman: The Animated Series* for the top spot among kids ages two to 11. Even Lucie Salhany's old pal Oprah Winfrey got caught in *MMPR*'s cross fire; in Los Angeles, where the show went toe-to-toe with the talk-show host at 3 p.m., it put up a 6.9 rating and 20 share to her 6.1/18.

By the second week of October, during which the heavily promoted "Green With Evil" five-part miniseries aired and brought sixth ranger Tommy Oliver into the mix, Mighty Morphin Mania wasn't just ready for liftoff—it was already halfway to Rita Repulsa's palace on the moon.

Loesch wasn't the only parent in disbelief at *MMPR*'s raucous sprint out of the gate. Across the world in a French hotel room while attending that year's MIPCOM—another TV conference hosted at the Cannes site—Saban Entertainment publicist Jeff Pryor delivered Saban the ratings report from the week prior, in which "Green With Evil" aired.

"He looked at it, and I remember him saying, 'Is this a joke?'" Pryor said. "He said to me, 'Is this a mistake?' The numbers, they just blew everything else off the charts."

Pryor faced his boss and for the first time saw something he hadn't remembered seeing: a look of satisfaction. But like a Monster of the Day swelled to epic proportions, its time on Earth was fleeting.

"That lasted for two seconds and then Haim became Haim the hard-charging businessman," Pryor said. "'This is a phenomenon. This is my time to shine.'"

CHAPTER 6

Green With Evil

The first episode of "Green With Evil," a five-part story, begins where many episodes of *Mighty Morphin Power Rangers* start: the Angel Grove Youth Center, a gym, juice bar, or whatever the script called for. Its generous owner-operator, Ernie, was originally intended to be the show's main comedy engine before Bulk and Skull were fully conceived. The late Richard Genelle, a foulmouthed New Yorker who makes no effort to conceal his accent, portrayed him. "I can't repeat most of the jokes he would tell us," Jason Narvy said. "They were always corny, but so much profanity. All the F-words. Working with him was always a blast."

That day, the Youth Center's palm tree–covered walls bore witness to the Angel Grove Martial Arts Expo; such tournaments were frequent around these parts. The Ranger teens, huddled together, offer words and acts of encouragement to their leader, Jason, as he prepares to face a challenger who's new to their quaint locale. We can hear a flurry of "Hiyas!" erupting from the throat of Jason's off-camera foe.

"Thanks guys, but it looks like I'm gonna need all the help I can get," Jason says as the scene cuts to a long-haired teenager sporting a headband and a cutoff shirt, both green. The first time we see Tommy Oliver, he's flying. Jason's opponent is in midair, performing a series of spinning crescent kicks.

"Man, that dude is pumped," says Zack as Billy nods in agreement. "Who is he?"

Trini correctly speculates that he's a new kid in school. Kimberly, wide-eyed, notes that he's "really cute," which prompts, arguably, the best acting display from Austin St. John in his tenure. He emotes dismissively toward Zack and Billy, then back at Kimberly and Trini, now amid a blushing powwow, before looking down and practicing a mini kata, doused in jealousy. Was it acting or genuine envy? The leader of the Power Rangers was handsome too, and more traditionally so than this newcomer—why wasn't Kimberly fawning over him?

The Pink Ranger wasn't the only one hit with instant infatuation. Through her personal telescope, Rita Repulsa is wowed by "that guy"—to this point, he hasn't been named beyond credit text introducing "Jason Frank as Tommy Oliver." She wants him to be her Green Ranger and delights her lackeys with a plan that involves destroying the heroes with "one of their own kind." Back on Earth, Jason and Tommy are midway through their duel, the score even at 1–1. Over the next minute and a half, an exemplary display of martial arts sees Tommy push Jason to the brink of defeat before the latter comes through in the clutch to score two points and end the match in a 4–4 draw. It's the first time that one of the show's heroes has nearly tasted defeat and analogous to the long fight ahead of them.

This all happens in the span of less than three minutes, but it drastically altered the course and cultural impact of a show that, in 16 episodes, already occupied the minds of millions of children. Now the show's soon-to-be-most-beloved character and actor had just crescent-kicked his way into their hearts.

The five-part "miniseries," conceived largely by Stewart St. John, itself received a unique series of on-air promotions that set the stakes and consistently reminded viewers of what was to come for each episode as it originally aired. Serialized arcs weren't exactly foreign in kids TV: *Transformers* in 1986 kicked off its third season with a five-part arc that follows the events of the animated theatrical film released a month earlier. But at the time, networks generally preferred airing episodes whose storylines didn't hinge on a child having seen previous ones. Former Fox Kids frontrunner *X-Men* was something of a trailblazer over the course of its first couple seasons because its producers insisted on tighter continuity at a time when the consideration was an afterthought; that's partly why the show attracted an older audience over time.

The *Zyuranger* footage used throughout "Green With Evil" initially was farmed out to several writers—including a young Gary Glasberg, the longtime showrunner on *NCIS* prior to his 2016 death at age 50—but the returns weren't great.

Stuntman Hien Nguyen (left) poses as Isaac Florentine performs a mock kick toward his face while airborne. Nguyen worked for two seasons of the show, often as part of the Putty Patroller crew, and donned the White Ranger suit for *Mighty Morphin Power Rangers: The Movie*. Florentine was a stunt choreographer and director through several iterations of *Power Rangers*. Courtesy Isaac Florentine

"Ellen [Levy-Sarnoff] had gotten some scripts based on it and it was just not what she was wanting," St. John said. "She goes, 'Can you just look at all this?' I read the scripts and I'm like, 'No, no, no, no, no, no.'"

For St. John, "Green With Evil" was a microcosm of what he believed the show could be at its best: an action-adventure soap opera for kids, rife with drama that extended beyond the confines of a single 20-minute sit-down. He patiently waited for an entire month to see what happened next to the Teen Titans; was it that much to ask a kid to wait 24 hours to see if Jason could escape from Goldar's clutches in the Dark Dimension? "It felt very comic-booky, and so I begged Ellen, 'Please call Fox Kids,'" said St. John, who was shocked when Ellen came back within the day, green light in hand. "This has got to be the most exciting thing kids have ever seen."

St. John remembers feeling like a kid again when he saw promos for the miniseries air for the first time on the Los Angeles Fox affiliate. He doesn't know where the tapes are now, if they even still exist, but he feverishly recorded every episode. Prior to broadcast, he felt like he'd helped create something special. In the short term, the suspicion was confirmed via runaway ratings. Three decades later, his story remains the only five-part episode in the show's history, and the character he delivered stands alone.

"It was everything that I loved," St. John said. "He's planted inside the group. There was the romance that I wanted between him and Kimberly, which was very much what I thought kids would respond to at the time having come out of comic books. I thought, 'Just let me bring something that takes it to another level,' within the boundaries of it being a kids show.

"I just had the most fun. And to this day, I'm always like, 'I'm the guy—I'm the guy that introduced the Green Ranger.'"

Tommy is an outsider. You're guaranteed to have a reaction, positive or negative, to his arrival before he ever dons green spandex because he disrupts the status quo. Kids at home watched *MMPR* for a month and figured out the formula; the mere existence of a new teenager turned Power Ranger was a massive curveball.

But as much as he had in common with the teenagers viewers already loved—he's good looking and a skilled martial artist and wears an easily identifiable color—Tommy had an edge to him. Following his bout with Jason, the next time we see him is when he white-knights for Kimberly; Skull makes unwanted advances while his partner in bullying, Bulk, eggs him on.

"Hey, didn't you hear the lady? She said 'no,'" says Tommy. His eyes send the message more succinctly. Bulk makes a threat, and then something happens that nearly defied one of the network's rules: through a series of kata, Tommy responds with a clear threat of his own. It's all performative—neither Bulk nor Skull receives a punch or kick—but the *threat* of teen-on-teen violence is enough to send them scurrying. Kimberly fawns over the demonstration, and Tommy goes from lion to kitten in seconds, showing us our first glimpse of the tender, mild-mannered young man underneath the long hair and longer kicks.

The comedown in intensity doesn't last long: wanting to be certain he is worthy of her Power Coin, Rita sends a team of Putty Patrollers to Earth to fight Tommy. The scene, directed by second-unit maestro Isaac Florentine on just his second day of work, was shot in an alley on West 7th Street in Los Angeles—used only in this episode and the next, making it one of the most exclusive locations in all of *MMPR*. The stunt work on display—highlighted by a Putty Patroller, portrayed by suit actor Erik

Betts, who gets struck with a garbage can lid and thrown backward into a stack of boxes—is some of the show's finest. Paired with the site and story beats, it all comes together to create one of the best fights in the show.

How good is it?

"When we shot it, I remember on the rooftops people were standing and cheering," Florentine said. On a plane later that night, he kept replaying their reaction in his mind and for the first time started to convince himself that the show might work. And if it did, he thought, the Green Ranger would *really* leave an impression on them. He was so confident in the character that, when he noticed the suit wasn't brought over for a publicity shoot with the stunt team near the end of their production schedule, he made a call and pleaded for someone to bring it over to the studio. There were only five stuntpeople on the shoot that day, so Florentine donned the costume himself. Within a year, the fruits of his labor were immortalized on VHS box art.

The Green Ranger's costume is most distinguished from the others by a gold shield and matching arm cuffs. The original Japanese adornments were composed of foam rubber, like most of the monster suits, which over time tends to stiffen and crack. That happened with haste to those pieces, prompting the Stateside costume department to deliver a solution for scenes in which the Green Ranger suit appears in American footage. That's why, front and center in the VHS release of "Green With Evil, Part 1," there's visible Velcro in the foreground. Saban Entertainment opted for a cloth shield and cuffs that were *inspired* by the original design rather than a faithful reproduction. The show already tested the limits of illusion building by juxtaposing an Americanized story alongside year-old Japanese footage shot on lower-quality film; this decision, purposefully or not, was an outright admission that the jig was up before it even got underway. The American Dragon Shield is a shiny wink to the fourth wall. That's watching it with the cold eyes of an adult, of course. It's not that kids *didn't* see the difference, but why linger and allow it to distract from the astonishing story about to unfold?

The Green Ranger's first act is terrorism. Since he has a Power Coin, he can enter the Command Center—and gleefully does so. There, he infects Alpha 5 with a virus and berates Zordon before disemboweling the computer terminals, severing the mentor's connection with the world. "Zordon has been eliminated, and the Power Rangers are next," says Tommy, laughing and standing amid fiery modules in a darkened Command Center, its alarms still buzzing with no one to heed them. The makeshift shield doesn't distract one bit from the horror that unfolds. If the Rangers were to overcome this threat, they'd have to go it alone.

Things continued to escalate. Tommy sends Jason to the Dark Dimension, a circular holding cell that, narratively and production-wise, is the Angel Grove Youth Center, but for Rita's crew. Clever camerawork makes the semicircle set feel enclosed and, combined with harsh light and fog machines, creates a claustrophobic effect. For a couple episodes, the Red Ranger and Goldar battle there, physically and mentally, resulting in the show's tensest moments to date; with no escape route and his Power Morpher in Goldar's possession, it becomes a matter of surviving, not defeating, the bad guy. Just as Goldar is about to destroy Jason in "Green With Evil, Part III," Rita sends the Green Ranger to take over; like his predecessor, Tommy spends too much toying with Jason, affording the other Power Rangers just enough time to pinpoint his location and teleport him away as a fatal strike was imminent.

This victory is short-lived; Jason gets enough time to recount his experience before a new recurring villain, Scorpina, joins the fray. By the time "Green With Evil, Part IV" begins, the heroes can't morph due to an energy surge related to their efforts to locate and bring Zordon back to his tube. Billy eventually produces a fix, but while the Rangers are distracted by Goldar—he's targeted Bulk and Skull, trapped on a stolen bus—Tommy returns to the Command Center to derail restoration efforts. This time, though, Alpha 5 was prepared for his hijinks and briefly traps him in an energy field before he flees and joins a decidedly one-sided battle. After narrowly saving Bulk and Skull, the Rangers' Zords fall into Earth, victims of a destructive spell and an incredibly melodramatic eulogy from their drivers.

Richard Genelle appears in more than 100 episodes of *Power Rangers* as Ernie, the owner-operator of the Angel Grove Youth Center Gym and Juice Bar. Genelle, who died in 2008, played the character for the last time in *Turbo: A Power Rangers Movie*. Screenshot, Author's Collection

All seems lost. Back at the Command Center, Jason reminds his down-trodden teammates that the smallest chance of victory is "enough of a reason for us to keep on fighting." Alpha 5 concurs and conveniently has some good news to share: while trapped in the force field, the Green Ranger's "interspatial bio-vibrations" were analyzed to build a visual ID of the person underneath. The reveal shocks our heroes, who spend the bulk of the arc's final episode trying to convince Tommy, in and out of spandex, to turn against Rita. He's having none of it; it's much more fun to take his newest toy, the Godzilla-inspired Dragonzord, out for a destructive spin.

Alas, because of *Zyuranger* footage and the nature of kids TV, Tommy's switch from spellbound baddie to do-gooder was destined. Zordon returns, exhumes the Zords, and informs the Rangers that Rita's hold on Tommy will end if they destroy the Sword of Darkness—a powerful weapon she gave him earlier in the miniseries. It's difficult to stick the landing on any "bad guy turns good" story, but doing so while weaving a sensible narrative conclusion around existing footage was a potential recipe for disaster. It isn't perfect: after four dramatic episodes, watching the spell be undone by a Blade Blaster shot to a flimsy sword is unsatisfying. But it succeeds as a mirror of the moment we met Tommy, when he and Jason sparred to a draw as civilians. The Red Ranger, as he did before, takes the final point, and both emerge victorious—Jason for breaking the spell and Tommy for choosing teamwork.

Back at the Command Center, Zordon lauds the effort displayed by the Rangers and Alpha 5 in his absence before reciting to Tommy the three basic rules of being a Power Ranger. The arc ends with a callback to the celebratory final shot of "Day of the Dumpster." Tommy, hesitant for just a moment, thrusts his hand into the circle of arms and joins the Power Rangers for a joyous leap.

The shot freezes, and Tommy is once again where we first met him—in the air, this time with friends at his side. "Green With Evil" works at its core as a simple "found family" story, one that's representative of the entire franchise. For as much as *Power Rangers* is about being and doing good, friendship is always front and center. The heroes usually have (seldom-seen) families, but the vast majority of 973 episodes revolve around conflicts and situations that strengthen and emphasize the bonds that exist among a group of teenagers—and sometimes adults—who vol-untarily come together for a shared purpose.

Tommy is a stand-in for any kid who ever felt uneasy in a new environment or had obstacles, legitimate or perceived, in their way of making friends. His turn from good to bad to good maybe isn't as emotionally complex as it might be in a show written for adults, but it's a universal plight. We all seek acceptance, even when we know we've messed up. We've all been brainwashed, or at least misled, and required a friendly soul to break our own Sword of Darkness that held us captive. Even children.

As *Power Rangers'* cool accessories and badass robots piled up over decades, Tommy persisted as the show's most popular and recognizable character. Sure, he had a cool shield and the Dragonzord, and that was part of it, but something else elevated him, at least among those watching in 1993. They made an active choice to forgive and accept him, just as their chosen heroes did.

"I was watching from the beginning, but when it cemented in my heart was 'Green With Evil,' because that mini-series got every single kid in my class talking," said Eric Berry, creator of *Ranger Command Power Hour*, one of the longest-running *Power Rangers* podcasts. Berry's family moved from Georgia to Illinois in the summer of 1993, which preceded his entry into middle school. It was a dramatic adjustment for the sixth grader, who struggled to make friends and found comfort in *MMPR*. Based on the conversations he hadn't overheard at school, he worried that none of his cohorts were watching the show. "Now I finally had something to connect with them and talk about. Maybe other kids were secretly watching *Power Rangers* too, cause it never really came up until 'Green With Evil.'

"Everyone says, 'Oh, *Power Rangers* taught me this, that and the other,' and yes, it taught me all those things too. But what it brought for me early on was a sense of community—that you can connect with people through a shared experience. That week of 'Green With Evil' was probably the greatest week of my sixth-grade life. It really helped me make friends and got me to open up with other kids in class. And I didn't feel so alone. Ever since then, I've been a lifelong fan."

Tommy's characterization, depending on one's point of view, was enhanced or dismembered because of the source footage. His counterpart in *Zyuranger*, freed from his own delusions, remains something of a loner and shows up to assist the core team only in times of heightened distress. Also, he dies! The latter was never going to be allowed on American children's television in 1993, but the Green Ranger's haphazard involvement and eventual disappearance from the story had to be accounted for. Kids might have short memories, but Tommy was going to be hard to forget—more so than anyone behind the scenes imagined.

The solution: Tommy often casually forgets that he's a superhero. He leaves his wrist communicator—watch-like devices designed by Yuda Acco and built by Mark Richardson off-screen and invented by Billy on it—in his gym bag while working out, ensuring that he won't be able to respond to a distress call from Zordon or the other Rangers. Other times, he's out of town at a karate meet. In the most forgiving circumstances, Tommy is cut off from the team through the intervention of Putty Patrollers eager to get their asses kicked. The bag of tricks was shallow but effective enough to navigate the footage issue; it just had the side effect of neutering a character who, mere episodes ago, was a one-Ranger army.

The conundrum also afforded a lot of civilian screen time for Jason David Frank, who was still very much getting his sea legs under him.

"None of the kids really had great acting ability . . . and the least of them was Jason Frank," said Robert Hughes,[1] who directed all five parts of "Green With Evil" and 15 others in the first season. "Jason looked great. He could *sky* as a martial artist. The kid was amazing. In fact, I think that Austin St. John was actually very threatened by Jason when he first appeared on the set, because he was so good. But [Frank] was very insecure as an actor. He would ask me after every take, 'How was I? Was I good? Can I do it again? Can I do any better?' I was just there to support and reassure him, and tell him, 'Look, if you can just be yourself, you are Tommy.' Most actors—I don't know whether it's John Wayne or Steve McQueen or Cary Grant, any of the great classic actors—movie stars aren't different from role to role. . . . I said, 'Look if you can be yourself and be natural on camera, the camera already likes you.' I think he really grew into the part and got better and better."

The source footage allowed for a story to be woven around a magical candle that de-energizes the Dragon Power Coin. In a two-parter with an on-the-nose title, "The Green Candle," the Power Rangers bid adieu to Tommy. At that point, he'd appeared in 18 episodes, already more than Frank's initial contract. Written well before the October 1993 airing of "Green With Evil," it was a fine enough send-off for the character and an actor for whom Saban Entertainment had different plans. Encouraged enough by *MMPR*'s initial access, Saban was eager to capitalize on footage from other tokusatsu shows acquired from Toei. *Cybertron*, a planned adaptation of 1987's *Choujinki Metalder*, would see Frank trade his spandex and green wardrobe for techno threads and a leather jacket. Based on the pilot, little seems to separate Adam Steele from Tommy Oliver—both are expert martial artists predisposed to issuing wisecracks—except for the overarching narrative: Steele is a solo hero whose long-missing father has bequeathed a cybernetic suit to fight the evil forces of Grimlord, an interdimensional being moonlighting as a tyrannical businessman. Steele even had his own comedic duo with which to contend, one-half of which was to be played by stand-up comedian Jamie Kennedy.

Frank, a lively, easygoing presence on set who was already familiar with the quirks of creating a show like *Power Rangers*, was a no-brainer to cast for another rushed pilot. Plus, in the words of Saban publicist

Jeff Pryor, Frank "looked like he just fell off a billboard or came from a surfing competition." For a show that hoped to capture a slightly older audience than that for which *MMPR* aspired, having a draw for teen girls was appealing.

There was just one problem: kids *really* loved the Green Ranger. Part 2 of "The Green Candle" first aired on November 18, 1993, a Thursday. The next week, network executives at Fox Broadcasting fielded hundreds of calls from parents whose children had goaded them into pursuing an answer to the question, "When is Tommy coming back?"

The short, factual answer: next week, in an uncredited cameo in "Doomsday, Part II," originally written as the series finale. Tommy shows up at a public celebration of the (morphed) Power Rangers and tells a group of kids, squabbling over which is the best, that "they're all totally awesome." After sharing emphatic handshakes with each of his former teammates, the camera zooms in on Frank's soft grin and lingers for a couple seconds. Months before anyone knew the show was going to resonate, director Terence H. Winkless nailed the coverage for a shot that cemented Frank as a star.

Fox Kids president Margaret Loesch later decreed a more fulfilling, long-term answer.

"Our poor receptionists are like, 'What do I do? What do I tell these screaming, heartbroken parents now that Tommy's gone?'" said Ann Austen, a programming executive with the network. "And Margaret said, 'Tell them he's coming back.'"

Loesch got on the phone with Haim Saban. Cybertron might have been able to defeat Grimlord, but he was no match for the distraught youth of America.

CHAPTER 7

A Pig Surprise

Ahead of Christmas 1993, VHS distributor PolyGram expected to ship 1 million units of its five *Mighty Morphin Power Rangers* tapes. Each featured a single episode—"Day of the Dumpster," "High Five," "Food Fight," "Happy Birthday Zack," and "No Clowning Around"—which collected a diverse swath of what the show brought to the table. Each cover featured an illustrated graphic of an original Power Ranger fighting the episode's Monster of the Day in the foreground, their personal Zord in the background and—most unusual—a five-headed panoramic graphic that shows the teen and Zord blending together to form the Ranger's helmet. There are a number of parallels that can be drawn between *MMPR* and *Animorphs*, a popular teen-centric Scholastic book series that started in 1996, but this artwork is uncanny. It elicits the same feeling of "curious discomfort" on which the covers of those books thrived.

"This is the zaniest, wackiest, craziest thing you've ever seen, but it works because kids get it and they know that their parents don't," Bill Sondheim,[1] PolyGram's senior vice president of sales and marketing, told reporters in December 1993. The company was selling more than 100,000 *MMPR* VHS tapes a week. "Kids want a product that their parents don't get."

The brightly colored lovechild of Margaret Loesch and Haim Saban now was a pop-culture obsession. Any mocking now came from outside the house—*Chicago Sun-Times* TV critic Ginny Holbert wrote that *MMPR* "is badly written, poorly acted and filmed with all the professionalism of an eighth-grade media project."[2] Hers was more representative of the media at large, but there were outliers like Kinney Littlefield, charmed by the show's "cosmic stir-fry of Spielberg, cyborg and the 'Wizard of Oz'" and its irresistible cast. "They may play Power Rangers, but Austin

St. John, Amy Jo Johnson, Walter Jones, Thuy Trang and David Yost are about as-to-die-for as anyone on 'Melrose Place.'"[3] Institutional takes didn't matter at this point: historic ratings were validation enough. And the holidays were kerosene.

Most coverage in the months following *MMPR*'s premiere focused on its unnerving appeal among children and their clamor for merchandise connected with the show—especially its toys. Why could PolyGram push out so many tapes aimed at making every day a "Mighty Morphin Day?" Because toys for the top-rated kids show in the country were sparse. Bandai America projected that the line would perform decently at retail, and toy-aisle receipts in July and August signaled that the show might work, but—like everyone else involved with *MMPR*—there was no reason for the company to believe it would become the hottest thing going.

At least 30 different action-figure lines were showcased in February during the 1993 Toy Fair, an annual exhibition for toy makers and retailers to rub elbows and forecast what's likely to blow up in the coming year. Event recaps by the *New York Times* and *Washington Post* didn't mention *MMPR*. Paul Valentine,[4] an industry market analyst for Standard & Poor's, told the *Providence Journal* in December 1993 that he couldn't even remember anyone talking about *MMPR* at the show. Toy distributor Stephen J. Sandberg told the paper that informational and promotional overload from the biggest players—Hasbro, Kenner, and Mattel—often begot ignorance about goings-on at "secondary companies"[5] like Bandai. Peter Dang, the American division's vice president of marketing, sales, and development, showcased clips from the show at that year's expo.

"The reaction from buyers was mixed at best,"[6] Dang said. "There were some pretty good indications it would be successful. But there was no indication of the breadth and depth of acceptance."

Whoops. Parents camped in front of Toys "R" Us stores waiting for inventory trucks to arrive, hoping to emerge from their sleeping bags fast enough to snag one of 18 unique products available in the initial toy line. The Deluxe Megazord and Deluxe Dragonzord, fully transformable versions of the on-screen robots, were the hottest commodities. Megazord retailed for a suggested price of $29.99, or about $63 in 2024 when adjusted for inflation. Dragonzord was a slightly better deal at $24.99, especially since it came packaged with an eight-inch scale action figure of the show-stealing Green Ranger. The other eight-inch Power Rangers—each sporting a far-from-show-accurate insignia of their Power Coin symbol in the middle diamond of their costume—sold for $7.49 apiece. Considering the hardness of plastic, larger-than-typical scaling, and overall tooling, these figures would still be a steal if they released today for their inflation-adjusted price of $14.64.

SORRY, WE DON'T MEAN TO PLAY HARD TO GET.

We at Bandai America would like to take this opportunity to apologize for any difficulty you might have experienced in finding Mighty Morphin Power Rangers toys. We are doing everything possible to produce enough Power Rangers toys to meet the demand. Thank you for your patience and understanding. We promise, we won't be hard to get for long.

AMERICA

When *Mighty Morphin Power Rangers* became an unexpected juggernaut, toy manufacturer Bandai America couldn't meet demand. Ahead of that holiday shopping season, it issued an "apology" ad via newspapers across the United States and elsewhere. Bandai America

Of course, there were eight-inch bad guys to beat up at playtime: Baboo, Squatt, Goldar, and King Sphinx made up the initial assortment of "Evil Space Aliens." Baboo and Squatt are peculiar inclusions since the two never actually do battle with the series' heroes, but they're in every episode along with Finster, who the following spring joined the assortment. Curiously missing was Rita Repulsa, who at one time was advertised as part of a fall 1994 assortment of five-inch action figures. That figure never materialized, and the original Power Rangers' archnemesis waited almost two decades to be plasticized.

The line's priciest item, ringing in at a gnarly $39.99, was Titanus the Carrier Zord, a large, motorized toy required to form Ultrazord—a combination of all the Power Rangers' giant machines. Often forgotten are the three "Battle Bike" toys, which retailed for $9.99 but had the most inherent playability of the line after the Megazord toys; available in red, blue, and black, each came with a four-inch scale figure, a Blade Blaster, and a motorcycle on which the hero could ride. Unfortunately, similar four-inch scale figures of the Yellow and Pink Rangers—represented only by sidecars on the Black and Blue bikes—never arrived. Even easier to forget is the five-inch-scale Megazord, more of an action figure than a transforming toy, though, at $9.99 and packed five in a case, it was easier to afford and find compared to its fully functional counterpart.

The best value, in the short term and as a long-term speculator, came in the form of a $16.99 role-play set that included toy versions of the Blade Blaster and Power Morpher. The Blade Blaster—here called the Power Gun/Sword, a super-rare instance where the brand uses the word "gun"—leaves a lot to be desired in terms of show accuracy but is a fun toy; it features lights and sounds and, like in the show, can seamlessly transform from blaster to sword. Even cooler was the Power Morpher, which also had electronics and came with all five of the original Power Coins. Aside from different sticker applications, it looked almost identical to the one used in the show.

That's because it was: Bandai provided prop master Mark Richardson with finished molds of the Morphers used for the *Zyuranger* toy line. The original toys featured four black stickers and two red stickers: a top one that read "Zyuranger" and a bottom printed with "Kyōryū Sentai." For the American toy, the black stickers were carried over, and the red ones were changed to "Mighty Morphin" and "Power Rangers," but in the show, the red stickers were split into "Power" and "Rangers," while the black stickers were removed to mitigate peeling. For the show, the "Power" and "Rangers" stickers were applied in a manner that lined up with how they appeared when lined up against their Japanese counterparts—that is, if looking directly at the Power Morpher, the red activation button is in the lower left. Not as much attention to detail was paid when the stickers were mass applied for the American toy, so the activation button is in the upper right. It's a single toy, but it embodies all of *MMPR*'s absurdity, chaos, and inconsistency.

Wildly, neither it nor the Blade Blaster received a rerelease after arriving as part of the initial assortment. There was never a "Tommy Edition"—his Power Morpher had matte gold paint versus the gray of the core five—or any variants released from the 1995 feature film, wherein each Rangers' device had a chrome finish with painted flourishes that matched their respective color. The eight-inch Power Ranger molds were reused and repurposed, sometimes with and without additional action features, all the way through 1998's *Power Rangers in Space*; that the original Power Morpher was confined to 1993 was a blunder that became readily apparent once eBay arrived. Opened and worn-out Power Morphers regularly commanded hundreds of dollars until Bandai released a higher-end version that came out in 2013. By 2025, several collector-aimed versions of the Power Morpher had been released, along with multiple Tommy Oliver editions too. After-market sales of used 1993 editions still regularly sell for about $100; sealed versions have gone for as much as $400 in the past couple years. It's hard to beat an original.

Naturally, some didn't buy the party line from Bandai that it was caught unaware by *MMPR*'s success. As far as parents were concerned, the relatively unknown toy manufacturer was a Grinch from the East, here to spoil Christmas for the entire family through the deployment of campy propaganda and intentionally short supply.

"Sneering clerks[7] in three stores behave as though I've asked for gold bullion when I inquire whether they have these items in stock," Anna Quindlen wrote in December 1993 as part of her Pulitzer Prize–winning *New York Times* column. "Driving home, I wonder who to blame: retailers, manufacturers or the child who waited until November to articulate a need more profound than the need for food or water."

As retail orders soared in the lead-up to the holidays, Bandai ratcheted up production—factories in China, Hong Kong, and Thailand were open 24 hours a day to boost manufacturing tied to *Mighty Morphin Power Rangers*—and began delivering more of its toys by air rather than sea, but it was far too late and too little to satisfy demand. National spokespeople for the biggest retailers warned that their chains didn't expect a steady supply of merchandise until January at the earliest. This is where Bandai flexed its marketing muscle: the company rolled out in-store signage and newspaper ads that effectively functioned as rain checks for guilt-ridden parents to put under the tree in lieu of a Megazord. Some featured art of the Red Ranger, who best matched Bandai's red-and-white logo, and a nine-word headline: SORRY, WE DON'T MEAN TO PLAY HARD TO GET!

"We at Bandai would like to take this opportunity to apologize for any difficulty you might have experienced in finding Mighty Morphin Power Rangers toys," the ad copy reads. "We are doing everything possible to produce enough Power Rangers toys to meet the demand. Thank you for your patience and understanding. We promise we won't be hard to get for long."

While it was nigh impossible to find his action figure, fans living in Los Angeles had an opportunity to meet Jason David Frank the week before Christmas. A hastily thrown together appearance at the Topanga Plaza mall in Canoga Park on December 18, 1993, drew a crowd of more than 5,000 people, including 11-year-old Brian Hansel, whose father drove him two hours to be the first in line at 7 a.m.

On the same day, only about 20 kids sat on the lap of Santa Claus. Jolly Ol' St. Nick would be there tomorrow, or Monday, or next year. The Green Ranger was more important.

"This is phenomenal,"[8] Frank told the Associated Press. It was nothing compared to what was around the corner.

No one involved with *Mighty Morphin Power Rangers* will ever forget how they spent Presidents' Day 1994.[9]

On February 21, the six Power Rangers actors, along with Jason Narvy and Paul Schrier, were scheduled to perform a series of shows—in their respective characters' costumes, sans helmet—on the stage of the American Tail Theater, a 2,000-seat venue at Universal Studios Hollywood. The night before, park officials started to think those accommodations wouldn't work, so they arranged for the shows to be held at its 6,000-seat namesake amphitheater. It was a prescient consideration but did little to ease the coming groundswell.

Margaret Loesch at the time lived in the Toluca Lake neighborhood of Los Angeles, less than a 10-minute drive to Universal City. Early that Monday morning, she received a phone call directing her to turn on her TV. "There was a reporter in a helicopter over the freeway that led to Universal Studios," Loesch said. "They showed a traffic jam like I had never seen in my life. It was unbelievable."

An eight-mile backup on the 101 Freeway prompted the California Highway Patrol to close two exits to the amusement park. The loftiest estimates put the day's total number of attendees at 50,000, while the lowest projected "more than 30,000." Depending on which estimate you believe, it either was or is the largest single-day crowd in the park's 60-year history; according to Universal's own reporting in 2017, more than 40,000 people who visited on January 2 of that year set the record. For $29.95, attendees received a day's admission and got to spend about 45 minutes watching the Power Rangers answer questions from the audience, perform light stunts, and heavily promote the values of staying in school, embracing teamwork, and abstaining from drug use (proceeds from the event supported the Drug Abuse Resistance Education program).

Ann Austen, the Fox Kids programming executive, had the unenviable task of warming up the crowd prior to each show.

"I won't say I was booed, but when I walked out and was doing my little spiel thanking everyone, I could just feel the, 'Get out of here, where's the Power Rangers?'" Austen said with a laugh. "That was the first time I saw children and the joy on their faces. The anticipation and the excitement. I was like, 'Wow, we have touched a nerve. This is really, really connecting with these kids.' That was powerful."

Amy Jo Johnson felt like a rock star and acted accordingly, shouting into the microphone before light scolding from park officials concerned for kids' eardrums. Adrenaline fueled her through the day's performances; alone with her thoughts that night, anxiety won. "It was too much for me," Johnson said. "I went home and had horrible nightmares."[10]

Hysteria sustained. A few weeks later, Frank and Johnson represented *MMPR* at Kids Stuff Expo, a trade show in Anaheim. About 20,000 fans showed up to see the on-screen power couple. Vendors took advantage of the captive audience: one toy merchant, Alan Saffron, moved more than 11,000 items that day. "All of a sudden it became mobs and mobs of people,"[11] Saffron told the *Orange County Register*. "We won't be able to come back tomorrow because there'll be nothing left." In October, 32,000 people showed up at the Toys "R" Us store in Manhattan to meet the Power Rangers; event planners had prepared to accommodate a sixth of that.

In September of the same year—barely 12 months after the show premiered—Frank, Johnson, and David Yost made appearances, out of costume, during a Labor Day event at Aloha Stadium in Honolulu. Their arrival time at Honolulu International Airport, 7:55 p.m. on the preceding Friday, and flight number were reported in the *Honolulu Advertiser*, the state's largest newspaper, along with language encouraging fans to bring leis.[12] More than 5,000 fans showed up to welcome half of the Power Rangers to O'ahu. Frank felt like they were the Beatles; Johnson felt like a beetle.

"We all were almost lei'd to death,"[13] Johnson said. "They put so many flowers on us. I couldn't breathe, I started hyperventilating. Jason turns around and looks at me, he has so many flowers, all you can see are his eyes. It was so crazy. . . . We got in the limo, and I remember just driving away and turning around and looking back—and Jason of course is hanging out the roof screaming—and there's just a sea of people."

The stratospheric success of *Mighty Morphin Power Rangers* made Saban fantasize about a world that seemed beyond even his ambitious imagination. Why couldn't Saban Entertainment be the biggest entertainment company on Earth? Disney, scmisney.

"That's our goal,"[14] Saban said in December 1993. "The question is level and intensity of expansion, and how do we best get there."

Of the many hurdles standing between Saban and his lofty goal, most immediate was the loss of fuel for his *MMPR* fire: usable footage from *Zyuranger*'s 50-episode run was exhausted through the first 40 episodes ordered for *MMPR*. In Japan, the characters, suits, stories, and other assorted paraphernalia changed every year, and while Saban firmly believed the helmets were the stars of the show—not the actors underneath them—he didn't want to do too much to rock the boat. It was crucial to keep the six suits with which kids had become enamored, even if they had to be mishmashed with a different *Super Sentai* series. *Gosei Sentai Dairanger*, set to finish its broadcast in February 1994, would be tapped for Zord footage throughout *MMPR*'s second season, planned for the fall 1994 broadcast window. In the interim, though, neither Saban Entertainment nor Fox Kids wanted kids to tire of Ranger reruns. In addition to a 52-episode second season, Loesch made a 20-episode "mid-season" order to extend the first.

"Doomsday" had been rewritten and reedited to provide open-ended closure; Zordon gives the teens a chance to relieve themselves of their world-saving responsibilities. They effectively say, "Thanks but no thanks." So, narratively, when the show picked back up in February 1994 with "A Pig Surprise," it wasn't all that jarring. After a three-month hiatus, fans at home were greeted with the return of their heroes and a popular Monster of the Day, Pudgy Pig, revived through the not-so-subtle recycling of battle footage already used in "Food Fight." A Megazord fight got cobbled together through the reuse of *Zyuranger* footage first used in the "Green With Evil" miniseries, making this possibly the most bastardized creation in TV history—and a great case study for how and why *MMPR* works.

Pudgy Pig's return was an exception. Most of the additional 20 episodes—and several at the top of season 2—featured footage of the team fighting monsters not found in *Zyuranger*. In the fandom, this footage, commissioned by Saban Entertainment and filmed by Toei in Japan, is referred to as "Zyu2" and for a while was the subject of a "lost media" hunt. Fandom historian John Green is also a rabid fan of *Power Rangers*' "Evil Space Aliens," and the unedited "Zyu2" footage[15]—uploaded to YouTube in 2014 by former stunt coordinator Jeff Pruitt—was a holy grail.

"The bad guys are where I feel the biggest opportunity for creativity exists in *Power Rangers*," said Green. "Ranger costumes last for a year or two. Same with Zords. While there can definitely be original stories or gems of originality within them, how seasons progress and even how the actual episodes play out is somewhat formulaic by necessity. But monsters? That's where the originality can shine. A lot of this leans on Toei, as the costumes themselves continue to amaze. But, on that foundation, *Power Rangers* gets to add a name, a voice and a character. Maybe the monster sounds like a previous monster, but its personality is different. Maybe the design isn't a clear home run, but the name is a great pun or play on words. Finally, the monsters are the underdogs. They always lose in the end, even if they briefly get to win."

Toei shot the "Zyu2" Megazord footage with the Dino Megazord suit, not that of the Thunder Megazord, which replaced the OG in season 2. This, of course, meant all the "Zyu2" footage had to be spliced together to create the illusion that the Thunder Megazord was in those fights. Editor Adi Ell-Ad felt his job was on the line when he was asked to make it happen. He didn't think it was feasible due to the number of close-ups. It would be impossible, he thought, to make it appear as if the suits were anywhere near the same jurisdiction, let alone fighting one another. He passed his best effort along to Shuki Levy, who within 10 minutes rushed into Ell-Ad's edit bay to alert him that Saban was on his way over to watch the edit. Ell-Ad had not yet met the man who signed his checks and briefly wondered if the checks might stop coming.

After a quick watch, Saban demanded to see it again. And again.

Among the most coveted items from the original wave of *Mighty Morphin Power Rangers* toys is this set, which for almost two decades was the only first-party release of the team's morpher and sidearm. Courtesy Kenn Glenn

"Haim back then knew the Japanese footage and our dailies that we shot. He watched everything," Ell-Ad said. "He knew every frame. And he goes, 'No way. How did you cut it?'"

Saban was exuberant. He and Shuki started talking loudly in Hebrew, indecipherable by anyone else in the room other than a few curse words directed at one another—personal terms of endearment. When English speaking resumed, Saban informed Ell-Ad that his effort had preserved footage of 10 monster fights the company anticipated were unusable—he'd made their investment more valuable. If you're eagle-eyed or pause quickly, you can catch glimpses of the Dino Megazord in a frame or two throughout season 2. If not for that, the sleight of hand might never have been revealed to anyone unfamiliar with how it came together.

"Haim shakes my hand and goes, 'What do you think?'" Ell-Ad said. "And I go, 'About the scene?' He goes, 'Hell no, about us.' I'm looking at him and Shuki and say, 'Only really two friends as close as you guys could talk to each other like that.'

"Haim goes, 'The scene you just cut, piece of crap. Welcome to the family.'"

The "Zyu2" footage also helped alleviate the show's other biggest problem: bringing the uber-popular Tommy Oliver back to the team. The two-parter "Return of an Old Friend," among the first of many episodes written by Levy's then-girlfriend, *General Hospital* star Shell Danielson, puts the character back in green spandex just 14 episodes after he supposedly lost his powers for good. The other Rangers' parents—most making their first and only appearance—get trapped in the Dark Dimension by Rita Repulsa. The Rangers hand over their Power Coins to Goldar as part of a ransom to save them, but the bad guy—shocker—doesn't oblige. Zordon, in an act of desperation, uses his own energy to temporarily recharge the Dragon Power Coin, which works but depletes him to the point of being wiped out of existence.

As a reintroduction of Tommy, it couldn't be much better—particularly in how it recontextualizes him as a fallible hero versus the unstoppable villain in his debut. He retrieves the Dragon Dagger from Goldar, halts a destructive spree by the Dragonzord, fights off a pack of Putty Patrollers, and, as his powers start failing, musters just enough strength to snag his friends' Power Coins before fleeing. Most impressively, he does it all wearing the cloth Dragon Shield. These episodes were the show's first to feature morphed fight footage produced in America and provided a glimpse into how *MMPR* would evolve over its second and third seasons. Keeping the characters in their original suits rather than adopting those provided by the annual *Super Sentai* changeover naturally would necessitate more original fight footage of the U.S. production team. "Return of an Old Friend" also sets *MMPR* on a path where it has a more definitive leading man than a wholly equitable show. Contextually, the two-parter functions as a much stronger season finale than any of the final 10 episodes that follow it, all of which offer standard-issue *MMPR* fun but nothing in terms of an end point or dramatic impact on the status quo.

Of course, they didn't need to at that point. *Power Rangers* was the biggest kids show on the planet. Its toys couldn't stay on the shelves. A movie was in the works. Nothing short of a space dumpster getting discovered on the moon, it seemed, could stymie the Mighty Morphin momentum.

CHAPTER 8

The Mutiny

"Success is often the first step toward disaster."[1]

Former Los Angeles Lakers coach Pat Riley wrote that in his memoir, *Showtime*. In 1980, the Lakers won the NBA Championship with a roster featuring four future Hall of Famers: Kareem Abdul-Jabbar, Spencer Haywood, Magic Johnson, and Jamaal Wilkes. All but Haywood returned for the 1980–1981 season, priming the Lakers to become the first NBA team to repeat in more than a decade. They lost in the first round of the playoffs.

Riley in the same book coined "the disease of more," describing a phenomenon where members of a winning team lose sight of the things they sacrificed in order to become champions—shot attempts, minutes on the court, cigarettes, cheeseburgers, money, and so on. The high of victory subsides, and a natural want for "more" overtakes it.

"I had a radio on my desk listening to what's being called out on the set," said Judd "Chip" Lynn, *MMPR*'s production manager. "They called me and said, 'The actors have walked off the set, you need to come down here.' I'm like, 'What do you mean? Have them come back? Are they off to wardrobe?' They're going, 'Nope, they've left the set, they're not working anymore.'"

It shouldn't have surprised anyone that the show's stars would call for a bigger share of a Megazord-sized pie. They were rookie champions who couldn't go anywhere without getting mobbed by ankle biters and their caregivers. Every time they turned on a TV or picked up a newspaper, they couldn't avoid the phenomenon they helped drive—or talk of the monster revenue pouring into Saban Entertainment. Kids loved Billy, Jason, Kimberly, Tommy, Trini, and Zack: though they'd signed away their likenesses before the show even had a final name, their faces remained valuable leverage. Or so they thought.

Haim Saban perceived actors as a means to an end. What kids *really* loved about *MMPR*, he reckoned, were the colorful costumes, over-the-top monsters, and larger-than-life robots. They didn't want to be Zack or Kimberly on the playground; they wanted to be the Black Ranger or Pink Ranger. They weren't clamoring for the return of Tommy but rather the return of the Green Ranger. Couple that perspective with a hardened distaste for Hollywood unions, and you've got a boss whose predisposition was to shrug and shout, "Shalom!" But Saban tried to bargain when the actors—and their freshly minted agents determined to help them make *MMPR* a SAG show—wanted to revisit their contracts if for no other reason that it would have been hypocritical not to; he himself had gone to Margaret Loesch to renegotiate the paltry Fox Kids licensing fee when the show exploded.

"Haim said, 'OK, let's see if we can find a deal that makes everybody happy,'" Lynn said. "And it made some of them happy, and some of them weren't happy."

Based on a *Variety* column from 1994, *MMPR*'s actors made about $60,000 a year,[2] equivalent to the purchasing power of about $130,000 in 2024. That was and is modest by Hollywood standards but is not as impoverished as some actors have made it sound over the years. Austin St. John said he "could have worked the window at McDonald's[3] and probably made the same money the first season." That might have been true if he owned and operated a McDonald's location; California's minimum wage in 1993 was $4.25, meaning the lowest possible amount one could have made working a 40-hour week at McDonald's at the time was $170, before taxes, or a yearly salary of $8,840.

Going union was about more than salary, though. None of them received residuals for a ratings juggernaut that, by the fall of 1994, was broadcast in about 100 countries. Most of them had already appeared in 60 episodes, enough to fill out three months of once-a-day weekday reruns in syndication, and were about to film 52 more episodes *and* a feature-length film. The same applied to merchandise—their likenesses were slapped on action figures, VHS tapes, and trading cards, but none of that revenue trickled down to the actors under the helmets. It was hard to see outsiders and Saban himself constantly describe the show as a potential billion-dollar franchise and not wonder, *Are we getting screwed?*

Beyond the money, a SAG contract would have drastically improved working conditions. Shoot days that started before sunrise and ended after sunset would be a thing of the past or, at least, better compensated. There would be health care benefits—something that, for some reason, a production that demanded frequent stunt work didn't initially provide. The addition of a stipend for actors to cover personal health-insurance premiums was granted after David Yost broke his nose in a bar fight while filming the first season.

"That instance woke them up,[4] but unfortunately never woke them up to deal with the union," Yost said. During a post–first season meeting with Saban that included all six Ranger actors as well as Jason Narvy and Paul Schrier, the matter of going union was raised for the first time by Walter Jones. Their boss's response was clear.

Alpha 5, Zordon's faithful robot companion, served up holiday cheer in *Alpha's Magical Christmas,* one of several direct-to-VHS specials produced during *Mighty Morphin Power Rangers'* heyday. Courtesy of Morphin Museum/© Saban Entertainment

"'Not a fucking chance in hell. We can't afford it,'" Narvy recalls Saban saying. To this day, Narvy admires Jones's gumption for initiating the conversation. "And it was not in a mean manner."

Therein lies the paradox with Saban: he was cold in his business calculations but the warmest personality in any room. When it came down to dollars and cents, he was happy to talk and listen, but there were hard limits. It wasn't in his nature to relinquish control, and beyond driving up costs, union oversight would limit what the actors could and couldn't be asked to do on set. Giving in to SAG would have a ripple effect on the production schedule and signal other unions—or people who could be part of them—to start grousing. As lean as the show's budget was, it was even tighter with people—many of whom proudly embraced that leanness. A person's title might suggest they do one thing, but anybody could do just about anything on the *Mighty Morphin Power Rangers* set given the right set of circumstances and a healthy dose of "want to."

"I played high school football and I was a bit big," said Bryan Cahill, a boom mic operator and sound mixer. "I would get mistaken quite often for Austin, the original Red Ranger, because from behind, with the broad shoulders and everything, we looked very similar." Once while shooting on the first unit, he'd overheard that the second-unit crew was going on location the next day and would be without a stuntperson. The first unit was off that day, so Cahill volunteered his services. "They brought me down to the beach and put me in a Putty Patroller outfit. I thought they were just going to have my legs in front of the camera so you really wouldn't see me, but the first thing they have me doing is flips off a mini trampoline on the beach. I can recall our first AD Chris Auer saying to the stunt coordinator [Jeff Pruitt], 'Should we really be having our boom operator doing flips on a mini trampoline?' And the guy says, 'I'm giving him the easiest ones!'"

Cahill survived and thrived, enough to be drafted on a couple more occasions. While the face actors had every right to be disgruntled by their own situation, the suit actors had even more reason to aspire for SAG governance. As demanding and anxiety-inducing as it could be, the faces at least got to experience exuberant fanfare on the road and, decades later, parlayed their days on the show into full-time touring gigs where they can hug fans and sign action figures for more than $60 a pop. Talented stunties like Erik Betts—a frequent Putty Patroller who also spent an extensive amount of time in the Green and Red Ranger suits—put their bodies on the line without any adulation.

"When I would do the high falls and stuff, you would hear me go, 'SAAAAAAAAG,'" Betts said with laugh. "Hoping and praying, hoping and praying. I hoped all those things would pay off one day."

Betts, also the first American to don a monster costume as Pudgy Pig in "Food Fight," says the spandex suits got so hot in the California sun that his boots pooled with sweat, enough to fill multiple 16.9-ounce bottles each day. He wore store-bought cowboy boots, painted to fit the suits.

"I'm trying to do fight scenes on dirt and stones, full-on gravel, wearing cowboy boots with no grip," Betts said. "That's an attestment to young Erik's skills, but also of his level of stupidity. I would never dream of doing that crap now."

"When you're working non-union, it's like working in the streets," said Hien Nguyen, another founding stuntman on the show. "You gotta know how to protect yourself."

Betts and Cahill are among those who carved lengthy film and TV careers following their time on *Mighty Morphin Power Rangers*. Both Betts and Nguyen briefly had turns as forward-facing stars in *WMAC Masters*, a martials arts fantasy show produced in part by Renaissance Atlantic Entertainment. They valued and still appreciate their experience on *Power Rangers*, but sticking with it longer than they did would have been to their detriment. Same for Pruitt, who came on as stunt choreographer after Florentine left to direct features, and his wife Sophia Crawford, with whom he got acquainted in between her stints as the Pink Ranger. The couple also worked on *WMAC Masters* before heading stunts for another burgeoning action series, *Buffy the Vampire Slayer*.

"It was one thing when it was under the radar, but it started becoming a big, big deal," Pruitt said.[5] "We were [making] shows for, like, between 165 grand per episode to 250 grand per episode, which is nothing. That isn't even a star's salary. . . . There wasn't anything like *Buffy* or the type of shows that you see nowadays. *Power Rangers* was the first time we had wall-to-wall martial arts fighting, every single day. So it was a good opportunity for me to practice and have fun."

After four years as a full-timer, Cahill occasionally freelanced for Saban Entertainment. Once while working as a sound mixer, he brought along a friend to do boom work. The typical day rate for freelance boom operators on *Power Rangers* at the time was about $125 for a 12-hour commitment. Cahill pleaded to get his friend the higher rate he'd negotiated for himself, $215.

"They're like, 'Who's worth $215?'" Cahill said. "I say, 'Well he was a boom operator on *Titanic*, and he's coming in because he's bored and doesn't want to sit at the house. So yea, I think we oughta pay him the $215 a day.'" The producer relented.

Alonzo Bodden, a stand-up comedian who won the third season of *Last Comic Standing*, got his start in entertainment as a driver on *MMPR*. Later, he did monster dubs. "There would be times where people would complain about food," Bodden said. "My first job, I worked in aerospace, and I'm thinking to myself, 'Y'know, at my last job I had to buy my own food.' Free food always tastes good. One of the things I felt there that I think you get on a good production, is a sense of teamwork, a sense that we're all doing this together. In some ways I was naïve because I was new to the whole production process . . . but I had a great experience. Jonathan [Tzachor], I'll always remember him because he was really supportive of my comedy career, which I really appreciated.

"I don't have any dirt for you 'cause it wasn't that kind of vibe. It was fun and funny."

According to former Saban Entertainment president Lance Robbins, the actors' agents sought 500 percent salary increases in addition to SAG recognition (and the benefits thereof). Caving to a union wasn't going to happen, but Saban offered them new contracts that included raises. They were also presented with gifts.

"Saban had given each of them a new Jeep or something like that, and of course their agents said, 'A new Jeep, what the fuck? You guys are making millions,'" Robbins said. "This is a business, and they had to realize that it's the costumes that they're buying, not the kids."

For three of the Rangers—Jason David Frank, Amy Jo Johnson, and David Yost—the new terms proved acceptable. Jason Narvy and Paul Schrier also stayed aboard. The others—Walter Jones, Austin St. John, and Thuy Trang—were steadfast in their demand for the show to go union. So a week after season 2 premiered on July 21, 1994, open casting calls for new Power Rangers were held in Dallas, Los Angeles, New York City, and Orlando. Auditions weren't advertised as replacement-motivated, and Saban Entertainment executive Elie Dekel[6] at the time declined to confirm how many actors were sought, but their intent was clear: identify three ethnically diverse actors—and quickly—to replace half of the leads on the hottest kids show in the world.

It's tough to pinpoint 30 years later why the Rangers' united front against Saban Entertainment dissolved. Frank was a budding star for whom Saban Entertainment and Fox Kids clearly had a fondness, seeing as they'd developed an entire pilot around him (*Cybertron* was reworked as another team-based tokusatsu amalgamation, *VR Troopers*); Johnson seriously approached her craft and career and likely perceived the value of a feature-film credit as outweighing the upside of jumping ship at *this* juncture; and Yost, the oldest of the cast at 25, had moved to Hollywood from Iowa in pursuit of an opportunity like the one he'd gained—how easy would it be to find a gig like *Power Rangers* again?

In the decades since, St. John and Jones have continued to defend their commitment. Jones says if he could do it over, he would have stuck around long enough to do a movie before bolting[7]—exactly as Johnson would do the following year. The only Ranger who had ample entertainment experience prior to the show also had the least trouble landing work in its aftermath. Bit parts on popular sitcoms *Step by Step* and *Family Matters* gave way to a recurring role on *Malibu Shores*, a short-lived NBC drama that starred a little-known 20-year-old named Keri Russell. Jones steadily continued to work since, but his biggest post-*MMPR* role came in another kids show, the Nickelodeon sitcom *Space Cases*. He received top billing as Harlan Band, the only Earthling among a group of space cadets who for two seasons did a preteen take on *Star Trek*.

"Zack was so close to my natural character because I grew up in a single-parent household, so I was used to being the man of the house, I was used to being the protector,"[8] Jones said. "It felt easy to be Zack, whereas Harlan I had to put myself in a different place. He wasn't just a teenager; he was a teenager in space surrounded by other space aliens taking on a whole world of discovery and having to figure out all these issues that were coming at him while trying to grow and deal with his own personal issues. . . . It took me to a different place that wasn't as simple."

In addition to their on-screen performances, every *Power Rangers* actor since day one has had to become a voice actor. In the early going, as seen here from Thuy Trang, that sometimes meant recording lines on location. Courtesy Bryan Cahill

Beyond a joint statement prepared by Saban Entertainment, Trang never addressed her exit from the show in an accessible forum. She warmly embraced having been a trailblazing Asian American superhero while making public appearances with Jones and St. John following their exits, though. While Trini wasn't devoid of insensitive stereotypes— "Plague of the Mantis," in which she has a burning desire to learn a style of Chinese kung fu, probably wouldn't make it to air now—she was largely defined by her intelligence, emotional as much as intellectual. A lot of that's a testament to Trang; generally, *MMPR*'s heroes were less fully realized characters than they were archetypes with personality traits of their actors impressed on them.

"I always felt very much a part of that world, I felt like I was always represented," said Simu Liu,[9] a *Power Rangers* fan who grew up to portray the MCU's first Asian American lead in 2021's *Shang-Chi and the Legend of the Ten Rings*. "It was very on-the-nose representation—black, black; yellow, yellow. It wasn't perfect, but it was definitely there, and it was definitely trying."

Tragically, Trang died on September 3, 2001, in a car accident while traveling as part of a bridal party. She was 27.

"It was intimidating, almost, to work with her on your first day, because she was so pretty and she was so poised, that she almost seemed stand-offish,"[10] said Narvy. "But when you meet her? She was the most open, loving person you would ever want to meet. It's a real loss that she's not around."

"I wish she were here[11] to experience some of the things that we experience from the success of the show now," said Jones. "Her career was just launching. I think she would've done some great things."

St. John has stuck closest to the guns he and castmates palmed in 1994. They agreed to unfair terms because they didn't know any better—or that the show would be one of the biggest in the world. If they couldn't take action while the iron was scorching hot, could they ever?

"[Saban's] idea of taking care of us was making sure we had a good spread on a catering table,"[12] said St. John. "I remember thinking, 'Screw it, I'll move into something else.' I didn't really have good representation, and I learned a lot about trying to go from children's TV into movies and things like that. It was definitely harder than I thought it would be." Over the next two decades, St. John appeared in two low-budget thrillers, *Exposé* and *Footsteps*, receiving little screen time in each as a detective. When he left Hollywood, he got a degree in exercise science from Concordia University in Canada and became a medic. At 18 years old, Austin St. John was reluctantly learning how to act like a hero; before he was 40, he'd saved real civilians in Washington, D.C., and soldiers in the Middle East.

"I was a late teenager, young man by the time I was leaving the show, and I had all these people who were looking up to me and expected so much,"[13] St. John said. "I don't think they understand how they inspired me to try and do something with my life that I felt was deserving of their belief and their adoration."

Whether it was driven by greed, a need for control, ego, or a combination thereof, Saban's insistence on keeping the show nonunion transformed it, literally and on a fundamental, big-picture level. Kids had spent the better part of a year bickering on playgrounds about which Power Ranger was the best—*Billy's a genius! Zack's the coolest! Trini's so nice! Kimberly is hot! Jason's the leader! Tommy is Tommy!*—and now three of them were about to be written off midway through 1994 and replaced with other attractive, physically gifted young adults.

The message was clear from on high: your face is fine, but the helmets matter more. To a degree, Saban was right—30 years of *Power Rangers* suggest that the cool suits and gizmos have an undeniable amount of influence on how people embrace, perceive, and remember the show. But *MMPR*'s characters—as archetypal and flatly developed as they were—resonated with kids more deeply than the mogul ever admitted. The raucous response to Frank's leave of absence should have been evidence of that; instead, Saban followed the precedent set by the dismissal of Audri Dubois, and the show officially put itself on a course to eventually do what *Super Sentai* did from the very beginning: replace the entire cast every time the suits change.

Producers and writers made efforts to soften the blow in-show. The replacements get introduced a few episodes before the changing of the guard. The holdover Rangers later receive some written communications from the outgoing trio, who are continuing to help the planet as part of a Peace Conference in Switzerland. But the trio's absence is still difficult to reconcile decades removed from the initial shock and with the benefit of adult-level awareness. It doesn't help that, because they left somewhat abruptly, scenes of multiple episodes had to be filmed with body doubles and blocked to prioritize the remaining three Rangers. Existing footage of Jason, Trini, and Zack was repurposed and carefully matched with ADR—some of it existing, some of it performed by folks around the office. A producer told postproduction supervisor Paul Rosenthal that he did a "pretty good Austin" impression, and that's all it took for him to read for Jason.

"It was like a Band-Aid that was lifted really quick," said editor Adi Ell-Ad. "We had to get on with the program."

The call to recast was Saban Entertainment's to make as the producer, but it made Fox Kids uneasy. "I almost had a heart attack," said Margaret Loesch. "But I supported it. Under the circumstances, I did support it, but I was nervous about it." Ann Austen, the director of programming, wasn't thrilled at all—it went against her instincts, both as a producer and as a person.

"Haim Saban said, 'It's about precedent, it's about money, it's about not letting the actors rule how we run the show,'" Austen said. "He assured Margaret that the show would survive—it wasn't about the actors, it was about the show itself. To some extent, I guess he was right. But it was very, very, very hard. And I personally did not approve of the way it happened. I looked at all the actors as my kids, and always have, and I did not like seeing that happen. But it's an industry-wide problem."

Multiple members of the cast have since speculated about how things might have transpired if all six of them remained on the same page and continued to lobby for SAG. Given the man whose mind they needed to change, it's unlikely it would have mattered. The nature of how *MMPR* was made afforded the creative team plenty of ways to dismiss the entire cast off-screen, if needed. It isn't difficult to imagine a hypothetical two-parter—let's call it "Face-Off"—wherein the Rangers are forced to remain morphed for two episodes while fighting a monster whose ability allows them to steal the faces of people. For whatever reason, after defeating it, a kink in the Morphin Grid alters all of the Rangers' appearances, a revelation made in the final scenes. It could be tied to a theme along the lines of "it's what's inside that matters most." That idea took me all of five minutes to generate and is no less believable than anything else that might have come up in preliminary discussions surrounding a total cast implosion. (Similar shenanigans were also used to replace a cast member in *Big Bad Beetleborgs*, a later tokusatsu adaptation produced by Saban Entertainment.)

More than 25 years later, the departure of Jason, Trini, and Zack served as a launchpad for alternative-universe stories told across multiple Boom! Studios comic-book titles released more than 25 years later. Author Ryan Parrott reimagines the Peace Conference as a well-intentioned white lie to cover up that the trio was recruited by Zordon for an off-world mission requiring them to don new powers as the Omega Rangers.

"In some ways [it was] a meta way of, like, giving them a proper exit,"[14] Parrott said. "Everybody knows about the way they left, and I always thought, 'That's not fun.' . . . The other thing that's really nice is once we do that story, it's not lined up with the TV show, so I can go anywhere, and they can meet anyone. That part has been really cool."

Although a product of greed and shortsightedness, watching one's heroes give up extraordinary power, the companionship of a tight friend circle, and the comforts of home to change the world without spandex is incredibly moving. Off-screen sacrifices by Jones, St. John, and Trang begot an on-screen sacrifice that stands out in delivering one of the show's core messages: you don't have to be a Power Ranger to do powerful things.

A cast shake-up was just another wrench in a season already littered with them.

Rita Repulsa's source footage had dried up with *Zyuranger*. How do you raise the stakes from a wicked witch predisposed to crushing head-aches? Bring in her boss.

"I am Lord Zedd, emperor of all he sees." These are the first words spoken by *MMPR*'s first American-made villain as he debuts in "The Mutiny, Part I." He's grotesque, flayed to the point that his brain is exposed through the remnants of what might have once been a helmet; it's got a visor similar to those of the Power Rangers, except it's even redder than his exposed muscle. The rest of his body is lightly protected by chrome metal caging and arterial tubing.

Lord Zedd reprimands Rita and immediately renovates her home through a barrage of lightning bolts; as the Moon Palace transforms around its occupants, its new head of household arrives on a throne, accompanied by a dread-drenched score and a live boa constrictor. Zedd transforms the snake into a staff topped by a large letter "Z."

A portion of a shooting script for "The Mutiny, Part II," used by Jason David Frank, who added handwritten notes. Originally written as a two-parter, the footage was expanded into three episodes. Courtesy of Jesse Lee Herndon

Robert Axelrod's exemplary effort on the mic brings Zedd fully to life. Like Barbara Goodson, Axelrod's tenure with Saban Entertainment predated *MMPR*, but he had already worked on the show too; he was also the voice of Rita's monster maker Finster in addition to various Monsters of the Day. (Axelrod's Goo Fish, a "Zyu2" monster first seen in "Something Fishy," isn't too far off from what Zedd would sound like.) He auditioned three times and had to convince producers that it was actually him, not doctored audio, creating the "husky, Marlboro-laden voice"[15] that became synonymous with the skinless antagonist. Axelrod worked, on- and off-screen, up until his death in 2019, but his 117 episodes as Lord Zedd are his magnum opus.

"Zedd had integrity, a word whose dictionary definition is 'wholeness.' He was wholly evil, intent on destroying 'The Power Twerps' and taking over the world . . . or at least Angel [Grove] City," Axelrod said. "I liked the stately quality of the character, similar to Darth Vader.[16] He wasn't stupid and always bounced back for more."

Stuntman Ed Neil—not the one from *The Texas Chainsaw Massacre*—added Lord Zedd in-suit performances to his ongoing Putty Patroller duties. The toughest part for Axelrod was timing up Zedd's dialogue to that of Neil, who uttered lines while shooting to help aid directors capturing coverage. "His body language was quite acceptable, but he spoke the lines too rapidly,"[17] Axelrod said. "I wanted to keep the character stately, slow in pace and impinging in tone, but he made that difficult. . . . I asked several times if I could be on the set to work with him, on my own time, but the opportunity never materialized. I let it go after a while."

There's no hint of struggle in Axelrod's performance, which blended with Neil's to create one of the most unsettling villains ever realized in children's television. To date, *MMPR* monsters had been just that, monsters—there was no mistaking Pudgy Pig or Eye Guy for something removed from fantasy. They might scare the youngest among us, but most fans could go to bed knowing that neither would attack them in their sleep. Same for Rita Repulsa, whose cacophony of cackles and complaints softened her ability to instill fear. Rita at least appears human, just one with a brave stylist. Zedd resembles someone who might have once been human, but those days are far behind him.

Despite her pleas, replete with foot kissing, Zedd re-imprisons Rita in a space dumpster and hurls her into the stars. She promises to return, but it plays like an empty threat. In one fell swoop, her successor proved himself to be the authority on evil—and he did it in front of a national prime-time audience.

"The Mutiny" was filmed as part of a two-episode cluster over the course of nine days in April 1994, to accommodate more on-location takes. "Introducing Lord Zedd was a big deal," said Ell-Ad. "Shuki [Levy] directed like it was a feature film, basically," and that called for everything to be bigger: the camera movements, the locations, and the audience. When Ell-Ad started his first pass on the footage, he felt there was "almost enough" to stretch "The Mutiny" across three episodes; it just needed a quick scene or two to set up an additional cliffhanger on which to end one of the parts. "I went to Haim with this and he said, 'Yes, let's do it, go to the set and direct the scene you need to do it.'"

Saban and Margaret Loesch worked out an arrangement where *MMPR*'s three-part season 2 premiere would first air in national prime-time slots over the course of three weeks in late July and early August. This decision had a twofold goal: bring in even more—and older—eyeballs but also encourage parents to watch the show more actively with their children. They wanted them to see the show for the campy action-adventure sitcom it was rather than the violence-laden romp some tried to paint it as.

Hard data suggested that, at least, their reach goals were met: "The Mutiny, Part I" premiered at 8:30 p.m. on Thursday, July 21, 1994, following a rerun of *The Simpsons*. It garnered a 7.2 rating with a 13 share, good for forty-ninth overall[18] among the 80 prime-time programs aired across the four broadcast networks that week. It finished third in its time slot behind ABC's *Matlock* (9.2/17) and NBC's *Wings* (11.7/22), an often-forgotten part of a "Must See TV" lineup that featured *Frasier* (15.5/27, fourth that week) and *Seinfeld* (16.2/27, No. 1 overall). With the help of Homer Simpson and Lord Zedd, Fox easily conquered CBS police drama *In the Heat of the Night* (5.9/11) that evening. Most of *Power Rangers'* other "victories" that week came against fellow Fox shows—two Saturday broadcasts of *Cops*, a narrow win over *The X-Files* (7.1/14), and a *Married... with Children* rerun (6.3/11) on Sunday among the highlights—but it also performed better than ABC's *Dinosaurs* (6.5/13) and short-lived CBS sitcom *Good Advice* (6.9/13). It also wasn't too far behind regional coverage of Major League Baseball games (7.8/15).

A move to Friday night virtually guaranteed a drop in performance for the final two parts of "The Mutiny." Part 2[19] had the worst showing of the three (4.7/10) but still beat six other prime-time broadcasts that week. The finale[20] ranked worse in its week (eighty-fourth of 97 broadcasts) but performed slightly better (4.9/10). The last two parts were paired with new episodes of another Fox Kids hit, *X-Men*. In both instances, the mutants slightly outperformed *MMPR*, another indicator for Fox brass that maybe this *X-Men* thing was worth milking further. Behind the scenes, Loesch had long championed the development of an *X-Men* feature film; nearly six years to the date of these midsummer airings, Bryan Singer's *X-Men* unknowingly sat in motion a multi-decade run of superhero dominance at the box office.

It's hard to say whether "The Mutiny" won over skeptical parents, but kids were still captivated in the summer of 1994. By December, despite much pleading by the critics, they'd all be dreaming of a white Christmas.

CHAPTER 9

A Monster of Global Proportions

In October 1993, when *Mighty Morphin Power Rangers* was still very much in its infancy, it grabbed the attention of a developmental psychologist at Cal State Fullerton who noticed his six-year-old daughter and her friends watching it after school. His first thought?

"God damn, it's violent," said Chris Boyatzis, who oversaw and designed a study along with two undergraduates, Gina Matillo and Kristen Nesbitt. It was a simple experiment: one group of 26 after-school day care students, ages six to 11, watched a randomly selected episode of *MMPR*, sans commercials; the next day, another group of 26 students would not. The team observed each child in each group for two minutes apiece to see how they played with one another inside the school as they waited for their parents to arrive, counting the number of "aggressive acts" performed in that time interval. The short verdict: *Power Rangers* made kids—especially boys—more aggressive.

For the purposes of the study, an "aggressive act" was defined as "any physical act that was done intentionally and seriously," such as kicking, hitting, shoving, or tackling, and also not something you'd expect from typical play fighting. In the experiment, boys and girls in the control group, as well as girls in the *MMPR* group, all committed a low number of aggressive acts; boys who watched *MMPR* committed, on average, about three aggressive acts in the time span, ultimately leading to a conclusion that boys who watched the show were seven times more likely to be aggressive toward peers.

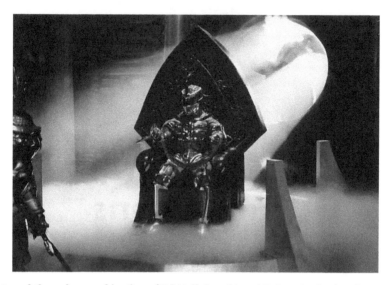

Portrayed through a combination of Ed Neil (in suit) and Robert Axelrod (voice actor), Lord Zedd was the first lead villain that originated from the U.S. production. Courtesy Yuda Acco

That kids might emulate "aggressive acts" after watching them wasn't a unique discovery. In the early 1960s, Stanford professor Albert Bandura conducted a series of experiments using Bobo dolls, the bowling pin–shaped toys whose combination of superheavy bottoms and superlight tops makes them bounce back up after being struck. These experiments were among the first to show that kids (in Bandura's study, three- to five-year-olds) who observed aggressive behavior from an adult model, live or recorded, would imitate that behavior. The experiments have been retested, reimagined, and rebuked many times since but remain among the most cited and influential studies in developmental psychology. They were instrumental in the construction of Bandura's social learning theory, which boils down to this: People learn social behaviors by observing and imitating other people.

Television in the Lives of Our Children, a collection of research published in 1965, found that "for *some* children, under *some* conditions, *some* television is harmful. For *other* children under the same conditions, or for the same children under *other* conditions, it may be beneficial. For *most* children,[1] under *most* conditions, *most* television is probably neither harmful nor particularly beneficial." Those conclusions were widely accepted in 1969, when the U.S. surgeon general started work on a 1971 report studying the impact of television violence. The report cites dozens of studies that reflect Bandura's theory as it relates to the imitation of aggressive behavior. But, to the dismay of some researchers whose data helped compose it and committee members who helped write it, the report generally arrived at this conclusion: except for children who are predisposed to aggression, TV is probably a net neutral. However, Surgeon General Dr. Jesse Steinfeld during a Senate subcommittee hearing in 1972 said the report showed "sufficient data"[2] to warrant immediate remedial action, which did not come; Dean Burch, then chairman of the Federal Communications Commission (FCC), acknowledged that action was needed but wasn't sure from whom—the government or the market.

Twenty-one years later, Boyatzis and his team conducted a study whose findings were well substantiated and that, by his own admission, was fairly rudimentary in its design. But it happened under meaningful circumstances. It came after the Children's Television Act (CTA) of 1990, long-coming legislation that limited the amount and allowable content of advertising shown during children's TV programming, as well as a related amendment to the Communications Act of 1934 that created the National Endowment for Children's Educational Television. By 1993, the CTA—lobbied for by children's TV advocate Peggy Charren since the 1960s—was under fire for light enforcement and the vagaries of its standards, which led some broadcasters to cite *The Flintstones* as an example of educational programming. *MMPR* became the poster child for its inadequacy.

"It's designed as a 30-minute commercial,"[3] said Charren, who died in 2015. "If everybody in the child's world has one, if it's talked about at school, then that's what a child will want."

Boyatzis and Charren weren't *MMPR*'s only critics, but they were the most visible, effectively becoming Lord Zedd and Rita Repulsa for Saban Entertainment and Fox Kids. Boyatzis's study was widely circulated by news media, including a *20/20* report by John Stossel broadcast in December 1994. Stossel's package noted the national unrest among schoolteachers who couldn't get kids to calm down because of the show. Boyatzis replicated his experiment for *20/20* and suggested that a bureau of TV standards—something like the Canadian Broadcasting Standards Council—be created to review broadcast shows; Stossel, who later in his career became more boisterous about his libertarian leanings, was dismissive of the idea as well as the thought that *MMPR* caused actual harm to children. He found at least a few parents who agreed. "The bottom line is that you have to know your child and you have to set appropriate limits," Roy Markowitz[4] said. "If you feel that your child is gonna rape and pillage after watching the Power Rangers, turn it to *Barney*."

Speaking of Canada: parental complaints led to *MMPR*'s removal from YTV, an Ontario-based children's network, in November 1994, but the show remained available via U.S. broadcasters as well as other Canadian broadcasters, to whom Saban Entertainment delivered cuts of the show that were further trimmed of action. The YTV "ban"—which lasted less than a year—came two months after New Zealand's Broadcasting Standards Authority successfully advised TVNZ to pull the show; that removal remained intact for nearly two decades. For two days, *MMPR* was pulled from broadcast in Denmark, Norway, and Sweden when it was briefly—and inadvertently—linked to the tragic death of Silje Marie Redergård, a five-year-old girl who died of hypothermia after three boys allegedly beat her to unconsciousness on a Norwegian football field. The boys, all between four and six years of age, claimed to have fended off the actual perpetrators—older children, they said—by kicking them in the legs "just like the Ninja Turtles."[5]

One of the most diverse surveys on *MMPR*'s impact came via the *Orange County Register* in Irvine, California. The newspaper compiled feedback from 50 callers who couldn't come to a consensus. Some—on both sides—were children.

"In the future, the 'Power Rangers' could be the most recommended show by everybody if they just cut down on the violence,"[6] said 10-year-old Shawn Susanka of Santa Ana. "I used to watch 'Ninja Turtles' when I was little," said Richard Stowers, a 13-year-old from Cypress. "I used to play. I never got hurt. No one else ever got hurt. I think it's stupid to go crazy over it."[7] One more, courtesy of six-year-old Ikagar Singh, a martial arts student who was photographed for the piece: "They fight all those monsters, those yucky monsters."[8]

Adult feedback to the paper was similarly divided. Schoolteacher Debra Weller (age 40) said kids had to be barred from playing Power Rangers because they were "trying to mutilate[9] one another." Paula Stewart (34) watched with her son and was offended less by the violence than by the show's stories. "The plots are stupid,"[10] she said. Tim Meryweather (38), Joan Lewis (30), and Rodd Weber (29), all felt the Power Rangers were good role models. Sharon Fry (53) referenced a son-in-law who was never allowed to play with guns as a child, then grew up and started hoarding firearms. "If they can't be little boys and play with that kind of stuff," said Fry, "they're going to grow to be big boys, and they're going to have worse problems."[11]

There was even a celebrity respondent. Saban Entertainment declined to comment, but actor Walter Jones chimed in with this bit of wisdom. "Kids fantasize about being heroes," Jones said. "They fantasize about saving the world, stopping the bad guys. That's better than fantasizing about being the drug dealer[12] down the street."

Calls for a content advisory system predated *Mighty Morphin Power Rangers* and were something that Loesch mostly dismissed when Fox Kids came under fire as *X-Men* took off. "I think that some of the heated-up discussion about violence may not be dealing with the real issues,"[13] Loesch said in July 1993, pointing to guns and criminal activity as more relevant matters than cartoon violence. Sure, she was defending her castle, but she'd also been weaned on the likes of Daffy Duck; if Loesch as a six-year-old in Mississippi could separate reality from fantasy in 1952, why couldn't a six-year-old in Mississippi do the same in 1992?

"I was going to ruin the children of America," Loesch said. "That's what I was told from a very prominent social scientist. I didn't believe it, but that weighed on my shoulders. . . . One of the messages I would often say to the critics [was] they underestimated our audience. They underestimate kids. They underestimate the fact that kids know it's not real. Give kids more credit. We never had any evidence that any episode of *Power Rangers* ever created problems for children. Not one."

Internal hesitance over *MMPR* helped Fox Kids preplan for a public blowback, to the point that it commissioned dozens of public service announcements (PSAs) to be aired alongside episodes. These PSAs made the show's heavy-handed moral lessons seem subtle and were produced with an adherence to the show's aesthetic and vibe, making them feel part of its world. It would have been easy to film these messages, all about 30 to 60 seconds in length, as bare-bones as possible—have the Power Rangers in costume, standing in front of a chalkboard spouting quick life lessons via ADR—and throw them out to the world to be immediately dismissed as the charade that most PSAs typically were. "It is naïve to believe that a majority of children will listen to positive messages," Dr. Robert Schumann[14] said.

But there was legitimate thought *and* filmmaking behind the PSAs—and sometimes even highlighted therein. Some of *MMPR*'s best PSAs illuminated how TV is made, like when David Yost (in character as Billy) and Thuy Trang (likewise for Trini) demonstrated how Trini's cousin Sylvia was "transformed" into a cardboard cutout in "No Clowning Around." Another one centers around an encounter between Paul Schrier, Jason Narvy, and a group of kids to whom the comedic duo must explain that they aren't the bumbling characters they play on TV. "Television is full of make-believe, guys," Schrier says. "In real life, Jason's my best friend." It's funny, wholesome, and the kind of thing that'll never air anew on TV again—not because it isn't necessary or valuable but because the children's TV landscape (and entertainment in general) is so far removed from what it was in the early 1990s.

A few years later, the Telecommunications Act of 1996 mandated the entertainment industry to develop a TV ratings system that could be used in conjunction with V-chip technology to help parents block undesirable content. Among those ratings was one practically tailored to account for the existence of *Power Rangers*—TV-Y7-FV. It indicates that a show is suitable for kids seven years and older but includes an amount of fantasy violence considered more intense than parents might find acceptable. Beginning with its fifth season in 1997, every *Power Rangers* episode broadcast on network TV carried this rating, and any parent—whether offended by plot or punches—could bar it from their home with the click of a button.

Despite the hoopla over *Power Rangers'* violence in the media, Fox Kids brass seldom received feedback from concerned parents. Much more common (or at least better remembered) were heartfelt communications—how *Power Rangers* helped autistic children develop consistent routines, how seeing a Black superhero on TV made a difference in a kid's self-esteem, and how a message about injury prevention helped a boy who was struck by a delivery truck and flung 15 feet away escape with just a few bruises—and those of perverted fans. "I get some crazy letters from some older women, some really weird letters,"[15] Jason David Frank said. "The strangest one said that she could feel my hair, I'm in her dreams, fate put us together and that I'm a 'gargoyle of God' to her." The female actors often received mail from prison inmates. Kids sometimes left their phone numbers on letters, eliciting funny calls from Narvy and Schrier, in character.

The most intense reaction ever received by Saban Entertainment from the public wasn't prompted by a kick, a pie to the face, or a strike from the Megazord's sword. At the end of "The Green Candle, Part II," Tommy and Kimberly share a kiss for about three seconds. Tommy has not only just fought his presumed last battle as a Power Ranger but also labored to find the courage to ask Kimberly to a school dance. Their kiss is the perfect tension cutter in a moment riddled with anxiety. It also drew the ire of prudes.

"We had a hotline at Saban where people could call in and complain," Ellen Levy-Sarnoff said. "When that kiss happened, the phones were ringing off the hook. We couldn't believe it. It was just a little innocent, first-love kiss. I'm telling you, parents went bananas. 'How could you have sex on *Power Rangers*?' I can't begin to tell you how much flak that caused."

PRODUCER: RONNIE HADAR
LINE PRODUCER: JONATHAN TZACHOR
U.P.M: CHIP LYNN
DIRECTOR: TERENCE WINKLESS

CAST & CREW CHECK MAILBOXES FOR CLUSTER 16

MMPR PRODUCTIONS, INC.
4000 W. Alameda Ave., Burbank, CA 91505
TEL: (818) 972-4800 / FAX: (818) 972-4895
STAGE: 26030 Ave Hall#3, Valencia, CA 91355
TEL: (805) 294-1912/FAX: (805) 294-1897

Title: "POWER RANGERS"
Episodes 58,59,60
Weather: Partly Cloudy & Cool Low 70s
Sunrise: 6:02A Sunset: 6:01P

CREW CALL
6:30A

Date: WEDNESDAY, MARCH 16-1994
Shoot Day #1 Day out of 11
Crew call: 6:30A (Black)
Shooting call: 7:30A
Location: VALENCIA STAGE

SET/SCENE DESCRIPTION	SCENES	CAST	D/N	PAGES	LOCATIONS
•INT - YOUTH CENTER "Raul, Rene, Angela's Birthday"	6001	3,5,6,7,8,9,10,Y	D-1	1 3/8	VALENCIA STAGE Mark Manes Studios
•INT - YOUTH CENTER "Tommy Gets Pointers From Ernie"	5803	1,2,5,6,7,8,9,10,X	D	2 5/8	26030 Ave Hall STAGE #3 VALENCIA, CA
•INT - YOUTH CENTER "Tommy Works Out With Rene"	5805	6,10	D-	4/8	805.294.1917
•INT - YOUTH CENTER "Tommy Doesn't Hear Communicator"	5818	6,10	D-	5/8	HOSPITAL: HENRY MAYO MEMORIAL
•INT - YOUTH CENTER "Jordan Provokes Telly-Finally" - 2ND UNIT -	5821	6,10	D-	5/8	HOSPITAL 23845 W. McBean Pky VALENCIA, CA
•EXT - JEWELRY SHOP "Zack Leaves In Disgust"	6006	3	D-	3/8	805.253.8000
		TOTAL PAGES	-	6 5/8	

CAST AND DAY PLAYERS	CHARACTER	MAKE-UP	SET CALL	REMARKS
1. AUSTIN ST. JOHN	JASON	7:30A	8:30A	REPORT TO STAGE
2. THUY TRANG	TRINI	7:30A	8:30A	
3. WALTER JONES	ZACH	6:30A	6:30A	
4. DAVID YOST	BILLY	H	H	—
5. AMY JO JOHNSON	KIMBERLY	5:30A	6:30A	REPORT TO STAGE
6. JASON FRANK	TOMMY	6:30A		
7. PAUL SCHRIER	BULK	6:30A		
8. JASON NARVY	SKULL	6:30A		
9. RENE GRIGGS	ANGELA	6:30A		
10. RICHARD GENNESSE	ERNIE	6:30A		

ATMOSPHERE AND STAND-INS		SPECIAL INSTRUCTIONS
15 YOUTH CENTER PATRONS IN @ 7:A		PROPS - BATTERED GUITAR, EXERCISE MATS, WEIGHT BENCH & WEIGHTS/DUMBBELLS (6001) "HOW TO PLAY FOOTBALL" BOOK (5803) Tommy's BACKPACK (5818,21)
10 YOUTH CENTER PATRONS IN @ 7:A		
		SET DECO - TACKLE MACHINE (5805) PRACTICAL EXERCISE BIKE - PRACTICAL (5818,21)
		WARD - BULK IN A BALLET COSTUME (5803)

COMMENTS
TUESDAY - AUSTIN OR DIFF DAY (PER CHIP) BEFORE CLUSTER #16 BEGINS ON WEDNESDAY

PRODUCTION MANAGER: CHIP LYNN 818.557.4797
FIRST ASSISTANT DIRECTOR: HAL OLOFSSON 213.931.3848
SECOND ASSISTANT DIRECTOR: NICK KELLIS 818.567.7785 Pager

A call sheet from a cluster in which footage was shot for the final three episodes of *Mighty Morphin Power Rangers'* **first season.** Courtesy Gary Moir

CHAPTER 10

The Power Transfer

About four and a half minutes into "White Light, Part II," Zordon, now voiced by the late Bob Manahan, promises that "a momentous occasion" is imminent for the group of anxious young adults before him—three of them filming some of their final scenes. Minutes earlier, they learned, thanks to inadvertent sleuthing and spying by David Yost's Billy, that Zordon and Alpha—mysteriously absent throughout part 1—snuck away to cook up something spicy: a new Power Ranger. Whoever could it be? Maybe the fan favorite who just happens to be returning home this episode after a brief vacation to clear his head following another loss of his powers?

In fairness, there was a half-hearted effort to plant red herrings leading up to the inevitable reveal. As "Zyu2" footage dwindled and Tommy's time as the Green Ranger ended again, writer Mark Hoffmeier introduced Richie—a Hispanic teen who worked for Ernie at the Angel Grove Youth Center—and Curtis, Zack's cousin from St. Louis who'd just recently moved to town. They're not particularly fleshed out or involved in the day-to-day happenings of the 12 cumulative episodes in which they appear but were around enough to at least get a naïve six-year-old to think, "Hey, maybe they'll become a Power Ranger someday!"

But the job was Tommy Oliver's to lose from the moment Fox Kids started fielding phone calls from parents whose kids threatened to go hungry when the Green Ranger went kaput.

"I present to you . . . the White Ranger," Zordon says as an oversized spotlight beams down and a Christ-like figure descends. Jason David Frank hoisted on a crane? Nah, a fiberglass model sculpted by artist Connor McCullagh and filmed as a silhouette as it slowly funnels to the floor; the static toy just *slightly* jitters as it careens downward in a shot straight out of the Ray Harryhausen playbook. It's one of several American-composed sequences that stand out in a two-parter helmed by producer Jonathan Tzachor, in the director's chair for the first time since shooting season 1's "Gung Ho!"

The figure lands in front of the power teens. They're sporting white spandex outfitted in gold trim as well as a large black shield adorned with a gold, embossed symbol of an indeterminate feline. Their helmet is a great departure from those worn by the heroes we've come to know: whereas those are fitted with subtle features of their prehistoric inspirations and have a mouth plate shaped like a pair of lips, this one is more overt in its tribute—a gold, white, and black pattern designed to look like a cat's profile, complete with a flat mouth cover flanked by a pair of fangs and three pairs of whiskers. Black stripes on the helmet's crown suggest that this cat might be a (non-saber-tooth) tiger.

Their new comrade slowly unclasps their helmet. Kimberly fainting into an ad break tells us all we need to know before Tommy, ponytail and all, emerges after the commercial. "Guess who's back?" he says with a smile before attending to his girlfriend. Zordon asks the teens if they're pleased with their new leader, which plays awkwardly as a viewer if you're oblivious to Jason's forthcoming departure from the team. The soon-to-be-former Red Ranger forces the kind of grin that screams, "Mom's making me take this picture."

Whether happiness over Tommy's return was feigned or genuine in front of the camera, it was nothing compared to the excitement in the *MMPR* C-suite. A full-time move to weekday afternoons at 4:30 p.m. had been a no-brainer coming out of the May 1994 sweeps period.[1] The show more than doubled the performance of its nearest competition (*Garfield and Friends*) for two- to 11-year-old eyeballs in markets where it aired in the afternoon (19.6 rating/46 share) and the few where it still aired in the morning (13.1/53). Interest among the narrower six- to 11-year-old demographic was slightly higher in both time slots (14.5/57; 20.5/46), and it ruled Saturday morning[2] with an 8.7 rating, ahead of six other Fox Kids programs. By the time it was a year old, one in five American kids watched *MMPR*. And just about every boy in the country tuned in to see who was under the White Ranger's helmet.

"We had a great marketing and promo department that really teased it perfectly," said Maureen Smith, Fox Kids' research guru. "There was a lot of buzz. There were adults calling us, 'My son has to know what's going to happen, you've got to tell me, you owe me some favors.' And we had to keep our mouths quiet. That episode delivered a 91 share of boys 6–11. Ninety-one percent of boys ages 6–11 watching TV during that time period watched that episode of *Power Rangers*. I just about fell out of my chair when I saw it. I'd never seen a number that high."

MMPR was unstoppable. Not only did the show have a bona fide star back in the fold, but he was in a brand-new suit, and he and his teammates were equipped with a bevy of new Zords to combat Lord Zedd's forces—all of which meant another holiday season with must-have toys. The transforming Tigerzord with accompanying eight-inch White Ranger figure (manufacturer's suggested retail price [MSRP] of $29.99) became the linchpin of a fall 1994 Bandai America lineup that also featured new transforming and combinable toys for the Red Ranger (Red Dragon Thunderzord, MSRP $14.99) and the remaining foursome (Thunderzord Assault Team, MSRP $24.99).

Jason David Frank's return as Tommy Oliver in the two-parter "White Light" was a ratings bonanza for the Fox Kids Network. The White Ranger suit was adapted from *Gosei Sentai Dairanger.* Courtesy The Morphin Museum/© Saban Entertainment

Molds of the eight-inch figures from a year prior were slightly retooled for the fall of 1994 to include "Karate" action features, but the true standouts were 5.5-inch scale "Auto-Morphin" figures. There was one for each of the six original Power Rangers, and all came with two unpainted weapons—a Blade Blaster and their respective signature weapon, all of which could be combined to form the Power

Blaster—as well as a tattoo of their dinosaur symbol. The main selling point: each figure featured a latch through which a headpiece of the character's face could be "morphed" into the respective helmet of a given Power Ranger. If a person has touched a *Power Rangers* toy, there's a great chance it was one of these iconic figures. Each sold for a mere $3.99—just $8.52 in 2024 dollars!—meaning that if you could find them, the entire team could be had for under $25, pretax. How great a value was that? When the exact same figures in 2018 were reissued as part of a collector-targeted line, they retailed for $19.99 apiece.

Bootleggers and opportunists capitalized on the phenomenon, which continued to spawn long lines at toy stores and frustrate parents who saw through the marketing machine but couldn't risk relenting. "I despise Bandai for what they've done," said Stefani Weiss,[3] a mom in Pennsylvania, in November 1994. "But what they've done is very smart business." By the end of 1994, *Power Rangers* was projected to have earned $1 billion in revenue in just 15 months of existence, far outpacing action franchises that preceded it.

Whether *MMPR* actually spurred bad behavior or merely got swept up in the moral panic of the 1980s and 1990s, it undoubtedly thrived on materialism. It wasn't a trailblazer—*He-Man and the Masters of the Universe*, *Transformers*, and *Teenage Mutant Ninja Turtles* all made haste in the toy aisle thanks to captive TV audiences—but *Power Rangers* became the torchbearer of its own achievement and those of its predecessors. He-Man walked so the Green Ranger could run, often right into the blank pages and film rolls of critics eager to take a whack at it for turning children around the world into plastic addicts.

Developmental psychologist Chris Boyatzis confesses to having lunchboxes celebrating *Batman* (1966) and *The Green Hornet* as a kid. TV shows have always pushed product, directly or indirectly, but the 1980s paved the way for overconsumption.

"A lot of kids TV programs were developed in the '80s to promote toy lines, so it's just the ubiquity and pervasiveness of this consumer culture that's always made me dislike most media for kids on several different levels," Boyatzis said. "It just basically trains kids to be little capitalist consumers. . . . There's a lot that I was critical about with *Power Rangers*, but it was symptomatic. It didn't create the problem, it was just symptomatic of the problem."

Regardless of good intentions from the production side of a goofy, action-packed show and a team excited to tell small-screen stories, *Power Rangers* on some level *was* a toy commercial. Its progenitor, *Super Sentai*, has been coproduced by Bandai Namco[4] since its humble beginnings in 1975. Bandai America, by way of Frank Ward, had an executive on the set to help do what his Japanese counterparts did: ensure that the narrative and toy line were harmoniously wedded to one another, especially ahead of peak shopping periods. Ward and Tzachor, *Power Rangers*' showrunner for its first 10 years, were simpatico.

"Some of the producers that Haim had on other shows . . . they think they're special," Ward said. "They think they're all creative geniuses, and it's beneath them. 'Oh, we don't need toys. We don't care about that, we're creators.' It's hard to describe how important Jonathan was, because he—well, Haim was calling the shots—but not a lot of people would be willing to have this guy representing the toy interests and the marketing interests in their hair all the time. But Jonathan was."

Meetings with toy producers continued to be common for various writers, producers, and staffers into the 2020s. Since *Power Rangers* lagged the most recent *Super Sentai* show by about a year, Bandai America could reuse molds and create new domestic toy products with a healthy head start because the core concepts were already developed. And if they had a concept for a toy that might sell better among U.S. kids—say, for example, special armor or a motorcycle—they'd work with the writing staff to see that it gets inserted into the show.

Jackie Marchand, a writer whose involvement with the show began during production of the second season and lasted into the late 2000s, notes that Bandai's level of involvement ebbed and flowed from year to year and that they were generally an easygoing partner. They'd meet annually for extensive strategy sessions.

"We would have these charts of, 'How many times can we use the blasters? When do they get this power-up? When do they get motorcycles?'" said Marchand. "We had a big, giant chart of all 50 (episodes) and then we'd plug in story elements and then the action elements. . . . We'd make sure we were representing the toy element as best we could. And sometimes we would say, 'No, that's too much,' or 'We're not going to do that.' That was more of a producer's call. If you meet with the toy company, they're definitely going to want you to put a new toy in every episode, and as a writer I'd push back. I'm like, 'That blaster or weapon that we introduced two episodes ago as the best thing in the world now doesn't work because there's a better one?' It's hokey. There is a tipping point where it becomes a show about toys, and there was always pushback from the story department."

As Margaret Loesch made a habit of saying in the 1990s, kids catch on fast.

The unenviable task of replacing three of the six most famous faces among elementary students fell to two martial artists and a singer from Dallas, Texas.

Karan Ashley (Aisha Campbell), Johnny Yong Bosch (Adam Park), and Steve Cardenas (Rocky DeSantos) emerged from the latest *MMPR* casting call. Like their predecessors, they were an incredibly attractive trio and just as ethnically diverse. One upside of the cast swap? It provided easy maneuvering away from the awkward perception of having cast a Black man as the Black Ranger and an Asian woman as the Yellow Ranger. While Cardenas (Hispanic) assumed the slightly diminished role of Red Ranger, Bosch (Korean American) and Ashley (Black) slipped into the Black and Yellow spandex, respectively. And literally.

"I look and it's like all this Black Ranger stuff and I'm like, 'Oh sweet,' and [they say] 'Here's your suit,'"[5] Bosch said, recounting his first wardrobe fitting. "'Oh awesome.' And I pick it up and I look at it. 'Oh, there's a tag.' It says Walter Jones." It was baggy, as was the one left behind by Austin St. John for Cardenas; the costume department had to create muscle suits for them to fill out the spandex. Ashley, whose foot was a full size smaller than Thuy Trang's, was told to wear extra socks whenever she had to wear the suit's boots.

Before ever sporting any stretched-out costumes on-screen, they were introduced a few episodes earlier in a three-parter, "The Ninja Encounter." The trio hail from Stone Canyon, a city near Angel Grove, and come to town for a martial arts competition. They first "meet" the existing Rangers—by this point, Jason, Trini, and Zack were portrayed through a combination of stand-ins, stock footage, and disguised ADR—during an extended chase sequence. If this weren't a show that features rubber-suited monsters, a sentient disembodied head, and six teenagers who have no squabbles with one another whatsoever, this scene would threaten one's suspension of disbelief. The new trio and the oldies, along with Bulk and Skull, attempt to catch a rogue baby stroller, apparently fitted with invisible rockets. The stroller rolls around Castaic Lake in Los Angeles for almost five minutes, ample time for the Stone Canyon trio to show off their cool rollerblading skills while in pursuit. The soon-to-be Rangers along with Tommy, Billy, and Kimberly converge just as the child is about to tumble over a cliffside. Friendships are quickly forged before Lord Zedd kidnaps the newbies in a bid to turn them into evil ninja warriors.

On-air public service announcements were accompanied by print versions, like this one featuring the White Ranger. Courtesy The Morphin Museum/© Saban Entertainment

Beyond the introduction of Adam, Aisha, and Rocky, "The Ninja Encounter, Part I" is distinguished as the series' first to feature zero Japanese footage and also the first in which none of the Rangers morph. Part 3 also was a series trailblazer: it was the first to have music expunged from future airings and home-media distribution. Buzz Clifford's hit "Baby Sittin' Boogie" originally played over a scene of Bulk and Skull tending to the needs of the baby from part 1 but later was replaced with Bulk and Skull's clown car–like theme music. (It's a rare instance where

Saban being a cheapskate worked out for the better because the Clifford song feels incredibly out of time with the show.) By the end of it too, the trio also haphazardly learn the Power Rangers' identities, becoming the first to do so without having the plot erase it from their memory. Zordon brings them to the Command Center to swear an oath of secrecy. Just a couple episodes later, in the two-part "The Power Transfer," they're back in the Rangers' base succeeding Jason, Trini, and Zack, who—minutes after completing their final mission as Power Rangers early in part 2— hand over their Power Coins and get teleported to the deus ex Peace Conference. It's not the cleanest on-screen transition, but for the show's first attempt to write off existing characters and replace them midstream, it's buyable on a basic narrative level—especially for a legion of viewers, at the time, not privy to the off-screen reasons it occurred.

Longer term, it became a stark dividing line. If you were a Jason devotee when Zordon demoted him in favor of Tommy, he was at least still part of the team. You might convince yourself that he could someday reassume command—Tommy has come and gone, but Jason has been a fixture from day one. But this change felt permanent; the former Rangers gave up their powers willingly. Kids spent the last year getting to know and falling in love with these characters, and half of them were gone. If you were consciously or subconsciously seeking a jumping-off point, "The Power Transfer" was an easy place to do it after a steady barrage of "new" was thrown your way.

Still, Saban was certain the helmets were the stars, and he was about to put that to the test in movie theaters across the globe. Assuming, of course, that his movie got made.

The original cast of *Mighty Morphin Power Rangers*, from left to right: David Yost as Billy Cranston, Thuy Trang as Trini Kwan, Jason David Frank as Tommy Oliver, Austin St. John as Jason Scott, Amy Jo Johnson as Kimberly Hart, and Walter Jones as Zack Taylor. Photofest

Power Rangers' progenitor Haim Saban was a big dreamer. But even he could not have expected the show to pave the path to his becoming a billionaire, a key figure in the U.S. Democratic Party, and a Hollywood Walk of Fame honoree. He's flanked here by cast and crew of the 2017 movie. From left: Ludi Lin, Becky G, Saban, Naomi Scott, Elizabeth Banks, RJ Cyler, Dacre Montgomery, and Dean Israelite. Photo by Stewart Cook/Variety/Penske Media via Getty Images

Margaret Loesch (left) and Stan Lee (right) attempted to adapt *Taiyo Sentai Sun Vulcan* while the two worked together at Marvel. Nearly a decade later in 1992, when Haim Saban pitched a similar adaptation to Loesch, she was the only person who didn't laugh him out of the room. Courtesy Margaret Loesch

Bandai America's first wave of *Mighty Morphin Power Rangers* toys, released ahead of the show's premiere in August 1993, featured action figures in eight-inch scale, several inches larger than the standard action figure at the time. Courtesy Richy Salgado

A small sample of the merchandise available to fans of *Mighty Morphin Power Rangers* at its apex, including popular videotapes from PolyGram that stuffed many stockings during the 1993 holiday season and the revolutionary "Auto-Morphin" action figures released in 1994. Courtesy Kenn Glenn

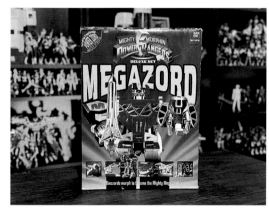

The original transforming Megazord toy retailed for $29.99, or a little more than $60 when adjusted for inflation in 2024. Courtesy Kenn Glenn

Mighty Morphin Power Rangers was a phenomenon with girls as much as boys thanks to the presence of female members in the Pink Ranger (right). During focus-group tests ahead of the show's premiere, girls said they liked that girls in the show "kick butt." Courtesy The Morphin Museum/© Saban Entertainment

The Yellow Ranger was gender swapped from her counterpart in *Kyōryū Sentai Zyuranger,* a tradition that continued for several years thereafter with other teams adapted from *Super Sentai.* The show's first male Yellow Ranger arrived in the show's 11th season, *Ninja Storm.* Courtesy The Morphin Museum/ © Saban Entertainment

The female Power Rangers proved so popular that they received their own line of dolls (left) to compete with **Barbie.** Author's Collection

Bryan Cahill, flanked here by Baboo (left) and Squatt, was a boom mic operator who occasionally filled in for the stunt team. Many former *Power Rangers* staffers liken their experience on the show to film school. Courtesy Bryan Cahill

On-set naps were a must, when possible, for cast members like Carla Perez, who joined the show during production of its second season to play an American version of the villainess Rita Repulsa. Courtesy Bryan Cahill

Concept art of Lord Zedd and Putty Patrollers in his chamber on the moon. Courtesy Yuda Acco

Jason David Frank (Tommy the White Ranger), David Yost (Billy the Blue Ranger), and Amy Jo Johnson (Kimberly the Pink Ranger) were joined by new cast members Johnny Yong Bosch (Adam the Black Ranger), Karan Ashley (Aisha the Yellow Ranger), and Steve Cardenas (Rocky the Red Ranger) for *Mighty Morphin Power Rangers: The Movie*. Photo by Frank Trapper/Corbis via Getty Images

Change was ramped up behind and in front of the camera by the time *Power Rangers Turbo* and its kickoff movie shifted into gear. Courtesy The Morphin Museum/ © Saban Entertainment

2001's *Power Rangers Time Force* was the last season produced by Saban Entertainment. From the left in this production still, its core cast consisted of Deborah Estelle Philips (Katie the Yellow Ranger), Kevin Kleinberg (Trip the Green Ranger), Erin Cahill (Jen the Pink Ranger), Jason Faunt (Wes/Alex the Red Ranger), and Michael Copon (Lucas the Blue Ranger). Courtesy The Morphin Museum/© Saban Entertainment

Decades before he oversaw adult animation at Netflix, Jermaine Turner (furthest right) was a Fox Kids executive and Disney executive who helped keep *Power Rangers* on the air until Haim Saban repurchased the brand in 2010. Photo by Natasha Campos/Getty Images for Netflix

The cast of *Power Rangers Samurai*, the first season produced by Saban Brands. From left: Erika Fong (Mia the Pink Ranger), Hector David Jr. (Mike the Green Ranger), Alex Heartman (Jayden the Red Ranger), Najee De-Tiege (Kevin the Blue Ranger), and Brittany Anne Pirtle (Emily the Yellow Ranger). Album/ Alamy Stock Photo

Longtime writer-producer Judd "Chip" Lynn returned as executive producer for *Power Rangers Dino Charge*, the cast of which was revealed at Power Morphicon 2014. From left to right: James Davies (Chase), Yoshi Sudarso (Koda), Lynn, Brennan Mejia (Tyler), Camille Hyde (Shelby), and Michael Taber (Riley). Photo by Rachel Murray/Getty Images for Saban Brands

Rojan Pandey (left) and Yusef Mousa Aryouib (right) dressed as the Red and Green Dino Charge Power Rangers, respectively, during a U.S. citizenship ceremony in 2016. Photo by Win McNamee/Getty Images

As part of a yearlong celebration for the show's twentieth anniversary, a legion of Red Power Rangers overtook New York City for a day. The festivities included a hoops session with local children and NBA star J. R. Smith. Photo by James Devaney/WireImage/Getty Images

Beginning with 2014's *Power Rangers Dino Charge*, the writer-producer duo of Becca Barnes (left) and Alwyn Dale (right) had a hand in most episodes of the show through *Power Rangers Cosmic Fury*, the thirtieth and final season in the show's original continuity. Courtesy Becca Barnes

From left to right, the primary cast of *Power Rangers Cosmic Fury*: Kai Moya (Ollie the Blue Ranger), Russell Curry (Zayto the Zenith Ranger), Hunter Deno (Amelia the Red Ranger), executive producer Simon Bennett, Jacqueline Joe (Fern the Orange Ranger), Tessa Rao (Izzy the Green Ranger), Chance Perez (Javi the Black Ranger), and Jordon Fite (Aiyon the Gold Ranger). Courtesy Simon Bennett

CHAPTER 11

Ninja Quest

A *Power Rangers* movie was in the works from the moment it was clear the show was a hit. Rights to develop a flick—negotiated with the help of David Greenblatt, a leading agent who a couple years later founded Endeavor Talent Agency with Ari Emanuel—were hotly contested by the end of 1993.[1] By April 1994,[2] they were won by 20th Century Fox, which seemed a natural fit from the outside looking in since *Mighty Morphin Power Rangers* aired under the News Corporation umbrella.

Steve Wang was brought on to direct. A special effects guru, Wang's biggest claim to fame was *The Guyver*,[3] a $3 million American adaptation of a manga series about a symbiotic bio-mech suit that starred Mark Hamill. Wang, a Taiwanese American whose fondness for the Japanese tokusatsu shows of his youth set him on course for a filmmaking career, codirected that film before flying solo on its sequel, *Guyver: Dark Hero*.

He drew up 300 storyboard pages, imagining ways to embellish the unique suits and environments that were already staples in *MMPR* while bringing some completely new flourishes to the table. A concept that most excited him: an action-packed opening scene that put the team on motorcycles.[4]

In between his *Guyver* stints, Wang met Koichi Sakamoto, who'd worked as a stuntman in the Japanese TV industry before immigrating to study film in America. Over time, Sakamoto befriended enough like-minded Japanese stunties to form a small stunt team, Alpha Stunts, which Wang hired to work on the *Guyver* sequel.[5] Wang and Sakamoto quickly hit it off, bonding over their shared love of Hong Kong action cinema and tokusatsu influences, and the pair couldn't wait to work together on the *Power Rangers* movie.

Alas, that dream was dashed about as quickly as it started. In July, halfway through preproduction on a film set to begin shooting in Australia that fall, Wang left the project over "major creative differences"[6] with 20th Century Fox. Among other things, the studio didn't want Wang to handle the second-unit action; they wanted seasoned Hollywood veteran Jeff Imada (*Lethal Weapon*). Wang at the time didn't know Imada but hoped they'd let the Alpha Stunts team—with whom Saban Entertainment had already been working on *VR Troopers*—work with Imada; 20th Century Fox barred Wang from communicating with Imada during preproduction.

"The sad thing was that Haim Saban and I were on the same page,"[7] Wang said. "Everything I wanted to do, he was like, '100 percent, this is great, I love this.'" But the studio—which paid a seven-figure sum for the license and bore the brunt of an initial $18 million budget—had the final say in just about every instance.

"It just got to a point where I just felt like, 'I have no control over this movie whatsoever. I don't even know[8] what I'm making,'" Wang said. "So ultimately, I just was like, 'I'm leaving, I can't do this film. I don't know what you guys are trying to do but I can't do it.'"

And thus, a turmoil-stuffed production was underway.

Bryan Spicer, a TV director and producer fresh off a healthy stint with *Parker Lewis Can't Lose*, succeeded Wang. He relished the opportunity[9] despite having no familiarity with the show and was particularly enticed by getting to work on a visual effects–heavy project at a time when computer-generated imagery (CGI) was just starting to revolutionize the industry.

By the time Spicer joined, the script was mostly realized. When the final credits rolled, it was attributed solely to Arne Olsen, who also received a treatment credit along with John Kamps. The earliest available versions, though, also involved sci-fi TV veteran David Kemper. Per IMDb, *Mighty Morphin Power Rangers: The Movie* was Kamps's first writing credit, while Olsen's only previous kid-friendly screenplay was *Cop and a Half*, a buddy comedy starring Burt Reynolds.

A Kemper–Olsen revised draft of the script, dated October 15, 1994, and first unearthed[10] by journalist and *Power Rangers* fan Shamus Kelley, is stuffed with oodles of dialogue and expository background that didn't make it into the final cut. It's interesting stuff to see from a movie production standpoint, but as Kelley surmised as part of his note-taking,

"The script itself is not much better than the movie as is. . . . It's still a confused as hell movie and barely resembles[11] *Power Rangers*."

Therein lies the core friction: *Mighty Morphin Power Rangers: The Movie* is a relatively expensive adaptation of a cheaply produced kids show adapted from another cheaply produced kids show. This movie had to look and feel as much like *MMPR* as possible while also distancing itself from the show in order to justify its existence and, at minimum, be tolerable to those outside of the two- to 11-year-old demographic. Given the parameters and expectations, there wasn't really a choice to approach the story differently than how the writers did: a generic kids adventure story with six protagonists differentiated mainly by the color of their clothes and nothing more. In their earliest TV forms, the Power Rangers are about as paper-thin as characters can get, but they feel completely fleshed out there compared to the versions here, who are mere action figures to be hurled out of airplanes and kicked and punched into oblivion until they find the MacGuffin that makes them able to kick and punch even harder. And it certainly didn't aid the creative effort that three of those six leads were effectively blank slates—at least Jason David Frank, Amy Jo Johnson, and David Yost were well established on-screen. Karan Ashley, Johnny Yong Bosch, and Steve Cardenas didn't have that luxury.

"You have actors that have been doing the role for a year and became famous with it despite what was intended by the production company or not, and you lose them for the film," said Jason Narvy. "I'm so grateful that the new cast came in because I'm as close to Steve Cardenas, I'm as close to Johnny Bosch really as I am anybody in this world excepting Paulie [Schrier]. But still, you got to wonder what that last-minute change did to how the film came out."

Ashley had performance cred. As a teenager, she was part of a pop group called K.R.U.S.H.,[12] which featured prominently on the platinum-selling soundtrack for the Daman Wayans film *Mo' Money*. But Bosch and Cardenas were, like Frank, charismatic martial artists whom producers felt could figure out the acting part later. When hired, all were told they'd be not only replacing some of the cast but also soon shipped to Australia to shoot a feature film. They moved immediately to Los Angeles in July 1994, started filming their first scenes for the TV show in mid-August, and by October were on a plane to another country to film a movie. That's a lot to put on a trio of young adults in any era, let alone a world that pre-dated smartphones and social media.

"My sister got married, I couldn't even go to her wedding in Vegas,"[13] Ashley said. "We had one month to shoot 20 episodes and we were whisked off to do the movie. And the movie was supposed to take three months."

The second edition of the *Mighty Morphin Power Rangers* team included, from left, Johnny Yong Bosch (as Adam), Amy Jo Johnson (Kimberly), Jason David Frank (Tommy), David Yost (Billy), Karan Ashley (Aisha), and Steve Cardenas (Rocky). Courtesy The Morphin Museum/© Saban Entertainment

Three months turned into six due to reshoots. Many stemmed from the exit and return of actor and model Gabrielle Fitzpatrick, who in the film plays a bikini-clad warrior named Dulcea. Dulcea sets the Rangers on a quest to retrieve the "the Great Power," which will afford them new Ninjazords and the ability to save Zordon, who's on his deathbed after a confrontation with the film's lead villain, Ivan Ooze. She's an overtly sexual, ass-kicking spirit guide; to this day, it remains unbelievable that such a scantily clad character exists in *Power Rangers.*

"I think Barbarella's a beautiful character and I felt a little Barbarella-esque, if you could say, in this one," Fitzpatrick said.[14] "And having been a model, the bikini wasn't a problem for me. I was always in bikinis at that age. It was no big deal for me to be in a swimsuit, I didn't even think about it cause Australians are always in swimsuits."

Fitzpatrick, making her feature-film debut after a few small roles in Australian television, was cast following a worldwide search and a meet and greet with producer Jon Landau, the studio's executive vice president of feature-film production (and who was also in the early stages of shepherding a little-known James Cameron picture, *Titanic*). While doing a camera test, Fitzpatrick performed a kick and fell to the ground writhing in pain. The shock and awe in the moment gave way to a rudimentary diagnosis: she'd developed an ovarian cyst, but it was large enough to force a break from work and prompt recasting. Mariska Hargitay, an American TV bit player, replaced her. Hargitay arrived in November, slipped into the loincloth bikini, and filmed quite a bit of material—including extended training sequences with the teenagers as they learn to improve their confidence and battle skills ahead of a dangerous mission without their morphers. None of that stuff, nor Hargitay, made it into the film.

"We were getting close to Christmas and they had me on hold a lot," Hargitay told Seth Meyers[15] during a 2019 interview. Hargitay flew home for the holidays, typically a shutdown period for the industry, and got in touch with the production on January 3. "I called them and I'm like, 'OK, I'm ready.' And they're like, 'Sweetie, you're good, don't worry about it.' And they fired me." The official stance was that Hargitay "wasn't quite right"[16] for the role and that her performance was too "logic-based for the character." Whatever the case, in the intervening period, Fitzpatrick's health improved enough that she was asked to return, and she happily did so. (Things worked out okay for Hargitay: as of late 2024, she was the only original cast member left on *Law & Order: Special Victims Unit*, which premiered in 1999.)

A perplexing aesthetic choice prompted other reshoots: the Power Rangers' visors and mouth plates were removed from their helmets to show the actors' faces. Decades later, photos surfaced of these shots, and they're about as goofy looking as they sound. Spicer said[17] this was to allow filmgoers to see the emotions expressed by the actors. While well intentioned, the choice spoke to 20th Century Fox's complete misunderstanding of *MMPR*. According to *Power Rangers: The Ultimate Visual History*, producers intervened on the basis that the heroes shouldn't have their identities revealed.

"The movie started out rough,"[18] said Tony Oliver, an uncredited consultant on the film. "So, Haim asked me to stay in touch and keep an eye on things. So I became the most hated person on that set, cause I would tell on them all the time." Through a third party, Oliver heard that Saban was so distraught by 20th Century Fox's handling of his IP that he called

Rupert Murdoch and threatened to pull the license. "That changed everything. After that, I was invited to set every day to look at the last night's rewrites and give my comments. I couldn't veto, but if I said, 'That sucks, you can't do it,' they usually didn't do it."

Safety concerns slowed shooting too. Alpha 5 suit actor Peta-Maree Rixon was briefly hospitalized[19] after suffering heat exhaustion because the material of their costumes made it difficult for air to circulate. Large fans were later brought on set to keep actors air-conditioned between takes. The Rangers' costumes, crafted by prosthetics artist Rob Burman and his wife Jennifer, were remnants of Wang's time on the film. Fox, based on designs administered to Burman via Wang, sought big, muscular suits, almost bubble-like. Neither man felt confident in that ask.

"We started to try and sculpt it looking like the original designs and he came in and said 'No, no, no, no, no,[20] this is never going to work, none of the stuntmen are going to be able to move in it," Burman said. Burman sold Wang on approaching them like "a skinsuit Ferrari," and that's exactly what the production got. They're 100 percent recognizable as Power Rangers but—literally—elevated. The Burmans' suits are among the most aesthetically pleasing in *Power Rangers* history but—despite their best efforts—were also the most immobile. Plans to carry the movie suits over to the show's third season were scrapped; they were just too restrictive and airtight to safely use. Burman tried to warn them when the costumer department presented him with bolts and bolts of fabric—double-processed vinyl on spandex—that would go underneath the polyurethane rubber armor.

"Basically, it forced us into making a suit that was like wearing a 45-pound layer of cellophane[21] over your whole body," Burman said. "If the actors complained, rightfully so. They didn't breathe." The approximate cost of each colorful death trap? $10,000. Thirty were made, five for each color.

A director leaving in preproduction. Executives headbutting. Life-threatening costumes. An extended stay in Australia. Months of reshoots. That's a lot of headache for a 90-minute kids movie.

As tumultuous as the production proved to be, a crucial win came in the casting of Paul Freeman as the villainous Ivan Ooze, a "morphological being" awakened after a 6,000-year imprisonment within a giant egg. Freeman, by far the most famous name attached after starring opposite Harrison Ford in *Raiders of the Lost Ark* a decade earlier, delivers a hammy performance that ensured that *Mighty Morphin Power Rangers: The Movie* would gain cult status regardless of whether the show survived beyond the 1990s.

Sporting a black and purple robe with appendages and other dressings evocative of his name, Ivan Ooze looks more like a weathered royal than a "galactically feared" and "universally despised" tyrant. The makeup department spent upward of four hours applying prosthetics to Freeman's face and hands as called for throughout filming (down from an educational trial run that took seven hours[22]). Ooze's horned head is something of a cross between Thanos and Medusa—complete with a protruding cleft comprised of two intertwining tentacles. "The only thing I could eat in this costume were smoked oysters,[23] which had to be dropped into my mouth," Freeman said. It was good fortune that he liked them.

Freeman, then 52, imbued Ooze with a level of theatricality that could come only from someone who came of age onstage. The classically trained Brit told the *Los Angeles Times* ahead of the movie's June 1995 premiere—the original Easter weekend release date was unrealistic by the winter—that his performance was "like nothing else you've seen in the last 100 years."[24] There will probably never be another like it in the next 100 years either. He drew inspiration from some of his favorite comedic forebears, American actor W. C. Fields and cartoon icon Bugs Bunny. Freeman's quips throughout the film—many of them written on the fly the day before or during production—enliven an otherwise ho-hum adventure. Ooze invades the Command Center and caps a short verbal standoff with Zordon by whipping out a flute and commencing a destructive tirade, interlaced with shoutouts to all the tragic events across history he missed while imprisoned.

"The Black Plague!"

"The Spanish Inquisition!"

And finally, with increased distress and tempered delivery, "The *Brady Bunch* reunion!"

At the time, Freeman worried that his effort would go unnoticed because of the makeup, and maybe it did on a professional level; this kid flick is his most notable role following *Raiders*. But with it came the adoration of millions of children who'd grow up with an unfettered fondness for the character, who embodied the spirit of what Saban imagined *Power Rangers* could be a decade earlier when he was sitting in a Japanese hotel room. Whether Ivan Ooze is *Power Rangers*' best villain is a matter of taste and preference, but he couldn't fit better into a "live-action cartoon."

A young kid at the center of the film's B plot, Fred Kelman (played by Jamie Croft), during the climax works to free his dad and other adults in Angel Grove from an evil spell.

This plot initially involved Bulk and Skull as proprietors of Ooze's spellbinding goo after answering a "Help Wanted" ad. Over the course of season 2, *MMPR*'s writers, along with Schrier and Narvy, worked to steer the bumbling pair away from being one-note bullies and into more developed characters in their own right. Going into season 3, the plan was to make them members of a junior police force, so it's likely the initial movie take was seen as too much of a step backward for the characters. The result, though, was a drastic reduction of Bulk and Skull's movie screen time as well as the complete elimination of Ernie, whose actor also had flown to Australia. "I think maybe you can see him in the background of one take, one shot," Narvy said. "We spent a lot of time together out at the bars in Sydney."

In the late 1970s, Peter Mochrie, who plays Fred's nameless father ("It was always 'Mr. Kelman' in the script," Mochrie said), kicked off a distinguished career in Australian TV and film with his role as an Olympic swimmer in the soap *The Restless Years*. Principal photography for the entire movie was shot in his country, and it is still one of the most expensive films produced down under.

"Australia hadn't had a lot of blockbusters come to town, and for this to come, it was mega," Mochrie said. "The Americans come to town with lots of money and everybody's going, 'Yea, ca-ching, ca-ching.'"

Extreme sports are as quintessentially 1990s as *MMPR*, and so—rather than the motorcycle showdown imagined by Wang—the film opens with the six Rangers, as well as Bulk and Skull, skydiving out of an airplane to raise money for the Angel Grove Fire Department. Green screens, high-speed fans, and wires were used to create close-ups of the characters as they descended to the ground, but a professional skydive unit performed actual dives that were captured for the film. They're an impressive lot, led by whoever's playing Tommy—the guy sky-surfs on a de-wheeled skateboard throughout his jump before nailing the landing on a target in downtown Sydney's Darling Harbour. That was Mochrie's first day on set.

"It's right next door to the city's central business district," Mochrie said. "They took over this entire park, and the first scene is these guys parachuting out of a plane. It was amazing, it was huge. They've got six, seven major Panavision cameras pointed on the sky making sure this was done. I think we had to do it in one take."

The movie begins in the sky and comes to a climax above it. Throughout, Ivan Ooze has used brainwashed adults to unearth a pair of gigantic robots against which the Rangers debut their brand-new Ninjazords, adapted from counterparts in the 1994 series *Ninja Sentai Kakuranger*. For the first time, the giant machines were created using CGI, and the results were rough.

In hindsight, it's easy to laugh at the film's dated graphics and chalk them up to being of the time, except they were dismissible then too. Although it cost one-third of the budget and took about eight months to come together, it inevitably drew unfavorable comparisons to the dynamic textures and lifelike realism on display in *Jurassic Park*, then two years old. Pixar's *Toy Story* released just four months later for the same target audience and cost just $10 million more—though it had years of work behind it. *Jumanji*, another CGI-heavy family film, carried a budget similar to *Jurassic Park* but was released a month later.

The climactic battle in *Mighty Morphin Power Rangers: The Movie* not only sticks out when propped against contemporaries, but also when juxtaposed with itself. For the better part of its run time, the film leans on impressive practical effects and stunt work. Until the end, its most apparently dated animations are delivered on the few occasions when Ivan Ooze transforms into a glob of purple goo—and the nature of the character lends itself to that working better than it should. But in the final showdown with Ooze, who fuses with the body of one of his giant machines to wage battle with the Ninja Megazord, the warts are too prominent. Whatever the film lacks narratively or as a character romp, it's a nicely paced adventure with incredible action set pieces. Its devolution into CGI sludge is as distracting as it was prescient for the future of a genre. "The half-life of CG technology is now so swift that watching a film made just a single calendar year prior is like seeing some laughable, fusty relic of a bygone era," said journalist David Jenkins.[25] "But the effects in the final reel of *Mighty Morphin Power Rangers: The Movie* have to be seen to be believed. Words lack the essential capacity to describe them. The passage of time has made the film feel like an avant-garde work that almost acts as a commentary on the modern blockbuster."

Critics described *MMPR: The Movie* as a plight through which the nation's parents would simply have to suffer. Pulitzer Prize winner Roger Ebert[26] wrote that it was "about as close as you can get to absolute nothing and still have a product to project on the screen" while offering backhanded praise for Ivan Ooze. "Some of his dialogue seems to have been slipped into the film by the writers as an antidote to their own boredom." Harry Sheehan offered one of the most diplomatic reviews. "In general, the movie is a model of professional dispatch,[27] delivering exactly what its presold audience would demand and then giving considerably more," wrote Sheehan, who perhaps too generously praised a final battle "produced through excellent computer effects."

The box office of *Mighty Morphin Power Rangers: The Movie* didn't match the small-screen boom, but it remains a cult classic thanks in large part to the performance of Paul Freeman as Ivan Ooze (visible in the background of this poster). © 20th Century Studios

Harsh words were easier to swallow than the middling box office. *Mighty Morphin Power Rangers: The Movie* opened to $17 million (inflation-adjusted $34 million) on 2,407 domestic screens, good for fourth place in a crowded five-day Independence Day window featuring *Apollo 13* ($38.5 million in its debut), Disney's *Pocahontas* ($23.4 million in its third week), and *Batman Forever* ($21.8 million in its third week). *MMPR: The Movie* clawed to a $66 million finish, likely strong enough to make back its budget (despite running afoul) and the costs of a marketing campaign that included, among other things, a trailblazing McDonald's toy promotion that didn't involve the purchase of a Happy Meal. But it wasn't even half the gross of 1990's *Teenage Mutant Ninja Turtles* ($135,265,915) or better than that film's sequel ($78,656,813). In a duel between cartoony, merchandise-driven martial arts franchises, the Turtles routed the Rangers.

"It wasn't the hit we hoped it would be," Margaret Loesch said. "We definitely thought it would do better. We were disappointed, I know [20th Century] Fox was disappointed. . . . We were a little frustrated about the decisions that the movie-makers were making because we weren't involved. Remember, Haim and I were involved—especially Haim, of course—every step of the way, every major decision [with the show]. And when you don't have that, you feel like, 'Ah! My baby! What are you doing?' But I'm not saying that's the reason the movie didn't work. I don't know. Maybe it just wasn't good enough or maybe the timing was wrong. I would have thought the timing would be right, but who knows?"

As the movie winds down, the city's children, along with Bulk and Skull, save their parents from walking off a cliff, and the Rangers revive their own surrogate father. It best mirrors the show in the final minutes. All our heroes converge at a nondescript lakeside hangout for a bite to eat. The Rangers laud Fred's accomplishment and convince him it's not impossible that he could be a Power Ranger someday, the same dramatic irony-laden banter that one might find at the Angel Grove Youth Center. Van Halen's "Dreams" fades in as an extravagant—and 100 percent practical—fireworks show leads us into the credits.

Its fiery centerpiece spells out "Thank you Power Rangers," a message from Angel Grove to its anonymous saviors. It just as easily could have been from the kids across the world ready to move on after this final adventure.

CHAPTER 12

Rangers in Reverse

Functionally, *Mighty Morphin Power Rangers: The Movie* works best as a coda following the show's second season, even if one must lean on suspension of disbelief to abstain from asking, "Why is the Command Center lit like a doctor's office?" or "Why do the Power Rangers' helmets have headlights?" In a perfect world, the suits from the movie would have carried over to season 3, and the movie would act as a bridge, allowing for the enhanced vibes to continue a little longer while the production team and Bandai plotted their next big shake-up: retiring the *Zyuranger* suits and adapting those of *Chouriki Sentai Ohranger*, Toei's 1995 series, to refresh the show as *Power Rangers Zeo*.

But that's not what happened. Between the suits' immobility (illustrated best by official promo shots wherein the groin of the White Ranger is torn) and Saban Entertainment's overall displeasure with the experience, the movie was left on an island, canonically. Decades before the MCU desensitized people to the concept of the multiverse, the masterminds behind *Power Rangers* unwittingly introduced the idea to eight-year-olds—at least the ones willing to stick around.

The movie's so-so box-office showing was foreseeable by the time June arrived. *MMPR* enjoyed nearly two full years of stratospheric TV ratings and toy-shelf dominance before its dip started in the spring of 1995, when production of the third season got underway. The show was still Fox Kids' top performer by a significant margin, but its average 8.7 rating[1] among kids was a demonstrable decline from its not-so-long-ago heyday, when ratings regularly charted in the teens.

Saban Entertainment didn't wait to see if the movie was a hit: the intended four-part premiere, "Ninja Quest," was filmed in April and essentially reimagines the movie's plot within the confines of the show.

In lieu of Dulcea, we get Ninjor, an import from *Kakuranger* and her polar opposite in every possible way: he's a beefy, blue android/genie-like ninja master voiced by Kim Strauss, who brings the goofy ally to life through a healthy Dudley Do-Right impression. Season 3 reveals Ninjor as the original creator of the Power Coins, and Zordon tasks his team with finding him after the destruction of their Thunderzords by a new recurring villain: Rito Revolto, a walking skeleton dipped in camouflage paint and Rita Repulsa's younger brother.

Rita, proving true to her word, returns with romance on her mind toward the end of season 2 in the three-parter "The Wedding." Through a combination of recycled *Zyuranger* footage and smoke and mirrors, Finster brings the diminutive dumpster dweller back to proper proportions, but, as he forewarned, she looks a little different. This altered Rita is portrayed on-screen by Carla Perez, but her voice sounds awfully familiar because it's still that of Barbara Goodson, who dubbed over Perez. Rita has Finster cook up a love potion, used to attract Lord Zedd. Their wedding brings out several previously disposed-of baddies and establishes that one or both of the chief evildoers are . . . Jewish? At least, that's a reasonable conclusion to draw thanks to the spirited rendition of "Hava Nagila" played on a pipe organ by Snizzard at their reception.

Some scenes for the "The Wedding" as well as "Return of the Green Ranger," another three-parter at the end of season 2, were filmed between stints on the movie set while in Australia. A school trip to Sydney is weaved into the storyline of "The Wedding," but these are the only episodes to acknowledge the Sydney backdrop. Others were written: one unproduced script penned by Tony Oliver, "Yo, Ho, Ho and a Bottle of . . . Rangers?," would have given viewers a sanitized history of Australia and colonialism as well as a fight with Putty Patrollers on a small boat. Ah, what could have been.

"Return of the Green Ranger" embraces chaos, throwing concerns about visual and narrative consistency to the wind. The teens return to Angel Grove High School by way of the Fox Studios Australia lot—hence why an entire green-space area of the school is never seen outside of this three-parter—before facing a scheme delivered by the enigmatic Wizard of Deception, an American original seemingly thrown together from whatever production could find in the nearest Sydney thrift store's garbage dumpster. The Wizard creates an evil clone of Tommy to turn into the Green Ranger and sends the rest of the team back in time to the 1700s, wherein this version of America the earliest colonial settlers apparently arrived via the Pacific Ocean. The Rangers confront ancestors of Bulk (a Benjamin Franklin send-up) and Skull (a commander of a redcoat regiment) in addition to a handful of ridiculous rat monsters that look cheaper than the deceptive wizard; they were originally commissioned for use in the feature film. It all ends tidily, of course, with the evil Tommy clone choosing to become good and taking up permanent residency as a protector of colonial Angel Grove. That this decision could have timeline-altering ramifications isn't ignored, as the true Tommy laughs while proclaiming, "I don't know if the history books are ready for this."

If it's possible for a show like *MMPR* to even have a jump-the-shark moment, "Return of the Green Ranger"—written and directed by Shuki Levy amid the hectic filming of the movie—is a strong contender. It's the second of three (!) multipart episodes that involve time travel in the a span of 13 episodes, preceded by "Rangers Back in Time," a two-parter in which Lord Zedd reverses Earth's rotation to turn the Rangers into children, and followed soon after by "Wild West Rangers," a two-parter wherein current Kimberly recruits ancestors of her friends to become Power Rangers. "Return" not only revives the Green Ranger powers once again but also creates a clone of the show's lead, who, by virtue of his magical origins, could still be alive in the present-day show. Throw in *MMPR*'s inherent cheapness and the chaos of a makeshift shooting schedule in another country, and it's about as kitschy as the show gets; all it's really missing is a farting, bipedal pig.

As the show approached a visual overhaul, a creative sea change happened in the background. Doug Sloan, an acting coach who worked extensively with Jason David Frank and who'd written several episodes following the initial 40-episode order, became supervising producer at the tail end of season 2. Jackie Marchand, a writer who'd worked under him as an assistant for a while, was elevated to assistant story editor. On set, Jeff Pruitt was forced to step away as the second-unit director after joining the Directors Guild of America, prompting the choreographers in charge of *VR Troopers*—Koichi Sakamoto and Alpha Stunts—to come aboard.

Ann Austen migrated from her seat at Fox Kids to the coproducer chair relinquished by Ellen Levy-Sarnoff, who left Saban Entertainment in June 1995 to launch a kids-focused block for UPN, a fledgling fifth broadcast network. The "Return of the Green Ranger, Part III" was the last of 106 episodes touched by Levy-Sarnoff, perhaps the most overshadowed architect behind *MMPR*. "One of the reasons I always liked working for Haim and on *Power Rangers*, too, is I've always liked start-ups," Levy-Sarnoff said. "He's from Israel and I'm Jewish. On Yom Kippur, which is the holiest day in the Jewish religion, Haim would call me up and say, 'This is a good day for a development meeting, there's nothing to do, we can talk about the show,' and I'd say, 'Haim, no, this is a good day to go to temple and contemplate your sins, OK? I'm not coming to a development meeting on Yom Kippur, I'll see you tomorrow.'" Saban laughed and gave up, which wasn't always his predisposition: while developing the show that would become *VR Troopers*, he was convinced it would be a much bigger hit with older kids and teens than *MMPR*, which, after initial across-the-board success, trended toward the younger end of its two- to 11-year-old demographic. Levy-Sarnoff didn't buy it, so she conducted focus groups with teenage boys in the 12- to 17-year-old demographic.

"They hated it so much," Levy-Sarnoff said. "It was still a kids show. But Haim was so set on creating this teenage version of *Power Rangers*." Saban wasn't able to sell Loesch on *VR Troopers* either, so it syndicated elsewhere. It didn't come close to *Power Rangers*, but it was a stronger performer in its first season than most other syndicated strips—among kids ages two to 11. Teens, who barely watched *MMPR*, still watched it more than *VR Troopers*.

Ellen Levy-Sarnoff, a key figure behind the development of *Mighty Morphin Power Rangers*, left the show to help lead UPN, a fledgling broadcast network. Photo by Andreas Branch/Patrick McMullan via Getty Images

Austen, who'd broken into TV as a secretary at Fox when it was broadcasting only on Sunday nights, had an itch for production going back to her time in Southern Cal's film school. "I always wanted to write, and I wanted to write in children's television," said Austen, whose dad encouraged her down the executive path because there was more stability in it. When presented with the opportunity to join *MMPR*—a show on which she'd given ample notes over its first couple years—she had to take it.

"I often joke it was because my notes were driving them crazy, so they thought if they hired me, they could sort of keep me under control," Austen said, laughing. "So there was probably a little of that, but I know Saban [Entertainment] appreciated what I was doing for the show."

The Austen–Marchand–Sloan trio, along with existing producers Jonathan Tzachor, Tony Oliver, and Paul Rosenthal, guided the show through a breakneck third season that, in addition to all the events of "Ninja Quest" and the "normal" chaos that came with creating *Power Rangers*, was tasked with the following:

- Cross-promoting *Masked Rider*, an adaptation of 1988's *Kamen Rider Black RX* that initially aired on Fox Kids. This led to "A Friend in Need," a three-parter filmed after "Ninja Quest" but officially preceding it as the season premiere.
- Establishing Bulk and Skull as junior police detectives and introducing a pseudo-mentor for them, Lieutenant Jerome Stone (portrayed by Gregg Bullock).
- Introducing a new villain turned hero, Katherine, who while evil can transform into a house cat. Point: bad guys.
- Pushing a *slew* of new merchandise. Beyond the Ninjazords and special Ninjetti costumes (a pre-spandex power-up), this season gives the Rangers a second fleet of Zords (the bipedal Shogunzords), some motorcycles modeled to look like sharks (possibly a response to the fleeting relevance of a would-be animated challenger, *Street Sharks*), and "metallic armor" (in execution, it's closer to glitter) to fend off another new villain, Master Vile, the father of Rita and Rito.
- Replacing *another* main cast member, Karan Ashley.
- Establishing Katherine as the successor to Kimberly after she leaves the team to go train in Florida for the Pan Global Games, an Olympics riff.
- Crafting a compelling arc that sets up the forthcoming—and drastic—transition to the *Ohranger* costumes.

Most of that occurs within the first 33 episodes of the season. The penultimate bullet was the most monumental: Amy Jo Johnson made it known that she was ready to move on following completion of the feature film. It was a much more amicable departure than the exodus of Walter Jones, Austin St. John, and Thuy Trang a year earlier.

Jerome Stone (Gregg Bullock, third from left) joined the cast as a series regular during the third season of *Mighty Morphin Power Rangers.* Courtesy of Gregg Bullock/© Saban Entertainment

"I was really good friends[2] with Shuki Levy, who was one of the owners, him and Haim," Johnson said. "I just went to him, as a friend, and said, 'I think I'm done, I think I'm ready to go try something else.' And he said, 'Awesome, great. I wrote this little movie called *Susie Q.* Will you do this and maybe like five more episodes?'" Johnson obliged. They shot *Susie Q*—a family fantasy-comedy helmed by *Power Rangers* and *VR Troopers* director/editor John Blizek—in Vancouver later that year, and Saban's Libra Pictures released it in October 1996. The film seemingly has met a fate like that of the title character portrayed by Johnson, who died on her way to prom in 1955 and gets revived as a ghost 40 years later. Throughout the late 1990s, it circulated on the Disney Channel, but since then, it's never been legally watchable or available for purchase in America.

Exit Johnson, enter Catherine Sutherland. Sutherland auditioned for Dulcea in Australia, and while she wasn't a good fit for what they sought from the bikinied baton wielder, Levy liked her and kept her in mind as a means to bring some international flair to the cast when Johnson departed. Less than a year later, she was walking the red carpet at the film's premiere, taking in the hundreds of fans cheering for the Power Rangers who had no clue she was about to wield the pink Power Coin. It was affirming after fleeing home to chase Hollywood.

"*Power Rangers* became my family after moving my life from Australia to become a part of the show," said Sutherland, whose character was named after her. "Shuki . . . took me under his wing. I was also very close to Doug Sloan and Ann Knapp, who were our main writers on the show. They definitely added elements of my own personality and life to Kat."

As for the transition to *Zeo*, the already-paid-for *Kakuranger* footage provided an out that could serve the interests of another MacGuffin-driven time-travel plot as well as action scenes that could get kids used to seeing completely different Power Rangers. "Rangers in Reverse," often packaged as the season 3 finale in streaming and home-media releases, ends with Master Vile reversing Earth's rotation to turn the teenagers into the same children we met in season 2's "Rangers Back in Time." (Hammering on the fourth wall, Lord Zedd proclaims, "This sounds like the re-run of a very bad movie.") The ensuing two-parter, "Alien Rangers of Aquitar," kicks off a 10-episode miniseries in which a team of Power Rangers from another planet are recruited to defend Earth. These Rangers—led by a female White Ranger, Delphine (Rajia Baroudi)—are scaly-faced humanoids whose home planet is made entirely of water. Their Ranger suits, those of the team in *Kakuranger*, are simpler than the *Zyuranger* threads: the spandex is mainly one solid color, accessorized with a belt, black-and-white wrist and calf coverings, and a unifying lightning bolt symbol emblazoned across the left breast. The helmets distill the suit into a tinier package: all one color save for a gold band that echoes their belt, perched atop a pure black visor outlined in thin white trim. They're a drastic departure from the Mighty Morphin Power Rangers yet feel at home in their world.

Meanwhile, the kid Rangers are sent further backward in time to retrieve shards of the Zeo Crystal, an extraordinary power source that they dismembered and distributed across history just a few episodes earlier. The child actors are thrust into very literal scenarios inspired by the ancestry of their characters, in all but one instance based on the ethnicity or nationality of the adult actor (Young Aisha is sent to Africa, Young Adam to Korea, Young Rocky to Latin America, and Young Katherine to Australia). As for Tommy? Turns out he's Native American, a revelation that'll get further explored during *Power Rangers Zeo*. In the short term, this side quest's most essential contribution was creating an easy out through which to write off the Aisha character. "I had gotten to the point where I was really unhappy,"[3] Ashley said in a 2005 interview, in which she also expressed appreciation for getting to be the show's first Black woman—and unabashedly so. "They let me get braids—they let me be the Black girl. For me, it was such an important thing to be a positive role model for young Black girls because I felt like we had never had that on TV especially that young."

Aisha's younger self stays behind in Africa, leaving her piece of the Zeo Crystal to a young Black villager named Tanya, who joins her new teammates back in the present. With all the pieces back in the 1990s, the Rangers return to their teenage state and bid adieu to their alien comrades. But their peace is short-lived: throughout the miniseries, Goldar and Rito have snuck around the underbelly of the Command Center planting bombs, to be ignited once they've stolen the reassembled Zeo Crystal. They succeed in their pillage and bolt right before the teens return. Seconds later, the explosions start.

Billy, who evaded the time-travel shenanigans through a combination of ingenuity and good fortune, leaps onto a sparking computer console—the same one whose buttons he touched the first time he teleported there—as it combusts, an attempt to shield his oldest remaining friend, Alpha 5, from harm. It's only right that Billy gets to shine in *MMPR*'s penultimate scene: he's the last of the five teenagers first teleported to the Command Center in "Day of the Dumpster" and is the farthest from how we found him. In the three years that have elapsed, his confidence has soared as his awkwardness has cratered. The Billy in "Hogday Afternoon, Part II" is as smart as ever, but his social intelligence is through the roof now too. He's long since shed the baggy shirts and suspenders in favor of clothes more flattering of his buff physique and given up his glasses for contact lenses—at Yost's behest. "I hear a lot of people that wear glasses say, 'I really wish Billy would have kept his glasses,'" Yost said. "I regret, as an actor, that I really pushed to get the glasses off. That was my mistake."[4]

Billy's bravery now rivals his curiosity: it's unfathomable to think that season 1 Billy would even consider putting his life on the life for "a fully sentient, multi-functional automaton." His heroism appears to be in vain. As Zordon urges, Alpha 5 teleports the Rangers away from the Command Center. They make it just far enough to see their base—their home away from home—combust from the outside. The blast knocks them—and millions of kids watching for the first time—to the ground.

Mighty Morphin Power Rangers doesn't end with a patented celebratory circle of freeze-framed hands raised to the sky. Its final shot is of six teenagers, assembled over the course of three seasons and 145 episodes, consumed with grief as they look at the vacant mountaintop where the Command Center once stood. There's no attitude here. Only remorse.

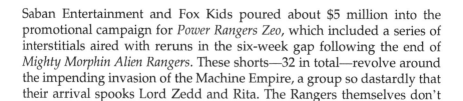

Saban Entertainment and Fox Kids poured about $5 million into the promotional campaign for *Power Rangers Zeo*, which included a series of interstitials aired with reruns in the six-week gap following the end of *Mighty Morphin Alien Rangers*. These shorts—32 in total—revolve around the impending invasion of the Machine Empire, a group so dastardly that their arrival spooks Lord Zedd and Rita. The Rangers themselves don't feature at all; the only friendly faces we see throughout the serials are Bulk, Skull, Lieutenant Stone, and Ernie. The shorts are tied together by a jingle, "Unleash the Power," that sounds similar to the *MMPR* theme and features a six-word call to action: *You gotta see it, it's coming.* There was also a sweepstakes whose winner was promised a truckload of toys—and the Ford Ranger in which they'd arrive. "It's certainly as big a push[5] as anything we've ever done in terms of on-air," Bert Gould, Fox Kids' executive vice president of marketing, said in 1996.

This was all part of an effort to reposition the show as the phenomenon waned. Retailers and licensees expressed concerns the previous summer after merchandise tied to the show and feature film sat on shelves far longer than anticipated. At the highest level, a total refresh of the property was considered, including the possibility of killing key characters and outright ending the storyline of the *Mighty Morphin* team. "We worked hard to identify the equity elements[6] of the show," said Peter Dang, Saban Entertainment's president of children's entertainment. "We also knew that every time we've introduced new elements, they've worked."

Nakia Burrise (second from left), who played Tanya, replaced Karan Ashley for *Power Rangers Zeo* the first major overhaul for the show. Courtesy The Morphin Museum/ © Saban Entertainment

Zeo issued shiny new spandex and helmets for our heroes to combat new robotic villains and returned the show closer to its roots—adapting suits from *Ohranger* meant being able to use *Ohranger* fight footage, a throwback to the first season. It did so while carrying on plot threads and overarching trends from the recent, more serialized seasons. *Zeo* brought back Austin St. John as Jason, who midway through the season gets a full-circle moment of his own when he assumes the powers of the Gold Zeo Ranger. It's often mentioned as a fan-favorite season—and for good reason: the confluence of core elements and level of experience behind the scenes jelled to create a 50-episode barrage that's incredibly familiar but with a lot more character building and narrative weight. Much of the season focuses on Tommy, now the Red Ranger, and his budding romance with Katherine (Kimberly sends him a "Dear John" letter from Florida about one-third of the way through *Zeo*). But everyone gets time to shine.

Take new Yellow Ranger Tanya, played by Nakia Burrise. It's not hyperbolic to say that within just a couple of episodes, her character is more fully realized on the page than both Trini and Aisha. Some of that's attributable to the nature of her "fish-out-of-water" arrival, necessitating that some early episodes revolve around the season's lone newcomer. But Burrise quickly fits in and takes advantage of richer material to work with than the actors who wore yellow before her. "The Shooting Star" and "Rangers in the Outfield," among the season's first six episodes, form as strong a double feature centered on "girl power"—and in a way that isn't patronizing—that you'll ever see in kids TV.

Another highlight of the season is a horror-movie riff, "It Came from Angel Grove," written by Joseph Kuhr and directed by Robert Radler. The gist: Adam falls asleep during a movie marathon and dreams his way through a series of vignettes in which his friends are classic horror monsters. *Power Rangers* has churned out more than a dozen Halloween-themed or horror-bent episodes, but "It Came from Angel Grove" stands apart.

"A lot of props in there are the actual props from *Bride of Frankenstein*," said Radler, who directed 28 episodes across *MMPR* and *Zeo*. "As many as they'd let me buy, I bought, so that's part of why it looks so cool. And we took a little more time [with it]. Kudos to Ilan Rosenberg, our DP, he's become a great friend and absolutely got it. We did a whole bunch of day-for-night and a lot of effects." At the end of his quest, Adam meets "Zordonicus," the sorcerer he's sought throughout an Oz-like quest. This version of Zordon is tinted red and has flames shooting in front of his tube. "We actually used the same chemicals that were used in *The Wizard of Oz* to make the fire happen. And it was quite illegal by then from what I understood. It was mentioned that we shouldn't hang out in the room afterwards."

Even Billy—now sidelined from battle—gets to shine in a pseudo-mentor role, though he wouldn't survive the season. Yost abruptly left the show, prompting a plotline where his character ages rapidly and must travel to Aquitar for a solution. There, the character once too frightened to fight a fish monster falls in love with a fish woman (eat your heart out, Guillermo del Toro). The Rangers say their good-byes via interstellar transmission, and that's it—the last remaining OG exits unceremoniously, complete with a poor voice-over imitation. As disappointing as it was in execution, the reason behind it is worse: in 2010, Yost said that he left the show over alleged homophobic behavior by members of the production. He later attempted gay conversion therapy—a practice rooted in pseudoscience and widely panned by major health organizations, including the World Psychiatric Association—and contemplated suicide.

"I was called faggot one too many times,"[7] Yost said. "I had just heard that several times while working on the show—from creators, producers, writers, directors. It's not that people can't talk about me or have an opinion about me, but continuing to work in an environment like that is really difficult. And I myself was struggling with who I was or what I was, and to be made fun of on some level or to be stereotyped or put into a category? Basically, I just felt like I was continually being told I'm not worthy of being where I am because I'm quote-unquote a gay person, and I'm not supposed to be an actor, and you can't be a superhero. . . . In order for me to get a handle on what was going on, I needed to leave when I left."

Some crew members—most publicly Scott Page-Pagter, who in 2010 called Yost a "pain in the ass" to work with—dispute that Yost was harassed over his sexuality, noting that others higher up on the food chain than him were openly gay. Regardless of what happened in the mid-1990s, that Yost felt like he had to leave the show and travel the path he took is, indisputably, disheartening—for any show but especially one that teaches five-year-olds that everyone matters.

"I think the characters we played gave a lot of kids hope, if nothing else, to go out and try things," Yost said. "To go meet friends. 'I see that they do martial arts, I'm going to do martial arts. I'm going to take dance, I'm going to take gymnastics.' A lot of people tell me, 'I came from a broken home, but *Power Rangers* was my one saving grace,' or 'I didn't have a lot of friends, but I saw that Billy had friends so it gave me confidence to go out and make friends.' There was something magical about everything that was involved in that, that has sustained—I think the original cast, for sure—for 30 years. It's so humbling, and it's such a blessing. I wouldn't trade it for the world."

While Fox Kids comrade *Goosebumps* usurped it as the network's top-rated show, *Power Rangers Zeo* kept the crown among syndicated strips with a 7.1 rating and 26 share in the May 1996 sweeps[8] period. The glass-half-empty perspective on those numbers: both the rating and the share were about 30 percent lower than those put up by the final episodes of *MMPR* season 2 during the May 1995 sweeps.

As much as one could attribute the ratings decline to the natural attrition that happens with most TV shows, *Power Rangers*—and every other show syndicated via the four major broadcast networks—also faced a rapidly ascending challenger in cable TV. Dedicated children's network Nickelodeon, especially, was a force with which to be reckoned; weekday reruns of its most popular show, *Rugrats*,[9] frequently garnered more viewership than premieres of most broadcast shows that weren't *Power Rangers*.

Saban Entertainment tried multiple times to duplicate the battle-tested formula of *Power Rangers*—marrying new American footage to existing Japanese footage—but shows like *Masked Rider* never had the staying power that their forebear did. Courtesy The Morphin Museum/© Saban Entertainment

Children's TV available via over-the-air broadcast also was once again under the microscope. In August 1996, the FCC adopted new regulations, to go into effect no later than September of the following year, that required all commercial TV stations under its watch to air, each week, at least three hours of "core educational programming"; that is, a program at least 30 minutes in length specifically designed to meet the educational needs of a child 16 years old or younger. No more history lessons as told by *The Flintstones.*

The current and projected landscape spooked Fox affiliates. Several wanted out of the weekday kids game altogether, reckoning that any adult programming would fare better. Most incoming Fox stations after 1993—acquired as part of an unprecedented affiliate realignment effort following Fox's landmark bid for NFL broadcast rights—refused to air weekday kids programming at all. They preferred news.

All this, just as the kids block was finally turning a profit.[10] In the blink of an eye, the castle that *Power Rangers* built was on shaky foundation. As its mother tried to shore up the place, its father was arranging a house of cards.

CHAPTER 13

Countdown to Destruction

If Haim Saban's dreams of a Disney-like empire weren't out of reach after the relative failure of *Mighty Morphin Power Rangers: The Movie*, they certainly were quashed by the abysmal showing of *Turbo: A Power Rangers Movie*—purportedly produced on less than half the budget (about $8,000,000) of the first film but yielding not much more than that over the course of its theatrical life. This time around, Saban Entertainment took the lead, and therefore it feels much more a part of the show than its counterpart. But its steward calling the shots did nothing to suggest *Power Rangers* should ever leap to the big screen again.

Essentially, it's the same movie as the first: a kid-centric adventure in which the Power Rangers use new powers to tackle a wisecracking enemy they've never met before. A pregnant Hilary Shepard Turner plays Divatox, a buxom pirate queen who lives with her bumbling crew aboard a submarine. The instantly recognizable *Mighty Morphin* suits are nowhere to be found, as this "sequel"—as it was often billed—actually occurs within the show's continuity and serves as the transition from *Zeo* to the next season, *Turbo*. The new powers aren't the MacGuffin sought here as they were in *MMPR: The Movie*; rather, they are handed over with little fanfare from Zordon to replace the *Zeo* powers—previously billed as the most powerful possible—because these are *more* powerful and will help the Rangers navigate the mission ahead. The new powers are also based on vehicles, giving the Rangers chromed-out helmets with legitimate headlights rather than the ones awkwardly forced into the first movie's helmets for a one-off scene. Even as a big fan of the *Turbo* aesthetic and the season in general, despite tonal whiplash on the heels of

Zeo, it's empty calories. The incredible narrative lead-up made the switch from *MMPR* to *Zeo* feel necessary. In contrast, the slapdash changeover to *Turbo* feels corporate and unearned. For anyone still disillusioned enough to think toys weren't a main driver, this film is the wake-up call.

Turbo takes a divisive swing that, as of 2025, hasn't been tried again by any on-screen iteration of *Power Rangers*: it puts an actual kid under the helmet. Shuki Levy, while directing the Saban-produced *Rusty: A Dog's Tale*, became so enthralled by an 11-year-old actor,[1] Blake Foster, that he asked him sans audition to join *Power Rangers* as a full-time cast member, beginning with the second movie. It served two purposes. First, it provided a quick replacement for Steve Cardenas, who decided to leave the show after a failed bid to get himself and his castmates equal pay for what they expected to be their final season. Second, it shook up the *Power Rangers* formula again while giving kids a sort of "Mary Sue" through which they could live vicariously.

In-universe, Foster's character, Justin, learns about the Power Rangers early in the movie after eavesdropping on a conversation while they visit Rocky, hospitalized with a severe back injury suffered in a martial arts tournament. Minutes later, he's recruited by Zordon to join the team and shows up to meet them in a big, blue Jeep. "Hey guys, I'm the new Blue Ranger!" And thus, Cousin Oliver is reincarnated as a Power Ranger. (To his credit, Cardenas played ball so that his character could be written off as gracefully as possible; he also cameos in the TV season premiere for *Turbo*, which recaps the events of the movie via a lengthy montage for the millions at home who, based on the box-office receipts, didn't see it.)

Foster's arrival was a tone-setter for the show's most disruptive year since the cast exodus in 1994. Jonathan Tzachor, a former fighter pilot who'd been the show's line producer from the beginning, had his hands all over the *Turbo* film, including some "second-unit" direction. Alpha Stunts' Koichi Sakamoto and Makoto Yokoyama, as well as production manager and occasional writer Chip Lynn, also shared in the second-unit shepherding. "It was nice because all of us had opportunities to do things on a movie that we couldn't do on a TV show because, of course, there was more money," Lynn said. "That was kind of fun, but it was a real challenge." These "second units" became so abundant that the production team started referring to them by colors, not number, to ID them. *Turbo: A Power Rangers Movie* shot in at least nine locations, including the Bahamas. "We were just all over the place," said Brett Born, the show's lone full-time accountant for nearly 10 years. "The script would change, there were production issues, and we had some unsavory types that we hired out to do certain specialty work. There were all these big problems. . . . We ended up spending twice as much as the original budget, I'm not even sure, and that wasn't even official because we had to use a little bit of the TV show [budget] to help fund the movie because it was getting so crazy." While Tzachor and Co. were busy keeping the film afloat, Ann Austen and Doug Sloan worked to keep production of the show moving—but not for much longer.

Saban Entertainment was eager to embrace Toei's philosophy of wholesale cast changes every season. Going into the second movie, Jason David Frank, the only remaining member of the season 1 cast and the only actor to that point whose absence from the show had elicited a notable outcry from children, made it known he was ready to move on from the program and already had some work lined up. "For me, it's a feeling in my heart,[2] to know that I've done what I had to do with the kids and move onto something else," Frank said in 1997. Saban Entertainment took this cue as motivation to replace not only Frank but also the entire cast except Foster.

"Johnny [Yong Bosch] brought a newspaper to the set, and we read that they were auditioning[3] for *Power Rangers*," Sutherland said. "And it was really shocking. . . . We really thought that we would finish out the season, and for whatever reason I think they were just done with replacing people."

"What made it even colder to me was that when we confronted one of the producers about it, they denied it,"[4] Burrise said. Theirs wasn't the only time on the show ticking down. Creative friction between Sloan and Tzachor worsened to the point that the former opted to pursue his own ventures rather than renew his contract; Austen joined Sloan, and the two remained writing and business partners for about a decade afterward. The final *Turbo* episode for each of them was the first half of a two-parter, "Honey, I Shrunk the Rangers." It's the final pair of episodes before another two-parter, "Passing the Torch," at the end of which Adam, Katherine, Tanya, and Tommy "age out" of being Power Rangers and hand their morphers over to four ever-so-slightly-younger teenagers they've chosen to succeed them. Narratively, their exit is as rushed as that of the trio that left in season 2—but the reason for it, in-universe, is far more indigestible. These four actors just delivered what might have been the best season of the show to date, and one was its superstar. Now they're too old to wear spandex? It was weak and reflective of a company in disarray.

"That was probably the low point of my time at *Rangers*, finding out that they were going to change casts, and they hadn't told the cast that," Austen said. "It wasn't really handled very well. Then on top of that, I was already starting to feel the tension of what was going on within Saban [Entertainment]. . . . Jonathan had enjoyed doing the movie on his own, had enjoyed having free creative rein, and he wanted that same creative rein on the series. So, I think that's what really came to a head. It was just politics. He really wanted to take over the show completely himself, and my contract was coming to an end, and it was just time to go. It wasn't the same fun place it had been when I started."

In 1992, as *X-Men* took off, Margaret Loesch approached Fox Television Group CEO Chase Carey with a suggestion: buy Saban Entertainment to have a proven in-house producer of kids television and leverage Saban's dealmaking prowess in the international marketplace as Fox sought to expand. By the time Fox was ready to pull the trigger, *Mighty Morphin Power Rangers* had become an unprecedented phenomenon and increased the value of Saban's company so much that an acquisition was unfavorable given News Corporation's sizable expenditures elsewhere (the company had recently landed an NFL package from CBS, acquired a slew of new affiliates, and was planning the launch of what became the industry's most valuable cable news channel). But there was a move to be made later: in September 1996, Saban Entertainment and the Fox Kids Network merged to form Fox Kids Worldwide, a 50-50 ownership situation with one of the owners, Saban, installed as CEO.

Loesch's biggest client was now her boss. For a little while, it worked. Loesch continued shepherding kids programming for Fox: in addition to the latest incarnations of *Power Rangers*, the 1996–1997 schedule was highlighted by the final season of *X-Men* and the first season of *Big Bad Beetleborgs*, Saban Entertainment's latest attempt to replicate *Power Rangers*' success by way of repurposed Japanese footage. It starred three preteens who, after saving a genie from a pipe-organ prison, are granted a wish to become their favorite superheroes. It was a mild hit,[5] outdrawing the afternoon strips that weren't *Power Rangers*, but between limited source footage and a quickly shifting landscape, it didn't last long. "I thought it would be more successful than it was," Loesch said. "I've thought a lot about this and tried to learn from it. Even though *Beetleborgs* had some unique elements . . . it was still a version of *Power Rangers*. All those other [shows] were spin-offs, in a way, therefore they were no longer as unique as *Power Rangers* at the time. They never could get the following among kids, they never had the symbiotic relationship with the cast of those shows like they did with *Power Rangers*."

By 1997, Fox Kids Worldwide had its sights set on a bigger prize: cable. The burgeoning ad market demanded the launch of an all-kids programming channel to challenge Nickelodeon and the Cartoon Network (and the Disney Channel, a far less meaningful contender at the time). In June of that year, after months of negotiations, Fox Kids purchased International Family Entertainment for $1.9 billion. The driving asset behind that purchase, the Family Channel, was already in about 70 million American homes. A quirk of the deal: Fox could program and rebrand the new network however it wanted, but it was required—in perpetuity—to air *The 700 Club*, an evangelical fundraising program headed by Family Channel founder Pat Robertson.

Producer Jonathan Tzachor had his hand in 545 episodes of *Power Rangers*, including every episode in its first 10 seasons. "I thought it was crazy; I didn't get it at all," Tzachor told the *Los Angeles Times* in 2001. "It was naive and simplistic, and it didn't look like anything else on TV." Courtesy The Morphin Museum/© Saban Entertainment

One would imagine that Loesch, who built Fox Kids into a behemoth, would be the ideal candidate to lead the exciting new venture. But in July, Loesch was instead "promoted" to vice chair of Fox Kids Worldwide and given a vague assortment of duties that, in practice, effectively led to her getting paid to do nothing. Not only was she not running point on the cable channel—something for which she lobbied—but she'd no longer have any real say in the creative happenings at Fox Kids. Saban's millions were now directly tied to the performance of the network and the forthcoming foray into cable, and he sought tighter control over how that money was spent.

Recurring characters Ms. Appleby (Royce Herron) and Principal Caplan (Harold Cannon), who occasionally appeared inside Angel Grove High School, made their final appearances in *Power Rangers Turbo*. Screenshot, Author's Collection

"Maybe it was naïve on my part or immature, but I felt that Haim and I made a fantastic team," Loesch said. "Because he was all about business, generally, and I was all about creative, generally. Together, we compromised at the very best places. He could make deals better and I could make shows better, and together we were formidable." Saban insisted that this outcome was beneficial, but Loesch no longer had influence on the man with whom she gambled her job in 1992. Saban wasn't incentivized to listen and had taken away her microphone. "The fact that he offered me big salary and an office and an assistant and I could do anything I wanted, I know from Haim's perspective, he thought he was being very fair and trying to make sure I was taken care of. It just didn't fit with my persona. I'm a builder. I'm someone who loves to fight the fight and go against the odds, try new things. And if I can't do that? I knew I'd be miserable."

Loesch turned down Saban's offer. *Power Rangers'* mother left Fox Kids at the end of 1997. "I was heartbroken," Loesch said. "It took me a couple years to come out of a funk. But, worse things have happened to people. Haim has been a good friend to me, in many ways, over the years. I know he still appreciates what I brought to the table."

Maureen Smith, whose performance in the Fox research department over the years made others take notice, was eventually tapped to succeed the

person who succeeded Loesch. On paper, Rich Cronin—a marketer for Nickelodeon who managed its late-night, retro-programming window Nick at Nite before founding TV Land—absorbed Loesch's old role at Fox Kids while assuming CEO duties for the Fox Family Channel, the new cable arm set to launch in 1998.[6] In practice, Smith, senior vice president of scheduling and planning, ran Fox Kids because Cronin couldn't join his new company until a nine-month legal blockade passed. Cronin was fired by MTV Networks in October 1997 after it discovered he'd negotiated a deal to lead Fox Kids Worldwide following the end of his contract with them in June 1998. As it turns out, that's frowned on.

Cronin's stay was short: Saban fired him in May 2000, less than two years after he joined Fox. The marketing muscle he'd flexed for 14 years at MTV Networks atrophied at the Fox Family Channel, which couldn't attract younger viewers at a fast enough rate to replenish the lost eyeballs of 50- and 60-year-old viewers who were, understandably, angered by the erosion of their once-preferred network. Fox Family had a shaky identity. It was billed as a "family" channel with a children's component, but its initial daily programming lineup was a potluck stuffed with Fox Kids retreads and sprinkled with imports fresh to American eyes. A couple of series got steady viewership—*Angela Anaconda*, a Canadian animated series, and *S Club 7 in Miami*, a British sitcom—but they couldn't challenge Nickelodeon's top dogs.

While *Power Rangers* continued to top head-to-head competition, the show again suffered a near 30 percent decline year over year in May 1997.[7] After a mid-season break ended in September and brought the monumental cast change, its ratings dropped again, this time by 42 percent[8] (3.0/20 share). After a four-year reign, *Power Rangers* was no longer the top-rated daily strip. The show was outclassed by the newest Saban Entertainment live-action superhero venture, *Teenage Mutant Ninja Turtles: The Next Mutation* (3.9/22 share).

Its star had faded, but *Power Rangers* was incredibly dependable. It still led in the toy aisle and remained a cheap-to-film procedural for kids—and was a successful known quantity for the advertisers who hadn't yet fled for cable's cheaper rates. Contrary to widespread apocrypha parroted by fans that the next season, *In Space*, was intended to be the last, there is no evidence *Power Rangers* ever was on the chopping block while under Saban Entertainment's purview. Smith certainly never considered canceling while she was in charge.

"*Power Rangers* is one of the few shows I've ever come across that had this feeling that 'this is gonna continue on and on and on and constantly find new viewers,' because the formula was just perfect," Smith said. "I didn't have to really worry about that show because it was running like a well-oiled machine." One of her few calls to shake things up for Fox

Kids' biggest franchise was to move most episode premieres to Saturdays to "eventize" the show. Another was the 1998 launch of "Power Rangers Power Playback," a rerun series capitalizing on a backlog of episodes that, by the end of *Turbo*, numbered 250. For many of the youngsters watching in 1998, this "series" was their first memorable exposure to the original *Mighty Morphin Power Rangers*. And it enabled Bandai to reissue old toys.

"Part of the thing about kids television, and I think *Power Rangers* was the perfect example of it, is every couple years certain kids grow out of the demographic," Smith said. "But you've got new ones coming constantly who now understand what they're watching on TV since they're of a certain age. For the kids who had never seen it before, it was fresh *Power Rangers* content."

The end of *Turbo* sees the four newest heroes—Ashley (Tracy Lynn Cruz), Cassie (Patricia Ja Lee), Carlos (Roger Velasco), and T.J. (Selwyn Ward), notably the first Red Ranger who's Black—leave Earth on a rocket after the Power Chamber is destroyed along with their powers (Foster's Justin elects to stay home). *Power Rangers in Space* opens at a celebratory gathering of the series' past lead villains, who've assembled before Dark Specter, a moon-sized big bad who oversees their United Alliance of Evil (casually name-dropped once before during *Zeo*'s premiere). He bears a striking resemblance to Maligore, the volcanic creature whom Divatox attempts to marry in *Turbo: A Power Rangers Movie*, because the costume was completely reused here ("You remind me so much of my fiancé!" she says). Soon, a spy—a Red Ranger—is ousted and flees after learning that Dark Specter has captured Zordon and is draining him of his energy. *Turbo*'s superb two-part finale ("Chase into Space") and the first six minutes of *In Space*'s two-part premiere ("From Out of Nowhere") combine to establish epic season-long stakes that go beyond simple "good guys versus bad guys" stuff.

The Red stranger, Andros, is a long-haired human (played by Christopher Khayman Lee) who hails from a planet called KO-35. When their paths collide, he reluctantly accepts the four earthlings and shares with them a new set of space-based powers. If that wasn't enough of a fait accompli, it turns out that the ship on which Earth's Power Rangers rode into space was specially programmed to combine with Andros's Astro Megaship to form a new Megazord.

Chip Lynn and Jackie Marchand, who'd led the writers room since Austen and Sloan left midway through *Turbo*'s production, combined to write all but two of the 43 *In Space* episodes. The Herculean effort paid off. Together, along with the production oversight of Tzachor and stunt lead Koichi Sakamoto, they conjured the first season of *Power Rangers* that feels intent on delivering a season-long story with connected subplots and extended character conflicts. It's all still done within the confines of

Power Rangers Turbo **replaced the show's longtime familiar faces with four new cast members mid-season. Blake Foster (center) was joined by Patricia Ja Lee (left), Roger Velasco (top), Tracy Lynn Cruz (right), and Selwyn Ward (bottom).** Courtesy The Morphin Museum/© Saban Entertainment

a cheap, footage-dependent kids show trying to sell toys, but it put forth a template for what *Power Rangers* could be as it moved forward. It also established a taxing precedent for the foreseeable future.

"We tried to use some writers but it's really hard to teach a writer to use footage and come up with a story that works for *Rangers*, so Jackie and I ended up writing a lot of them ourselves," Lynn said. "She's a really pleasant person and a good writer, and we had a great time writing together, so eventually we just gave up trying to find other writers and just wrote the lion's share of things ourselves. In some seasons, we wrote the entire season. And that was it. Everybody liked what we were doing so that became the new normal, even though it was a lot of work." Fantastic production design from Julie Bolder, who succeeded Yuda Acco during *Turbo*, bolstered an elevated narrative. Bolder's interiors for the Astro Megaship are as slick as anything you'll find in adult sci-fi, in part because the series' budget only kept going up thanks to its steady performance. "We had big budgets and we didn't have a lot of oversight, because we had good relationships with our Fox execs," Marchand said. "We were able to build our own models, our sets were like *Star Trek* sets. Giant, elaborate. Those years, we were able to really have a lot of the budget on-screen."

Throughout the season, Andros searches for his long-missing sister, Karone. We eventually meet her kidnapper Darkonda, as vile-looking a monster as has ever appeared on the show, and learn her whereabouts: Karone was brainwashed over time into becoming Astronema, the season's primary antagonist (played by Melody Perkins). The reveal happens a little more than halfway through the season, and while easy to foresee if you have any understanding of tropes, for most seven-year-olds, this qualified as mind-blowing. So too was Astronema's willingness to join and help the Rangers save Zordon, only to be captured and brainwashed again a few episodes later. Five years and six seasons in, *Power Rangers* still had tricks up its sleeve.

Christopher Khayman Lee (center) joined the existing cast for *Power Rangers In Space*, the final season of the "Zordon era." Courtesy The Morphin Museum/© Saban Entertainment

Everything comes to a head in the two-parter "Countdown to Destruction," the season finale against which all others continue to be measured, perhaps unfairly. The episodes conclude not only *In Space* but also the nearly 300 episodes that precede them. It does it with aplomb, putting a coda on a five-year run—retroactively referred to by fans as "the Zordon era." A satisfying finish is achieved, in part, through assisted suicide. Aboard Astronema's ship, Andros discovers a depleted Zordon, who implores the Red Ranger to destroy his energy tube, his last remaining tether to the physical world, in order to release energy that will destroy all evil in the universe (until next season). Astronema intervenes, and while defending himself, Andros mistakenly kills her. He somehow finds the courage to help Zordon save the world the only way he can now: by sacrificing his own life. "I will be gone, but my spirit will forever live in all that is good." Moments after taking his sister's life, Andros purposefully ends Zordon's and the ongoing fight across the galaxy.

Shouldering the weight of losing a mentor and sister, Andros carries Astronema's lifeless body off the ship and lays her on a street in Angel Grove—replete with teammates and citizens who'd been celebrating a remarkable victory. Tears fall before Zordon's words ring true: his spirit survives in all who are good. Astronema is dead, but Karone lives.

From a certain perspective, the true stars of *Power Rangers*' first six seasons are not any of the actors who morph but, rather, Jason Narvy and Paul Schrier. Theirs are, after all, the only two characters who appear in every season of the Zordon era. And they underwent just as many transformations as their spandex-clad counterparts: they were archetypal bullies, amateur detectives on the prowl for the Power Rangers' identities, junior police patrol members, professional detectives serving the public, primates (really), and odd-jobbers. Although their screen time dropped considerably during *In Space*, there they assisted a dim-witted, alien-hunting scientist, Professor Phenomenus (played by Jack Danning, who died in 2005).

Wait, primates? Narvy and Schrier were in the thick of working on a Bulk and Skull spin-off pilot that didn't get picked up, so in the first half of *Turbo*, their characters get turned into chimpanzees, for which they provided voice-overs (they could still communicate with each other). Former police lieutenant and detective Jerome Stone, now owner-operator of the Angel Grove Youth Center, cares for the strangely familiar rascals. "That was a kick, working with those two," said Gregg Bullock. "Sometimes it was a little scary because, the little one, he'd freak out sometimes and they'd have to come and get him, and I didn't want him to tear my head off or tear my arm off. They were pouring juices on my head, and I'd have them in my arms, and they'd have to do that several takes. It was crazy, but it was fun."

Gregg Bullock monkeyed around with "Bulk and Skull" during his final season portray-ing Jerome Stone. Courtesy Gregg Bullock/© Saban Entertainment

Jerome Stone was written off the show after *Turbo*, but Bullock was encouraged to audition for Professor Phenomenus, a much older character. "I put on this crazy wig, gray hair, a big fluffy beard and glasses, and I did a German accent." Bullock wasn't surprised that he didn't get the part but was taken aback when his agent informed him that casting agents didn't seem to care that he'd been on a popular kids TV show for almost three years. "I thought to myself, I've had a good run," Bullock said. "So I went and got a real job." He worked in occupational safety services for over 20 years before retiring in 2025. "I'm happy."

As late as May 1997, while *In Space* was still in development, Bulk and Skull would have featured more prominently as the founders of a "Citi-zen Force Group" to defend Angel Grove[9] while the Rangers were away. The spirit of that idea survives in "Countdown to Destruction," wherein Astronema addresses a large group of destruction-weathered citizens about to meet their end.

"Wait!"

The crowd parts, and Bulk, sporting a trademark bandana, steps into the frame. "I am the Blue Ranger," he continues.

Skull nervously looks at Professor Phenomenus before joining his best friend's side. "I am the Black Ranger." Phenomenus follows, insistent that he's the Red Ranger. Suddenly, everyone in Angel Grove is a Power Ranger. The actual heroes soon intervene, but the message is loud and clear: Angel Grove's citizens are ready to fight for their home.

More than a thousand *Power Rangers* stories have been told across a variety of media since "Countdown to Destruction." If it *had* been the end of the show, it would have gone out sending its greatest lesson, the one that—across all superherodom—*Power Rangers* delivers better than all.

Bulk and Skull lock eyes and hands before leading the charge. There's no spandex in the frame, but there damn sure are heroes.

CHAPTER 14

A Parting of Ways

Haim Saban publicly glowed about the Fox Family Channel's outlook. He said no group was better positioned than his to duplicate the hysteria of *Power Rangers*, which he once described as an "Attila the Hun[1] phenomenon." The problem: rebranding a cable network to attract people of all ages was a whole different game than repackaging a TV show to wow kindergarteners.

The slow trickle of eyeballs to the revamped cable channel might have been easier to stomach if not for growing broadcast-side dilemmas. Fox started to up the demands of its affiliates in January 1998. Among the asks: assist in the payment of a heavily increased NFL licensing fee, take on more marketing and promotion, and invest more in or, in many cases, launch local news broadcasts. At the same time, the profit-participation agreement tied to the Fox Kids Network was up for renegotiation. Some affiliates stocked up on syndicated sitcoms and local news anchors who could fill time on their airwaves and attract higher ad spending, positioning themselves to drop the weekday kids block. Newly acquired stations just didn't bother with it at all. Besides the potential for advertising growth, the heightened government oversight of kids programming and Margaret Loesch's abrupt departure created unease. Local buy-in of Fox Kids was dwindling.[2]

Saban at the same time neared the end of a heated battle with SAG. In early 1997,[3] extended talks between the union and Saban Entertainment amounted to nothing. The company position boiled down to the economic model of kids TV being fundamentally different than that of prime-time TV, for which the SAG agreements were designed. "*Power Rangers* was so high profile, and it was the first time that a non-union show had gotten so big," said Dave McDermott, Ann Austen's young protégé who succeeded

Haim Saban is widely credited as *Power Rangers'* creator, but it might never have existed if not for the extraordinary vision of Margaret Loesch. Courtesy Margaret Loesch

her as the show's network executive when she joined production. "So suddenly it was like, 'Why aren't they union and paying these kids SAG rates' and all this stuff. And Haim had just never done anything like that in his entire career."

By late January 1998, SAG called on its members to boycott Saban Entertainment productions and mounted a "public education program,"[4] distributing news releases to hundreds of media outlets shedding light on the circumstances under which cast and crew on *Power Rangers* were working. "In an extremely cynical manner, he has made hundreds of millions of dollars marketing his programs and ancillary merchandise to children worldwide, while exploiting the talent, material resources as well as the hopes and dreams[5] of child actors and their parents," SAG president Richard Masur said in 1998. A Saban representative dismissed the allegations, but within the next week, the two entities came to an accord, on a couple of conditions. The first: Masur had to issue a face-to-face apology to Saban. The second: Saban Entertainment would become a full signatory for everything *but* live-action children's programming, for which a carve-out was made to allow for contracts "reflective of the economic realities." Even when he lost, Saban won.

By the end of February 1998, the Fox Kids impasse appeared to be resolved: Fox Kids Worldwide and Fox Broadcasting bought out the affiliates' stake in the block for $100 million. As part of a 10-year agreement, the affiliates had to air 19 hours of children's programming each week and heavily promote the Fox Family Channel. An anonymous insider suggested the buyout was a precursor to Fox getting out of kids programming on its broadcast network—and soon. Saban at the time scoffed at the notion. "Whoever told you this is stupid,"[6] Saban said.

He was right: Fox continued to broadcast kids programming through 2008. It was Saban who got out.

Up-front advertising for children's TV in 1998 was a mixed bag for Fox Kids: it paced the four broadcasters with an estimated $120 million,[7] down from $160 million the year before. While it was fresh off its sixth straight win in the February sweeps period—led by *Ultimate Goosebumps* (6.6 rating) and Steven Spielberg–produced *Toonsylvania*[8] (5.3)—the market was cool, especially for the staid networks. By July, ABC's Saturday morning kids block, bolstered by a slew of new Disney toons, overtook Fox on Saturdays. Fox still led the weekday charge over the air, but basic cable ate everyone's lunch: according to Nielsen, it accounted for more than 80 percent[9] of kids TV viewership by the end of 1998, and Nickelodeon on its own accounted for more than half of total viewership. At 6.6 percent of total kids TV time, Fox was an embarrassingly distant third behind Nickelodeon and the Cartoon Network (28.4 percent), and its debt-riddled cable offshoot was nipping at its heels (4.5 percent). By the same time in 1999, Fox Kids had fallen to fourth (4.7 percent) and Fox Family to fifth (3.6 percent) in total kids viewership, passed by Kids WB thanks to its wunderkind, *Pokémon*.

Fox Kids fans who stuck around through 1999 were treated to *Power Rangers Lost Galaxy*, a bridge between the Zordon Era and everything after it. The established continuity of the show carries on, but the heroes at the forefront are all brand new and, notably, young adults rather than high schoolers. Their adventures take place on and around a mobile space colony, Terra Venture, in search of a new world to populate. It's an amalgamation of many new things and a few old things—these Rangers use the Astro Megaship and befriend an Alpha unit. It even brings Karone back into the fold as a Pink Ranger halfway through the season; actor Valerie Vernon, who portrayed Kendrix, the season's Pink Ranger, was diagnosed with leukemia during production and had to undergo regular chemotherapy. Kendrix, in an act of heroism, dies in the show—the first Power Ranger to meet such a fate—but gets revived by season's end. "I think that it actually made our series maybe a little bit more interesting than other Ranger shows, because it was something unique and shocking,"[10] said Vernon, who won her battle with cancer.

The show was in a strange spot: ratings were in consistent decline year over year, but millions still watched it, and merchandise continued to perform extraordinarily well for licensees. Spirited efforts in the marketing and promotions departments supported a steady demand for all things *Power Rangers*. George Leon, hired in 1994 as Saban Entertainment's senior vice president of global promotions, came aboard right as things were heating up for the brand and wasn't sure he'd be able to cut it; Saban had a reputation for not suffering fools very long, so Leon opened a separate bank account to pay himself an emergency salary just in case he was perceived as one. To this day, Leon still keeps what he calls his "shit-canned" account despite founding and running his own business, Cakewalk Entertainment.

Koichi Sakamoto, who grew up in Japan watching *Super Sentai* and similar shows, began working on *Mighty Morphin Power Rangers* during production of the second season. He continued to work on the program through 2010's *Power Rangers Samurai.* Courtesy Tyler Waldman

"We didn't know how well, or even if it was gonna work," Leon said of *Power Rangers*' annual reinventions. The space-based seasons were his favorites and featured some of the more, ahem, out-of-this-world promotional experiences. A touring virtual reality ride propped up *In Space* toys at Walmart stores in 1998, and the next year was followed by *Power Rangers Lost Galaxy: Intergalactic Encounter*, a touring inflatable stuffed with slides, mazes, strobe lights, and music. Parking lots from Los Angeles to

Atlanta welcomed the 5,000-cubic-square-foot behemoth, crowned by a gigantic Red Ranger. "We had thousands of kids lining up to go into the world's biggest moon bounce," Leon said. "It was an incredible experience, and to this day, every time there's a Guinness World Records book, I always go to the index to see if somebody beat our record, and nobody has to date."

Those promotions and others also helped move *a lot* of merchandise; overall licensed products soared 400 percent,[11] and toy sales went up 40 percent. "Your Walmarts and Targets and Kmarts—they were only interested in things that had a brand associated with it," said Eric Thomsen, coordinator of product development from 1998 to 2000. "And *Power Rangers* was hot. Every little kid wanted *Power Rangers* on their product. If you had a *Power Rangers* license, all you had to do was stick them on something and it was gonna sell. It was one of those beautiful situations where demand was so high, there was very little risk." It wasn't until his next stop—Sony Pictures Entertainment, where he followed Leon and the two stirred the Tobey Maguire–led *Spider-Man* franchise into another mighty merchandise machine—that Thomsen learned things weren't always so rosy. "It was a great time to be working [at Saban Entertainment] and to get my start; if anything, it gave me a false sense that licensing was easy."

Thomsen may very well be the first fan of *Power Rangers* to work in affiliation with the show. His initial exposure came while he was an intern at NBC in 1992. One of his friends interned at Fox, and Ann Austen helped coordinate an exchange where the two got to spend a day observing the rival's programming studios. "We went into an editing bay and they were working on promos for the Saturday morning block of programming," Thomsen said. "She said, 'Yea, we're working on this thing, it's a show that's from Japan and they're filming American actors and then they're gonna splice it together.'" Five years later, Thomsen joined Saban Entertainment by way of a temp agency. He wasn't as into *Power Rangers* as, say, the typical six-year-old, but he'd been keeping up with it as a fan of science fiction. He continues to watch it.

"It really captured my imagination," Thomsen said. "Even though in those early days it had a cheesy look to it, the monsters, robots and a team of heroes? It was just fun. I still get a kick out of it. I love the teamwork aspect of it. . . . It's certainly not highbrow entertainment, but that doesn't bother me. I've always been one that all you have to do is ignite my imagination, and I'm ready to follow you and be a fan."

One of the last major promotional ventures coordinated by Leon and his associates was Fox Family Worldwide's last McDonald's Happy Meal promotion—and arguably its finest. From late April to mid-May of that year, kids technically received one of 11 toys, but each was really two toys in one. Four-inch figures of each of the six Rangers in *Lightspeed*

Rescue were housed in transparent clamshell cases that could combine to form a 12-inch "Megazord" along with five individual "Rail Rescue" trains that contained a pull-back vehicle. In conjunction with the Happy Meal toys, a VHS tape was sold with the purchase of adult combo meals: *Power Rangers in 3-D.* The "3D" movie—flimsy, fickle paper glasses included—was just a combined cut of a late-season two-part episode, "Trakeena's Revenge." But the episodes didn't air until November of that year, meaning anyone who picked it up from McDonald's would get to see the *Lost Galaxy* Rangers join forces with the *Lightspeed Rescue* team in advance. As a promotional swan song for Leon and several others, it couldn't have delivered much more in terms of hype.

"*Power Rangers* is more than a show," Leon said. "It was a cultural phenomenon, and part of a cultural phenomenon is about living off the screen. It's kids pretending that they are the Red Ranger, and buying the Red Ranger, and playing as the Red Ranger, and then going to see the Red Ranger on TV. It's the reason why it's been able to live on so long."

Fox Kids' weekend performance saw an uptick in May 2000, with viewership among two- to 11-year-olds up 10 percent year over year. *Lightspeed Rescue* was the top rater among kids in its 8 a.m. time slot on Saturdays. If *Lost Galaxy* was a bridge from the Zordon era, *Lightspeed Rescue* was a logical destination. It's a clean break, the team-up with *Lost Galaxy*'s heroes serving as the only tether between it and the past seven seasons. A fitting logline for the season, which revolves around a group of adults recruited into a military-like organization: make a prime-time action drama—but for seven-year-olds.

"That was probably one of our biggest budget years," Marchand said. "I couldn't believe the sets that we were able to make and the locations that we were able to go to. And the pyro—that was an expensive season. . . . Jonathan [Tzachor] was able to say, 'We're gonna film downtown, we're gonna blow shit up.'"

Power Rangers was the wily veteran in a boys-centric block also anchored by a cartoon that served as cross-promotion for one of Fox Broadcasting's key partners (*NASCAR Racers*) and an anime dub, *Digimon: Digital Monsters*, that sought to ride the coattails of *Pokémon*, the inheritor of *Power Rangers'* kid-culture throne. While a strong success in its own right, *Digimon* couldn't touch the Kids WB rival. Although its broadcast ratings never approached *Power Rangers'* insane peaks, *Pokémon* soared while most kids shows on broadcast TV were in a free fall. And elsewhere, the video game–led franchise became a monster much larger than any pocket could contain. As of 2024, the *Pokémon* franchise is believed to have grossed more than $100 billion in revenue, by far the most of any entertainment property of all time. *Power Rangers* is estimated to have generated about one-tenth of that.

Weekday numbers for Fox Kids continued to tumble into the pits, and Fox Family viewership[12] struggled to even dig itself out from underneath them. Fox Family Worldwide, saddled with $1.7 billion in debt after its takeover of the Family Channel, operated at a loss of $86.4 million between 1999 and 2000. If not for a drastic reduction in production and programming costs and a cash loan with 20 percent interest from Fox Broadcasting, Fox Family Worldwide would have fallen into technical default[13] on a $710 million loan.

A press photo signed by the cast of 2000's *Power Rangers Lightspeed Rescue* From left to right: Alison MacInnis (Dana the Pink Ranger), Keith Robinson (Joel the Green Ranger), Sean Cw Johnson (Carter the Red Ranger), Michael Chaturantabut (Chad the Blue Ranger), and Sasha Williams (Kelsey the Yellow Ranger). Courtesy The Morphin Museum/© Saban Entertainment

Saban denied repeatedly to the press that he would exercise it, but there was a way out: the ownership agreement between him and News Corporation allowed each side to trigger "puts" of their shares, effectively forcing the other into buying out their stake at a market value determined through investment appraisers. In the summer, Saban delivered a valuation that suggested Fox Family Worldwide was worth $6 billion, meaning he could get approximately $3 billion from a hypothetical sale. In December 2000, Saban stopped denying and started forcing Rupert Murdoch's hand: Fox could own the debt-riddled company outright, or they could offload it together to the highest bidder.

As Murdoch mulled what to do with his stake, Saban drummed up interest. The November sale of BET—a private company whose cable channel catered to a growing audience of Black viewers—to Viacom for $2.3 billion[14] further motivated Saban. The transaction begged a logical conclusion: if a network that is in 20 million fewer U.S. homes and that targeted 13 percent of the population could fetch that price, maybe Saban's valuation, dismissed and ridiculed, wasn't so far off. Saban hoped Murdoch would keep the company. "We're too small to be big because we're competing against Disney, CBS-Viacom and AOL Time Warner, and we're too big to be just a small unit producing shows," Saban said in March 2001.[15] "This company really belongs inside the News Corporation."

By late July, there was a buyer, but it wasn't Fox: the Walt Disney Corporation agreed to purchase the entirety of Fox Family Worldwide for $3.2 billion and the assumption of its debt, which by then had ballooned to about $2.3 billion. The rebranded ABC Family Channel, Disney president Bob Iger projected, would become something of an "ABC2," affording it to better leverage its existing shows at a time when media giants were just starting to figure out how to make cable work for them. Disney chair Michael Eisner described the acquisition as a "safety net."[16] Several business analysts called the deal, valued at 35 times Fox Family Worldwide's annual cash flow, extravagant.

The deal closed in late October for about $100 million less than the first agreed-on price. Pocket change. Twenty years after falling in love with *Choudenshi Bioman* and less than a decade after conquering TVs and toy aisles with *Mighty Morphin Power Rangers*, Saban traded in his small empire and walked away with $1.5 billion in cash. At 57 years old, he became a billionaire while Mickey Mouse morphed into a reluctant stepfather.

CHAPTER 15

Fighting Spirit

After replacing Ann Austen at Fox Kids, Dave McDermott remained *Power Rangers'* network executive into the final years of Saban Entertainment's control. By that point, creation of the show was so well practiced that those involved felt network notes were more a formality than something to be seriously considered. By the time McDermott moved into a position of influence, he had little over *Power Rangers*.

"My mentor in the executive suite there was [*X-Men* producer] Sidney Iwanter, who was known far and wide as a cantankerous individual," McDermott said. "I thought, 'Well I'm gonna be cantankerous too.' Turns out, when you're dealing with Haim Saban and Shuki Levy? Shuki was like, 'We appreciate your comments, we're gonna do what we're gonna do.' I was like, 'What the heck?' so I went to Margaret [Loesch]. . . . And she's like, 'Yea, that's pretty much it.' But after a while, I got into the swing of it and got used to how the production was going. By the time I took it over, it was already a smash hit. I learned to roll with it. I loved what I loved about it and, once in a while, there was a thing where I'd go 'Ehhhh?' but it is what it is. You can't gloss it up too much, because it's got to be just dumb, crazy, action, fun, which is what's beautiful about it."

Power Rangers Time Force, the final season produced by Saban Entertainment, cost about $30 million to make in 2000. (Longtime production accountant Brett Born said episodes of *Power Rangers*—budgeted by season, not episode—cost somewhere between $500,000 and $1 million to shoot. This estimate splits the difference at $750,000 an episode.) While a close adaptation of *Mirai Sentai Timeranger*, it boasts an incredible amount of original footage and brought in *Mad Max* veteran Vernon Wells to play the season's sympathetic antagonist, Ransik, a mutant from the year 3000 whom that season's team, a group of time cops, pursues to the year 2001. As an unintended swan song, it's fantastic.

Chip Lynn and Jackie Marchand, *Power Rangers'* longest-serving writers, left after *Time Force*. Producer Jonathan Tzachor was famously efficient with the show's time and budget, and there was a healthy respect for what he brought to the table—perhaps from no one more important than Saban himself. But creative inclinations sowed division. "His strengths as a producer were not in the creative realm, in my opinion," said Marchand. "He always wanted to stick as close to the *Sentai* as possible and wasn't extremely receptive to original ideas. He had a lot of admiration for the *Sentai* and thought we should stick very, very close to that. That was always his preference."

Throughout *Time Force*, its Red Ranger, Wes, and Pink Ranger, Jen, develop a forbidden "will-they-won't-they" romance: Jen is from the year 3000 and Wes from the year 2001. Wes, played by Jason Faunt, is an ancestor of Alex (also Faunt), to whom Jen, brought to life by future Hallmark Channel queen Erin Cahill, was engaged before his apparent death at the hands of Ransik. It gets wilder: Alex returns from the grave midway through the show, and Jen breaks off their engagement. In the show's final scene, Jen and Wes confess their love for one another before separating. Stewart St. John's decade-old dream of a spandex-draped soap opera was fully realized, but not with the bow Lynn and Marchand wanted.

"The whole theme of the show was destiny," Marchand said. "Wes choosing his own destiny, that was his through line. . . . And then at the end, he doesn't choose his destiny. We had a big fight with Jonathan about that finale. I was like, 'They have to stay together, we've been creating this relationship for the whole season,' and Jonathan argued if they stay together, it ruins the space-time continuum. He got scientific about it, like the butterfly effect and all that. I'm like, 'Dude, I don't want to diminish kids' intellect, but they want a happy ending, the kids want the couple to stay together, and we'll come up with some reason why they can do that and not ruin the folds of time.' We argued for so long about that, and we lost the argument and I'm still mad about it to this day because I think it was the wrong choice. . . . It was still a good finale, but it was more of an example of how Jonathan wanted to exert his own opinions into the storylines, and that was kind of worrying."

Lynn grew weary of the pace at which he and Marchand worked and felt like he could be doing more for the show than he'd been allowed after nearly a decade on staff. "I would drive to work and look at the exit and think, 'Ah, some day I won't have to get off this exit, I can keep driving,' and that day came," Lynn said. "A lot of people who are writers or editors or directors, they're creative, and it gets to a point where they say to themselves, 'If I was to make this decision, it would be a different

decision,' and 'If I was in charge, it might be a slightly different show.'"
After he left *Power Rangers*, Lynn started building houses and flying his
personal plane more often. "Being on the show for as long as I was maybe
wasn't the best, but I made up for that by having other hobbies that could
distract me from it. It was a very intense relationship, between me and
the show."

On the small screen, Disney chased tween girls who devoured age-
appropriate sitcoms and made-for-TV movies on the Disney Channel, which
had slowly emerged from cable obscurity. Tzachor's extensive history made
him a short-term asset to the company, which had little understanding of
what it just purchased. So it took notes as he and remaining crew members
cooked.

Disney slashed the budget of *Power Rangers Wild Force*, the show's
milestone tenth season and the first made on its watch. For the first time, it
wasn't clear that there would *be* a next season. It also wasn't clear during
production where *Wild Force* would air since the Saturday morning block
formerly anchored by *Power Rangers* was leased to 4Kids Entertainment—
the producer behind *Pokémon*—in January 2002 for a four-year sum of
$101.2 million.[1] The final episode of *Power Rangers* to air on Fox Kids, "The
Master's Last Stand," is the twenty-sixth of 40 in the season and ends on
a tease for the season's endgame; cleverly, the first episode to premiere
a month later on Disney's Saturday morning broadcast block, ABC Kids,
was titled "Unfinished Business."

But it was an episode that premiered a couple weeks later, on October
5, that highlights *Wild Force* and may be the show's most memorable
outside of *Mighty Morphin Power Rangers*. A decade before Sam Jackson's
Nick Fury brought together the Avengers to save Manhattan, Tommy
Oliver led a group of Red Rangers on a mission to the moon.

Episode 452 of *Power Rangers*, "Forever Red," is a one-off romp that
unites 10 of the previous Red Rangers—all but Steve Cardenas's Rocky.
While recent seasons of the show made a habit of bringing back past
teams to join forces against a powerful threat, this took the idea to another
level. Leadership and the color red are synonymous in *Power Rangers*.
Here, 10 leaders gathered to overcome some familiar threats: surviving
members of the Machine Empire who've dug up Lord Zedd's long-
dormant Zord, Serpentera.

Fittingly, it was written by a fan. Amit Bhaumik was in high school
when "Day of the Dumpster" premiered. He thought it sucked. That same
afternoon, he ended up at Toys "R" Us and happened on a group of kids

singing the theme song. Bhaumik thought he should give it another shot. He watched *Mighty Morphin Power Rangers* in passing until the "Green With Evil" miniseries hooked him for good. Fast-forwarding a few years, Bhaumik is a film student at USC with steady internet access and decides to do something that so many in the nascent home-internet era did: create a fan site.

Bhaumik's site joined just a handful of others dedicated to *Power Rangers* in the mid-1990s. Oceanographer Erik Olson launched the first web page dedicated to *Power Rangers* in 1993 while studying for his PhD at the University of Washington. The bare-bones site, simply titled "Power Rangers," has just one image—a black-and-white GIF of the original Green Ranger—followed by a self-deprecating reflection on the show's first season and a list of its monsters. That's all it needed to attract hundreds of page views each week despite being built on a lark while Olson created a website for his true passion, tropical fish.

"In the lab we gravitated towards watching afternoon kids TV as a break from our work," Olson said. "Seeing *Power Rangers* for the first time was one of those mouth drops." Olson stuck with the show until the season 2 cast change but has occasionally watched episodes of newer seasons with his children. In recent years, he's binged several *Super Sentai* seasons, including *Zyuranger*. "I could not imagine being able to do that in 1993."

The Morphing Grid, webmastered by Manuel Perez, was a bit more robust and one of Bhaumik's favorites, and it inspired him to learn web design. On a campus server, he created Power Rangers Online Archive, which housed encyclopedic information and fan fiction, written by Bhaumik and others. It shuttered in 2000, and seemingly so did Bhaumik's connection to *Power Rangers*. A year later, he was writing for the show.

"After college I went to work for an entertainment magazine, dotcom kind of thing, so I was always writing," Bhaumik said. "I came on as an assistant story editor with the idea being I'd fill Jackie's position and they'd hire a new Chip. Eventually, me and Jonathan just kind of hit it off and really vibed." Tzachor named Bhaumik story editor, though functionally, Tzachor was as much the head writer as Bhaumik. "He was there in every story meeting, every writing meeting, worked on every script, supervised and had changes and notes for every draft." Koichi Sakamoto, the longtime Alpha Stunts head who had coproducer credits since *Lost Galaxy*, also had a heavy hand in *Wild Force*. "This is how it is in most TV shows: when you see the 'written by,' if it was really truthful, it would be like seven names."

It's unfortunate that "Forever Red" never aired on Fox Kids, because it was 100 percent created for fans who'd been with *Power Rangers* from the beginning. Andros (*In Space* Red, Christopher Khayman Lee) surveys the worsening moon situation before we cut to Earth, where Bulk and Skull—now the owner-operators of a resort bar—receive an important phone call intended for a frequent guest, Tommy (*Zeo* Red, Jason David Frank). From there, Cole (Ricardo Medina Jr.), an anxious Tarzan riff and *Wild Force*'s Red Ranger, gets recruited for "an important mission" by *Lightspeed Rescue*'s Red Ranger, Carter Grayson (Sean CW Johnson). The two convene at an airport hangar where *Time Force*'s two Red Rangers, Wes and Eric (Dan Southworth), reacquaint themselves with Cole (a two-part *Time Force* team-up aired 10 episodes earlier). They all soon meet T.J. (*Turbo* Red, Selwyn Ward) and Andros, who informs them that another "veteran Ranger" has assembled them. Tommy, whose short, spiked hair is a far cry from his long teenage locks, steps into the hangar before a commercial break. "He's a legend," T.J. tells Cole after intermission. The seven Red Rangers start to depart—via Astro Megaship Mark II—before Andros wonders aloud about another Red Ranger on Earth. "I guess he couldn't make it," Tommy says, disheartened. Then we hear the sound of an engine. A motorcycle approaches the hangar. Aboard it: the original Red Ranger, Jason (Austin St. John). "You guys weren't gonna do this without me were ya?"

If you poke beyond the surface and start asking too many questions, "Forever Red" becomes a headache. The oldest Rangers—Jason, Tommy, and T.J.—technically shouldn't have access to the powers they're using, as they were all destroyed or decommissioned. No members of the Machine Empire should still be alive since Zordon's sacrifice should have turned them all into dust. If one wants to get *really* trivial, you could cite an often-memed quote from Zordon in season 2's "Wild West Rangers"— "Too much pink energy is dangerous!"—to decry the entire episode's premise. To dedicated fans in venues like RangerBoard, the most prominent discussion forum for the show, these kind of continuity errors or unexplained moments have yielded untold hours of lost sleep. To anyone else young or old with any interest in the show? It's just the fun kind of crazy that can be delivered only by *Power Rangers*.

Bhaumik for a while felt cold toward the episode because its contents were spoiled online well before it aired and due to some of his own nitpicking. No one had a contact for David Bacon, the actor for Aurico, the Red Ranger from Aquitar, so his character joins late in the episode and never de-morphs. The same was initially true of Danny Slavin, the actor behind *Lost Galaxy*'s Leo, whose interactions with the other cast after joining them on the moon seem off. "We wrote it, filmed it and everything, then like a month or two later we were able to talk to Danny Slavin and he wanted to do it," Bhaumik said. "Koichi and Jonathan were really determined to bring him back, and I think they made the right decision. I didn't understand at the time that there was a way to kind of make him fit." Through a combination of solo scenes and early 2000s digital compositing, Slavin snuck in.

Bhaumik wrote the script for "Forever Red" in just a day. The only major alteration from his original draft was the threat: originally, a group of cultists aimed to revive Maligore, the villain from *Turbo: A Power Rangers Movie*. Sakamoto nixed that in favor of a Machine Empire angle because there were "robot suits" available to use. They were a mix of heroes and villains from *Beetleborgs*. "I wasn't aware until I saw them on set," Bhaumik said with a laugh. "That's another classic *Power Rangers* thing, where you just feel the cheapness." He also worked in a line of Tommy dialogue—"Aw man, that's one ugly Zord!"—that referenced an early internet fan hoax. Bhaumik lent the voice for Tommy in "Scorpion Rain," an alleged five-part serial that bridged the gap between *Zeo* and *Turbo*. "I never considered it canon, I just got a chuckle thinking, 'Oh man, I can't wait until fans see this who know about 'Scorpion Rain,'" Bhaumik said. "Koichi had a lot of notes on it and he argued with me like, 'That's kind of a silly line. If this thing is about to destroy the Earth and it's taking off, who cares if it's ugly or pretty?' I explained to him it was an inside joke."

To its great benefit, the show was written and shot before a full-fledged handoff to ABC and its broadcast standards and practices department. *Wild Force*'s final 10 or so episodes received notes that bamboozled production, such as *Can the Power Rangers not use weapons?* and *Why are they punching bad guys?* One of Bhaumik's most infuriating exchanges came amid work on "The Soul of Humanity," which premiered the same day as "Forever Red" but came well after it in the production pipeline. Midway through the episode, several civilians get piled under rubble from an explosion and abandoned by others who'd been near them. As a villain mocks the Power Rangers for protecting such selfish people, those who fled return with tools and other people to help lift the debris. It's a powerful moment that ties into the season's overall themes of pollution and negligence and spotlighted not so subtly by Cole: "Humans sometimes make mistakes, but in times of need we humans will do whatever it takes to help our friends." It concerned ABC.

"They were really pissed about that," Bhaumik said. "They're like, 'We're gonna need some policemen and firefighters to come because there are people in danger and people in trouble.' I'm like, 'Do you know what kind of show we're making? The superheroes are the first responders for this show.' The final compromise was sirens in the background, so little Timmy watching at home will say, 'Oh I can rest easy, the paramedics are on their way.'"

Tzachor's mastery of the unique *Power Rangers* machine was put to the test throughout *Wild Force*'s production. "Jonathan ran that show since it started," said Born, who'd worked with Tzachor for nearly a decade at Saban Entertainment. "He was proud of the show, so he didn't take kindly to [Disney's] remarks and innuendo. It was just a big power play, and they were gonna win anyway." Tzachor's intolerance for interference caught up to him, but he left the show with most relationships in good standing and, perhaps more important, an incredible track record in terms of managing all its moving parts. "There's just these people out there who kind of know the money in their head—roundabout, close enough, y'know—so that they don't have to get a detailed report every couple of days," Born said. "They already know. They might want to see something and double-check stuff, but they already know. Jonathan knew that show like the back of his hand. You couldn't have had a better person running it from that standpoint, for sure."

Outside of some quotes published in the *Los Angeles Times* in 2001, Tzachor has never spoken on the record about *Power Rangers*. He politely declined—multiple times over three years—to be interviewed for this book.

"Sometimes guys like that can be very quiet but at the same time very disciplined and very, very efficient," said director Robert Radler. "He was your original nice-guy producer. He never broke character, even when I was getting 'spanked' for whatever it was I had done that particular day. . . . I can't say enough for him. Even when there were difficult situations, he was always calm."

"He was very much into the action of it and getting to it as quickly as possible, so any kind of 'writer's wank'—stuff like the wonderful emotional beats—it was like, 'No, we sorta need to get rid of that,'" McDermott said. "He may be difficult to work with, but he always struck me as a really nice guy. . . . Disney just milked his brain and then got him out of there quickly, and that was a little bit of a bummer. But that's why they did that season, just to see how the sausage was made."

The merchandising juggernaut[2] behind *Power Rangers*—propelled by a Bandai toy line still recognized as the No. 1 Male Action Toy Brand, ahead of other stalwarts like *Pokémon* and *Star Wars*—encouraged Disney to continue producing the show despite frustration with its eccentricities.

Between its popular feature films and tween content, Disney struggled to attract boys with its consumer product lines, and *Power Rangers* presented an opportunity to diversify its portfolio through a proven hit. "It was literally all princesses, whatever the movies were and Mickey Mouse in terms of their strongest performing IP," said Jermaine Turner, another Fox Kids holdover. Turner's stay with Disney was lengthy—he remained there in various roles through late 2020, when he left to become the director of adult animation at Netflix. He and Shawn Tarkington, a production assistant during *MMPR*'s first season who'd graduated to production manager by *Wild Force*, became the show's network liaisons—and the people tasked with figuring out how to keep it going. They had an edict: make this cheap show more cheaply.

Peter Jackson's Academy Award–dominating *Lord of the Rings* trilogy kicked off in December 2001 with *The Fellowship of the Ring*. Jackson filmed all three movies in his native New Zealand, the diverse, lush, sprawling landscapes of which had been largely untapped by the American film industry. Pre-Jackson, its most notable export was arguably *Xena: Warrior Princess*, a 1990s action series. Those films were made, collectively, for less than $300 million, a fairly paltry figure in hindsight, even when adjusted for inflation (for comparison, Sony's original *Spider-Man* trilogy helmed by Sam Raimi cost something in the neighborhood of $600 million to make in the same time period). Access to local talent with experience handling pulp TV action and a far more stretchable dollar made moving *Power Rangers* to New Zealand seem like a no-brainer. There were some logistical hurdles, though, like the extended storage and maintenance of costumes, helmets, and props delivered from Toei and those commissioned locally in Los Angeles toward the end of Saban Entertainment's run. The many skills and facilities developed in conjunction with the show would not follow it across the pond.

"There were some very specialized components that required very specialized infrastructure," Born said. "I don't know how many teams on TV have ever had a monsters department, but we had a monsters department. The materials and cost and all that stuff, we had it set up here in L.A. and had Ivory Stanton making it. You take things to New Zealand, all of a sudden it's 'Where's your infrastructure? Where are you getting the materials to make and repair this stuff? Who's going to do it for you?'"

"You don't think about things like prop houses," Turner said. "There were no prop houses in New Zealand, so every prop had to be made from scratch. We had to literally build everything from the ground up, except for the toys we got from Bandai and the monster costumes we got from Japan. It was intense to have to expand out all that stuff."

Sakamoto's Alpha Stunts team followed production to its new country, so that aspect remained relatively intact except for locations. The tried-and-true deserts, quarries, and streets in and around Los Angeles were no more. The services of Iris Hampton, who'd cast the show since *In Space*, were no longer needed because Disney elected to forgo the makeshift agreement Saban had with SAG and instead cast nonunion international talent. For the first time, however, *Power Rangers* was produced under a Writers Guild of America (WGA) contract. Disney was determined to "age up" the show so that its characters and situations would better align with the other tween- and teen-skewing content it put on TV, ideally broadening the show's appeal to the higher end of kids ages two to 11 and possibly beyond. All their historical data indicated that interest in *Power Rangers*—the show and its merchandise—subsided around the time kids turned eight or nine.

Ann Austen (née Knapp) started working for the fledgling Fox broadcast network right out of film school. She eventually became an executive producer for *Power Rangers* in the early 2000s following an abrupt exit from the show in the mid-1990s. Courtesy The Morphin Museum/© Saban Entertainment

A couple of folks who knew a thing or two about *Power Rangers* led the charge: Ann Austen and Doug Sloan. Since leaving Saban Entertainment, they'd gotten into a fruitful relationship with Disney, for which they'd produced two made-for-TV movies, *Motocrossed* and *Johnny Tsunami*, that leaned into action sports and performed well on the Disney Channel. "When we got that call, it was, 'Wow, OK.' And then when they said it's going to be in New Zealand, 'Oh, that's even more fun,'" Austen said. "We already knew the Disney system, I guess, which had its own challenges of course, but we were really excited to do it. And it was WGA, which was a huge step up." Thanks to the WGA contract, Austen and

Sloan could bring aboard a couple of other *Power Rangers* veterans to work alongside them, Mark Hoffmeier and Jackie Marchand. "We knew they wanted to up the quality across the board—even though, I don't fault the quality we achieved [in the 1990s], I think we did a pretty good job," Austen said. "The writing was of its time, but this was 10 years after the show launched. Disney just wanted to evolve it a little bit."

Power Rangers Ninja Storm is swiftly distinguished from preceding seasons because it starts off not with five Rangers but with three, a wrinkle carried over from *Ninpuu Sentai Hurricaneger*. Beyond that, a heavy infusion of extreme sports, dialogue seeped in sarcasm, and an array of stunning backdrops jell to set *Ninja Storm* apart from its older siblings. It goes heavy on humor, the best of it delivered by New Zealand TV pioneer Grant McFarland, who pulls double duty as the *lucha libre*–inspired antagonist Lothor and the Ranger's sensei, transformed into a guinea pig for most of the season. Lothor's adult nieces, Marah (Katrina Devine) and Kapri (Katrina Browne), serve as comedic foils in the spirit of Baboo and Squatt but are much more conventionally attractive.

"One of my favorite episodes with them, I think they had a giant mosquito monster and I had them have a monster beauty contest," Hoffmeier said. "I asked if I was allowed to do that, thinking they would tell me no because it was such an out-there idea, and they said, 'Yea, do it!' They're putting a sash on this mosquito monster and giving it flowers, 'You've won the right to go attack the Power Rangers.' It seems so stupid, but it worked."

The heightened comedy, following multiple seasons of more "dramatic," serialized adventures, rubbed some longtime fans the wrong way. To them, the "Disneyfication" was too much. Sloan, who first perused RangerBoard under the screen name "nsbigcheese" before adopting "Dino Dude" ahead of his and Austen's next season, *Dino Thunder*, often quarreled with fans as new episodes premiered. A common reminder he issued: *Power Rangers* was made for people who had, at their oldest, just started puberty.

"*Ninja Storm* is what it is," Sloan wrote in 2003. "I think there was some great stuff in it and some stuff that could have come out better. But I stand by it as a CHILDREN'S series. It may not be what you adults would have wanted in a *Power Rangers* series, but that's life. Ever look under the tree and not get the G.I. Joe you wanted? That's what this is like." In case you needed further evidence that online fandoms have always been a touch absurd, in the same thread—titled "Disney must die"—a user unironically argues that the content of *Power Rangers* was never meant for kids, only marketed to them, and compares the show's complexity to that of the comic strip *Calvin and Hobbes*.

"I know there are people that are like, 'Oh, it got too goofy,'" Hoffmeier said. "It got too goofy? These are people in suits fighting giant monsters."

Dino Thunder, like *Ninja Storm*, begins with three protagonists and leans even further into trappings that reflect the time and corporation behind its production. The series' lone female Ranger, Kira, is modeled after Avril Lavigne and comes equipped with legit tunes, delivered by actor Emma Lahana, though much closer to Disney teenybops than Lavigne's pop-punk. Blue Ranger Ethan, played by Kevin Duhaney, is a computer and gaming geek with a predisposition for standing up to jocks, like soccer star and eventual Red Ranger Conner (James Napier). Collectively, they're a far cry from the five wholesome kids who kicked off the franchise. It's not clear right away that they'll ever even like one another, let alone become friends. After more than a decade, *Power Rangers* finally had something Zordon asked for in the original theme song: teenagers with attitude.

Dino Thunder is *Mighty Morphin Power Rangers* but reimagined for the 2000s. Obviously, the dinosaur motif was a driver, but so was timing. The youngest kids who could have seen and remembered *MMPR* were approaching high school age. The oldest among them would now be in college or entering the workforce. Couple those factors with two head honchos who were there from the beginning, and you've got the right mix for an homage that delivers a more dynamic narrative experience than the original ever was allowed to. And *Dino Thunder* wasn't done paying tribute to the show's history.

For *Power Rangers Dino Thunder*, the third Disney-produced season, executive produc-ers Ann Austen and Douglas Sloan brought back an old friend to mentor the newest Power Rangers. Courtesy The Morphin Museum/© Saban Entertainment

"Legacy of Power," the season's fourth episode, is the show's five hundredth—a milestone achieved by only three other live-action scripted children's TV shows in the United States as of 2024. (The others are all educational originals from PBS: *Mister Rogers' Neighborhood, Sesame Street,* and *The Electric Company.*) It opens with a superimposition: "Commemorating 500 episodes, may the power live on forever." The episode largely is a series-celebrating clip show framed around the kidnapping of the team's mentor. The three teens stumble on a video message from him. "If you're not me," he says, "then something is seriously wrong. This video diary is a confidential record, only to be viewed in case of an emergency. What you're about to see is a history of my life. My history as a Power Ranger."

To them, their guide is a high school science teacher whose college degree and knowledge of power-granting artifacts suggest he could make a better living elsewhere. To those in the know, Dr. Tommy Oliver is, as T.J. would say, a legend. The episode bridges into the next, "Back in Black," which concludes with Tommy becoming the series' Black Ranger. "I may be old," says the soul patch–sporting 28-year-old, "but I can still pull it off."

"We were looking for a stunt of some kind, and it just came up: let's bring back Tommy," said Austen. Frank was down, but his participation came with hurdles. Between his chain of karate businesses and family obligations, Frank was wary about traveling to New Zealand for an extended stay. An arrangement was worked out where he could film most of his scenes, do the bulk of his ADR work from the United States, and then return later to complete filming. His winnowed-down availability required a series of plot devices that result in his character being stuck in a morphed state and then, briefly, turned invisible for 13 episodes— about 34 percent of *Dino Thunder*'s allotment. The facelessness pays off come episode 27, "Fighting Spirit." Completely conceived and written by Marchand and mostly unchanged[3] from its original draft to filming, it puts Tommy—now comatose—face-to-face with his most challenging foe yet: himself.

Over the course of 20 minutes, within his mind, he spars with three past Ranger selves: *Zeo* Red, *MMPR* White, and, finally, *MMPR* Green—all while unable to morph. "I'm still as tough as ever," says *Zeo* Red. "The question is, are you?" Tommy goes blow-for-blow with him and *MMPR* White before *MMPR* Green finally overpowers him. On his back and with the Dragon Dagger poised to end him, Tommy declares he'll never give up. All he had to do was show that his will to live was stronger than any power bestowed on him by a Power Coin, Zeo Crystal, or Dino Gem. Tommy wins his battle and reemerges in the real world to help his mentees win theirs.

"Fighting Spirit" is widely regarded as one of *Power Rangers*' best episodes. The action pieces are among the finest the show's ever delivered, thanks to the show-stealing blend of Koichi Sakamoto's direction and Frank's decades of martial arts training. While the show's actors still did some of their own stunts, *Power Rangers* by this point preferred to cast legitimate actors who could learn to occasionally punch on camera rather than highly skilled fighters, gymnasts, and dancers. Frank was a dinosaur in that respect.

"Any time we'd come out to set, he'd say, 'Oh I wanna do this, I wanna do this, Koichi let me do this, let me do this,'"[4] Sakamoto said. "It was always fun working with him, 'cause we'd come up with great ideas and he'd come up with ideas. We shot so many fight scenes together. It was really fun working with him [in the 1990s]. Then when he came back for *Dino Thunder*, he was older and more mature now. But when it came time to do fight sequences, he was the same Jason Frank. 'Let's do this, let's do this!'"

Great fights buoy a message that goes far deeper than the typical "lesson of the day." In a social media post on November 20, 2022,[5] Marchand described "Fighting Spirit" as "a not-so-veiled metaphor about battling your inner demons." The post was prompted by news of Frank's death by suicide a day earlier. He was 49.

"I remember the first time I saw him when I was still at Fox and he had just been cast, and he was coming to meet the team at the network," Austen said. "In walks this shining star. Some people just have 'it,' you know? They just walk in with an inner glow that you cannot quantify. Throughout my career, I've met a few of those, but he was the first, and really the clearest. He had a charm and innocence and vulnerability, but also strength. He was a really charming kid, and so very smart. He learned fast. He was a great learner."

He was also, in his final years, *Power Rangers*' greatest ambassador. Beyond additional cameos, he was a convention centerpiece who consistently attracted thousands of fans to cities by himself. He wasn't the first *Power Rangers* actor to take to the convention circuit, but he embraced it to a degree and with fervor that was unrivaled. His social media following was incomparable among *Power Rangers* actors, even those whose post–*Power Rangers* acting careers bore much richer fruit. Likewise, so were his activities—long before social media was a fixture among once-famous stars, he interacted one-on-one with fans online, held frequent giveaways and contests, and starred in three seasons of an online reality TV show, *My Morphing Life*. Frank's most famous role is Tommy, but the performance for which he should be best remembered is Jason David Frank.

"I like to entertain people," Frank said in March 2022, eight months before his death. "[In my lines], you can wait but also be entertained. I appreciate people's time, because that's all we got at the end of the day. We've got 86,400 seconds a day. That's it. So we've got to make every second count. . . . Stuff happens so fast, and life is just so short. What are you going to leave behind? Are you going to leave behind a legacy where [people] remember your agent saying, 'Oh, you got to pay for an interview.' That's not what I want to leave behind. I want to leave behind, 'Hey, I got a chance to talk to this dude and not one time did he rush me off the phone, not one time did he do this.' That's the legacy I want to leave behind."

"Once darkness has entered your home, it's hard to get it out," said Jason Narvy, who remained close friends with Frank up until his death. "He struggled with it for a very long time, and I think the last couple years he was really on a downward spiral. When Frank was at his best, he was great. Our business is the worst place to suffer that sort of thing, because all the worst pitfalls of mental illness are both preyed upon and exacerbated by the nature of our business. Mental illness is about looking at one's place in this world and wondering if you are alone and belong. That's every actor's journey. 'Am I good enough?' The idea that I need to play the game. I remember once, Frank—completely unrelated to mental illness—when we started doing conventions, he was doing really well and he said, kind of self-deprecating, 'Yea baby, I'm faking it 'til I'm making it.' He wasn't faking it, he was doing well at that point and felt a little guilty about that. He was doing well and didn't want to be a complete braggart. In Hollywood, you do fake it until you make it. 'Oh, things are going good, I got projects, I got this thing I'm doing now.' Well, isn't that the perfect subterfuge to say, 'How are you feeling?' I'm feeling good—we're told we have to say that.

"When someone is *really* going through it, they've already been trained to keep people at a distance and try to deal with it on their own, pretend that it doesn't exist. Even people that aren't in this business pretend that there aren't mental health problems. So somebody as strong as Frank, who loved his family and friends dearly, to leave us all? That will tell you just, yes, how much he was suffering, but also how not himself he was at the end. He wouldn't do that if he was himself. He would take on the burdens of other people. He's fucking hooked us all up solid, and when bad shit has happened, he always let us know he was there as much as he could. He gave himself to everybody, and everybody wanted a piece of him. But when he was there, he was *all* there. For you."

CHAPTER 16

One Last Second Chance

Two years was enough time for Ann Austen and Doug Sloan to get Disney's *Power Rangers* operation going in New Zealand. They again left the show, this time on much better terms and with a fresh reminder of all the quirks that make *Power Rangers* a production unlike any other.

"Every season of *Power Rangers* is completely different, full of new challenges and hurdles to overcome," Sloan said. "No EP has as much control as you think they do. We basically do what the powers that be tell us to do and attempt, as best we can, to get as much of our creative voice into the show as possible, and it ain't always easy."[1]

"They essentially did us a favor," said Jermaine Turner, the Disney programming executive. "They had successfully moved on from that era of their career. We asked them to come back, and they said, 'OK, we'll do it for a minute.' We knew that we wouldn't have them for the long haul."

Bruce Kalish, like Austen and Sloan, had a preexisting relationship with Disney when he was tapped next to helm *Power Rangers*. He wasn't too far removed from having produced *The Famous Jett Jackson*, a Gemini Award–winning kids action sitcom, for the Disney Channel. The son of producer-screenwriters Austin and Irma Kalish had decades of TV credits under his belt, spurred by his parents' unwillingness to hire him until he got his own foot in the door as well as by an accusatory high school teacher. "She failed me, saying that my parents wrote the script and that I would never amount to anything," Kalish said. "Whenever I got paid, for years and years and years, I sent a copy of my check stub to her." The teacher never wrote back.

Kalish brought on a renowned creature effects artist, Greg Aronowitz, to copilot the show that became *Power Rangers S.P.D.* Disney wanted "a new look," and Aronowitz was the vessel through which much of it was generated. "I've worked for Roger Corman and I've worked for Steven Spielberg," Aronowitz said. "With my stuff, I try to strive for what Steven's able to accomplish but pull it off for what Corman spends." Jackie Marchand didn't have as much direct creative input on *S.P.D.* as the seasons before and after it, but she was integral to bringing the newcomers up to speed on *Power Rangers* and its inner workings. Writer John Tellegen, hired during *Ninja Storm*, also stayed aboard.

Aronowitz and Kalish conspired for nearly six months of preproduction while *Dino Thunder* was mid-shoot and generated a story where aliens and humans, for the most part, coexist peacefully. From petty crimes to world-threatening monsters, an intergalactic police force led by teams of Power Rangers—Space Patrol Delta—protects the planet. That all of this takes place in the year 2025 is a stretch. "I wanted to project it into the future, but they were like, 'Well no, it has to be where kids can understand,'" Aronowitz said. "It should have been like 2300 or something. . . . There were a lot of stressful arguments over the dumbest little things like that."

In his lone season as an executive producer, VFX and prop extraordinaire Greg Aronowitz poured hundreds of extra hours into making *Power Rangers S.P.D.* look and feel unlike any other season. Courtesy Greg Aronowitz

While future-minded, *S.P.D.* thrives on practicality. It deploys a Lego-like set that could be quickly reoriented and refurnished to turn what in most seasons would be a static hangout set into a dynamic area that could become a variety of rooms. The adapted version of Doggie Kruger, the season's mentor and whose *Super Sentai* counterpart would feel more at home in *The Muppet Show*, is part human and part animatronic. Aronowitz spent eight weeks working on a sculpture with lifelike textures to place over the head of actor John Tui. It required some tinkering for use in New Zealand: their power system's voltage is double that of the United States, so Aronowitz had to modify it to run on a battery.

That worked smoothly until the first day of principal photography, Aronowitz's directorial debut. "Everyone except Walt Disney is standing behind me waiting to see what happens with this thing that I built," Aronowitz said. "I go 'Action!' and the camera pushes in, the chair turns around perfectly, and his nose is right in the frame and smoke's coming out." The battery got so hot that it was melting the foam shoulder pads of Tui's costume. "It caught on fire and we're like, 'Son of a bitch,'" said Turner.

Discussions turned to creating a prosthetic, or simply painting Tui's face blue for the show's duration, to keep production moving. Aronowitz had created a foam replica of the animatronic, painted exactly like it, in case of emergencies, so that was used in the interim to capture some coverages that day. That same night, he and a friend took apart and rebuilt the animatronic. It never caught fire again, and within a week—thanks to big lifts from Simon Riera, director of photography, and Koichi Sakamoto's second-unit team—he was able to capture the shots nixed by flames on day one. "Once it was edited in, they had all forgotten, but in that moment, they wanted to buy my ass a ticket to get out of New Zealand," Aronowitz said.

The show's lead protagonists are the "B-Squad," forced to defend Earth when the top unit goes missing on a distant planet. A-Squad's helmets were repurposed from those used for the Rangers from *In Space*, fitted with a few extra bells and whistles to make them more police-like. The B-Squad Blue Ranger, Sky (Chris Violette), is a stodgy, by-the-books type whose father was a former Red Ranger for S.P.D.; flashbacks to his dad show him wearing the same suit and helmet as the Red Ranger from *Time Force*, just with an S.P.D. logo slapped across the right breast. These retrofits provide good fodder for fan theories to this day, but they were merely a product of engineering cool ideas as cheaply as possible. Aronowitz designed fully original helmets for A-Squad but was afforded the ability to only half execute them. "Disney had all this old stuff and were like, 'Just use this helmet, repaint it and stick stuff on it,'" Aronowitz said. "I didn't realize that, for the rest of my life, people would be saying, 'Wait, that's so and so from *In Space.*'"

While every season of *Power Rangers* strives to distinguish itself from others, *S.P.D.* went to even greater lengths—arguably to its detriment. Aronowitz admits that the season starts to sag before picking up at the end. A-Squad's return in the finale, but as traitors working for the series' lead villain, is more rushed than it should be after 30-plus episodes of absence. Consequently, a historic reveal—that their Red Ranger, Charlie (Gina Varela), is a woman—gets underserved. "It was an opportunity that could have been used better elsewhere, or given more spotlight with how important it was," said Marchand. "That was just my thought. She didn't have much going on except that she was a female Red Ranger. We didn't flesh it out."

S.P.D. was Aronowitz's only turn on *Power Rangers*. He stepped away of his own accord, in part exhausted by the process and reliance on Japanese footage, the need for which he frequently called into question—and more loudly so as he observed what Sakamoto and second-unit director Akihiro "Yuji" Noguchi, who started working on *Power Rangers* as a stuntman in the 1990s, were doing in New Zealand. The *Super Sentai* production team around that time had even started to lean on that crew to do things for them. "Their whole opening and everything for *Magiranger*, we did that while we were doing *S.P.D.*, because they were loving what we were doing," Aronowitz said. Budget, of course, was often brought up as the reason why things had to be done as they'd always had but never got mentioned when the crew was asked to re-create existing *Super Sentai* scenes to comply with American broadcast standards. "The sensibilities were different," Aronowitz said. "In Japan, it's almost like comedy. It's something for parents and children to watch, and it has a silliness to it. They intend to do that, that's why sometimes the monsters are a giant cup of noodle soup and stuff like that. Even in previous [*Power Rangers*] seasons, they still might be a little tongue-in-cheek, but they were still always trying to make a superhero show. It was never a comedy show."

Kalish ran point for *Power Rangers*' next three seasons, *Mystic Force*, *Operation Overdrive*, and *Jungle Fury*, and Marchand and Tellegen continued to shepherd scripts. Marchand took on story editing duties once again beginning with *Mystic Force*, a magic-themed season that hoped to leech some of the buzz created by the latest cultural tour de force, *Harry Potter*. Finally, she also received a well-earned coproducer credit. In practice, she was the acting executive producer for *Operation Overdrive*, the show's fifteenth season, because Kalish was entrenched in the development of an action-adventure spy show, *Aaron Stone*, at Disney's behest.

The animatronic (left) and stunt head for Anubis "Doggie" Kruger of *Power Rangers S.P.D.* Courtesy Greg Aronowitz

Unfortunately, budgets and episode orders ticked downward—starting with *Mystic Force*, Disney's final four seasons each had 32 episodes—while executive oversight heightened. "*Operation Overdrive*, that was one where Disney was putting their foot down on everything, just not letting us do anything," Marchand said. It was conceptualized as *Indiana Jones* meets *Power Rangers* but barely gets to scratch beyond the surface of an exciting premise. "Every writer says, 'The network notes are ruining us,' but they really did have some terrible interference."

Operation Overdrive is best remembered for two things: an anniversary team-up celebrating the show's fifteenth season and a twist involving the Red Ranger, Mack (James Maclurcan). Marchand wrote the two-parter "Once a Ranger," which reunites four of the New Zealand–era Rangers—Tori (Sally Martin, *Ninja Storm* Blue), Kira (Emma Lahana, *Dino Thunder* Yellow), Bridge (Matt Austin, *S.P.D.* Red, promoted from his series' Green), and Xander (Richard Brancatisano, *Mystic Force* Green)—along with a longtime vet to lead them, Adam (*MMPR* Black). Johnny Yong Bosch had returned to the show once since leaving for a cameo during *In Space*. He hadn't suited up in a decade before joining forces with younger faces in 2007 to fend off Thrax, the grotesque offspring of Lord Zedd and Rita. Between stints in black spandex, Bosch launched a prolific career in voice acting, mostly for dubs of Japanese animation, imports of which had soared in popularity since Saban Entertainment was toiling away on them in the 1980s. He also started and fronted for a modestly successful rock band, Eyeshine.

As for the twist: Mack, son of season mentor Andrew Hartford (Rod Lousich), at the start of the season takes the Red Ranger mantle that Andrew intended to assume himself. Much later, when it's revealed that Mack is an android, not a human, Andrew's concerns about his son becoming a Power Ranger seem more valid. "That was mainly Bruce's idea, to have the kind of Pinocchio robot situation," Marchand said. Kalish shielded the reveal from Disney as long as possible to ensure they could do it. Kalish was accustomed to Disney's way of doing business and usually was a good soldier, but he too lost some battles that seemed like winners. He fought to have a teenager in a wheelchair be part of a *Power Rangers* team, but that was a nonstarter for Disney—it was just a bridge too far to have a paralyzed person wield the kind of powers that had been used by, among others: a 12-year-old, a set of alien triplets, and a literal ball of light. "They didn't want to give false hope to some kid in a wheelchair, and I thought, 'Oh my God, how lame can you be?'" Kalish said. "He could walk or run or whatever if he was in a suit, right? But what difference is it from anybody else who, once they put on the suit, they have super powers? Why would you not want to do that? But they wouldn't let me. It's my biggest regret."

Kalish also drew ire for reaching out to a young boy whose parents died in an accident. They'd been shopping for *Power Rangers* toys. "I was able to contact the family, and I wanted to send them a lot of toys from *Power Rangers*. I also put together a clip, during the reunion show, where we ran the cameras for a couple minutes after and had the actors say hello to him. Disney got so pissed at me for doing this, like how dare I do that without asking them. I sent it to the kid, and he loved it. It helped him. He was like seven years old. . . . The kid's parents died buying him *Power Rangers* gifts. Where's your humanity? Disney was like that."

Despite the best efforts of various executives, producers, writers, cast, and crew from multiple continents, *Power Rangers*' performance as a TV product worsened under Disney.[2] After a strong mark posted by *Ninja Storm* (average 1.42 rating/6.86, slightly higher than *Wild Force*), average ratings for each season fell—for the first time—below the one-point threshold on both broadcast and cable. By the time *Power Rangers Jungle Fury* premiered in 2008, it averaged a 0.60 rating and a 3.07 share on ABC Kids and fared just slightly worse on small cable channel Toon Disney (0.56/2.97).

Disney's problem was unchanged from the one it inherited: the show steadily lost most of its audience by the time they were eight years old, and toy sales were dominated by purchases made for kids freshly graduating from toddler toys. "[The audience] just kept going younger and younger and younger, to the point where I was in Japan having dinner with the Bandai and Toei guys, and one of the guys said to me, 'Why don't you just put *Power Rangers* on in your preschool block?'" Turner said. "I'm like, 'I can't put *Power Rangers* next to *Mickey Mouse Clubhouse*.' That doesn't work. . . . In terms of the biggest sales, there was a disconnect. The sales were for 2–5 [year-olds] and we were trying to make a show for 11-year-olds. It's hard to square that, but we tried."

The production of *Jungle Fury* was hampered—though, unlike most scripted American TV shows, not halted—by the Writers Guild of America strike in 2007. Its first 15 episodes, as well as the final four, were written by one of Kalish, Marchand, Tellegen, or David Garber, a friend of Kalish's. When Marchand and Tellegen politely informed Disney of their intent to strike, the company nudged Kalish to return to New Zealand as part of a "wink-wink" arrangement, expecting him to write and change things as needed to keep the show moving in the direction his team wanted it to go. "I went over there and just sat on the set," Kalish said. "They paid me my salary, and I didn't do a thing. I went fly fishing every weekend."

Judd "Chip" Lynn, one of the very few people in the world who could fill the void without a crash course in how to write *Power Rangers*, came to Disney's rescue. He wrote the remaining *Jungle Fury* episodes and oversaw production. "They'd heard through the grapevine that in the past I'd written most of the scripts, and they called me up and said, 'Hey, would you like to give it a shot and see if you can keep the show going?'" Lynn said. "I think they were a bit skeptical of me because there were four or five people on strike, and they're asking me to take the place of all of them, and I was like, 'Sure, no problem.' I jumped on a plane to New Zealand and had a great time."

Marchand loved developing *Jungle Fury*. They'd ended up with what she felt was one of their strongest casts, and the season delivered the right blend of comedy and action that, to her, was quintessentially *Power Rangers*. It's one of her favorite seasons and one in which her influence was heavy but also marred by Lynn's intervention—not from a quality standpoint but from a personal one. He reached out to let her know he was considering it before he crossed the picket line.

"It just didn't sit well with me," Marchand said. "I know if the tables were turned, I would not have [done it]. It hurt. It hurt most because he was a friend. That really chilled our relationship." Lynn at the time wasn't in the union, but he later joined it following the strike. In 2014, he was named to the WGA West "financial core" list—a sort of "scarlet letter" for dues-paying members who've been identified as disloyal to union causes but from whom the union still collects dues in exchange for the same benefits granted to fully compliant members.

"The crew came to me privately many times," Lynn said. "'Thank you for being here, we really need to keep working.' That made me feel good about it. Our crew was anywhere from 90 to 130 people, and all those people faced unemployment because of, in this case, a handful of people who were striking in Los Angeles. It seemed a little unbalanced."

Disney called on Lynn again the following year to spearhead the back half of its final fully original season, *RPM*. Set in a dystopian future where most of the world's remaining population is housed in a bubble city, it's in some ways the kind of season Aronowitz aspired for *S.P.D.* to be compositionally. Its average footage breakdown per episode, 87 percent American to 13 percent Japanese,[3] was the highest in favor of original footage since *MMPR*'s third season. The result is a fan-favorite romp that takes suits and Zords from the rather goofy *Engine Sentai Go-onger* and places them in an apocalyptic adventure rife with self-referential and meta comedy. It's also a season that pushed the show to the brink of cancellation—and one of its biggest champions over the edge.

Marchand initially got offered the role of executive producer with the caveat that another Disney cohort, Eddie Guzelian, could cochair alongside her, effectively acting in a role similar to what Aronowitz had been to Kalish. She was cool with that but not with the proposed salary: Disney wanted to take the full executive producer allotment and split it evenly between the two. She remained in her old role, with her previous, higher salary, and continued to be subordinate to someone who not only was brand new to *Power Rangers* but this time completely green to live-action TV production.

Guzelian for more than a decade had written for animated Disney TV shows, and recently codeveloped *American Dragon: Jake Long*, an action-adventure hit for the Disney Channel. He was charged with the same edicts as those before him—make the show appeal to older kids, make it look different, and make it more cheaply—and told that he had "nothing to lose," as this would be the show's final season regardless of performance. After 16 years on the air, *Power Rangers* would be gone—so why hold back?

"Disney told him to swing for the fences, but they didn't give him a bat," Marchand said. "He wanted to do all this stuff, because he's a super creative guy, and I think a *really* good writer, but as a producer?" Guzelian's distaste for Marchand's scripts slowed production to a near standstill, to the point she became a scapegoat. She was sad but not surprised when Shawn Tarkington, with whom she'd worked since he was a production assistant on *MMPR*, called to deliver news of her termination.

"I was like, 'I get it, you're throwing me under the bus, but he's not going to be able to produce the show on time. He's underwater,'" Marchand said. "And then they fired him like a month later because he wasn't writing producible scripts to feed the machine. It was a disaster. I was so destroyed."

Guzelian, in a 2009 message board Q&A[4] conducted before the show premiered, acknowledged his culpability in a near shutdown of the production but claimed his dismissal occurred after that was rectified. He was let go the day after Christmas. "On my official termination papers with Disney, the cause is listed as 'Creative Differences,' which is a strange choice of words," Guzelian wrote. "I thought that I had a very open and collaborative relationship with the execs at Disney who were overseeing the show, including being very honest and up-front regarding everything, including the late scripts. When the time came to fire me, I think even these executives would admit that it was not handled in the same spirit."

Lynn is credited as an executive producer for 26 of *RPM*'s 32 episodes, while Guzelian is credited on 18. The general vibe of the show established in the first half remains intact, but how it wraps is completely removed from whatever Guzelian's vision was, as he had just pinned down where he wanted it to go prior to his firing and was given no opportunity to pass along his ideas to Lynn.

"It was Eddie's first time doing a live-action show, and it's tricky," Lynn said. "And *Power Rangers* is a tricky show anyway because it's low-budget and there's a lot of moving parts. I think he did the best he could and that he put together a really good season. I came in and did the best I could to catch up and keep up. It was a little dark for me—it felt more like it was for teenagers than for little kids—so I had to recalibrate and gauge what I was used to doing, but it was a great season with a great cast and crew, so many of whom had worked on the show for years.

"That is one of my favorite things about *Power Rangers*. You have so many people who were so experienced with what they were doing. You give them a design or a deadline or something and, somehow, they would do the impossible and make it happen."

CHAPTER 17

The Master Returns

Whether *Power Rangers* was or wasn't canceled by Disney depends on one's interpretation of the word.

The writing and filming of new episodes based on Japanese footage was suspended, but money was spent to produce "new" episodes for broadcast in 2010 and to promote Bandai's newest wave of toys—brand-new assortments, not reissues, based on the show that gained it a foothold in stores across America: *Mighty Morphin Power Rangers*.

Simply rebroadcasting *MMPR* wasn't feasible for two reasons. Its age showed considerably against that of other reruns, Disney Channel sitcoms like *That's So Raven* and *Hannah Montana*, with which it would share time on the decaying ABC Kids block. The bigger issue, though, was the haphazard length of episodes. By its second season, most *MMPR* episodes achieved a then-standard length of about 20 minutes, but run times in its debut season, produced in a laxer broadcast era, were all over the place. The shortest episode, "Doomsday Part II," clocks in at 18 minutes, 44 seconds, more than three full minutes fewer than the 22-minute standard for a 30-minute window in 2010. Twenty-two episodes of *MMPR*'s first season clock in at under 20 minutes.

Studiopolis, a Los Angeles postproduction studio, was tapped to standardize and glamorize *MMPR*'s first 32 episodes, matching recent-season orders. The company had recorded and dubbed several of Disney's animated projects, including its most recent adaptation of *Digimon*, the rights to which it also acquired in the Fox Family Worldwide purchase. And it had a big *Power Rangers* fan on staff in Dan Evans, a former development and programming manager for Fox Kids. The resulting product, christened by fans and later officially called a "re-version," is stuffed with comic-book panel-style graphics and lettering, brightened colors for high-definition broadcast, and edits to audio and visual effects intended to improve continuity and bring the footage closer to modern tastes. Evans made some other proactive changes, like placing pop-ups over areas that vaguely showed brands with which Disney didn't have partnerships. Others were born from a hilarious process in which episodes approved for TV almost two decades prior had to undergo rigorous review from Disney's standards and practices liaison. "And we would get notes back!" Evans said. "'Please change this, the language is offensive.' There was some note that said, 'There's too much leg showing' or something and I'm like, 'No, those are leggings. She's wearing shorts under her skirt.' We would have to go in and do color changes and stuff just to appease her."

The final re-version episode, "A Star Is Born," stretches the run time through the deployment of an almost minute-long montage of scenes from across the series as the show comes out of its final commercial break. "At the end, I thought it should all be a big valentine to the fans or whatever," Evans said. For the most part, they blasted the re-version on message boards and, increasingly, popular social media platforms. "My Twitter feed, all of a sudden, people are like, 'You suck! What are you doing? Why do you hate the Power Rangers?' I'm like, 'I'm just making a show. It's the same show, just prettier and with a couple graphics. It isn't really going to change your life.'" Uncouth feedback, thankfully, didn't weaken Evans's love of the franchise. "Even though it's formulaic to a degree, it's still a lot of fun to watch if you just go turn it on, get some popcorn or a big bowl of cereal, and let it just wash over you."

Sports broadcast preemptions and local decisions to air the show as early as 4 a.m.—problems that plagued much of the ABC Kids era—spelled doom for *RPM* and the *MMPR* re-version. So did the head-scratching decision to not air them on Disney XD, the new action-adventure kids channel that annexed the space once occupied by Toon Disney. "It was really hard for parents to square the Disney brand with *Power Rangers* because it was so violent," said Jermaine Turner. "And when the revenue started to drop, it was just harder for [Bob] Iger to justify having it as part of the umbrella, knowing that parents—not all, but a vocal amount—were so against [it]. That's why you never saw *Power Rangers* on Disney Channel."

Perhaps, in the interest of Bandai, additional re-version seasons might have been commissioned for the years leading up to 2013—the show's twentieth anniversary and a peg around which Disney considered a substantial marketing effort and the possibility of a new TV production—possibly produced without *Super Sentai* footage. "They wanted to have this big thing where they were like, 'Hey, Power Rangers!'" Evans said.

While ratings for the live-action show fell and disgruntled parents yelled, Turner internally guided the development of something else to refresh and reignite the property: an animated series. It would be a drastic departure from what *Power Rangers* had always been, but competition in the form of big-screen superhero films—often supplemented by cartoon adventures aimed squarely at kids—was on the uptick; suddenly *Power Rangers'* biggest distinguishing factor wasn't so unique. Going animated, in theory, could check a few boxes: scale down costs, attract different audiences, and expand the scope of storytelling (and toys that could be manufactured).

By the end of the 2000s, it was the internal Power Rangers project that most excited Disney's higher-ups. Turner and animator Mike Moon, developer and coproducer for the acclaimed Cartoon Network show *Foster's Home for Imaginary Friends* and later a Sony executive who helped develop *Spider-Man: Into the Spider-Verse*, worked with California artist Brandon Ragnar Johnson to create designs, storyboards, and animation tests.

"Our pitch internally was if you want to 'age up' *Power Rangers* and still be true to the brand, and expand consumer product offerings, you need to go animated," Turner said. "We got the buy-in, so we spent the money. It was fucking beautiful. The shit was beautiful." There was only one party who didn't love the idea: Toei. "They were very stringent about what you can do with that IP. . . . We knew if we didn't get Toei, there was nothing we could do, we'd be dead in the water. And Toei, politely and in a very Japanese way, was like 'fuck off.'

"Culturally, they are traditionalists. They don't like to fuck with what's working. At the time, the live-action show was working. They were getting checks and everything was good. They're like, 'Why are you gonna fuck with it by trying to do this animation thing that might not work,' even though we knew it would. They're like, 'You don't for sure, and we're not going to mess with a good thing.' It was a bummer for sure. We had these big poster boards with all the characters lined up, we had 'em hanging on our walls. We were so proud of them. Then it all went away."

If a cartoon couldn't rejuvenate *Power Rangers*, perhaps a cartoon schlepper could.

"The Power Rangers have come home," Cynthia Littleton[1] wrote for *Variety* on May 12, 2010. On that day, Disney sold *Power Rangers*, along with less noted brands like *Digimon*, to Saban Capital Group, the fledgling investment firm headed up by immigrant-turned-entrepreneur-turned-billionaire Haim Saban.

The sale price was just north of $40 million, or about one one-hundredth of the $4 billion Disney paid to acquire Marvel Entertainment, through which it believed it could finally gain the audience of older boys it long failed to attract. That transaction, announced in August 2009, expedited a sale of *Power Rangers* that had been explored for at least a year. It was an admission by Disney, which over the next decade would transform C-list Marvel superheroes into household names, that it couldn't figure out *Power Rangers*.

"We did some good seasons under Disney, so I do want to acknowledge that," Jackie Marchand said. "And we had some great partners over there. But it's such a giant machine and they have all these franchises, so they have different objectives. With *Power Rangers*, I think they wanted to see if they could fold it into the Disney brand and it never really fit. And once it didn't fit, they decided to phase it out. There was definitely much more oversight—many more executives giving notes, more input from Disney consumer products, a lot more meetings with toy companies. That's the way they run their shows, they're very hands-on. It wasn't just Haim saying, 'Go make a stupid show.' It was a different beast."

"They never really could figure out what is the 'boy version' of Disney until they landed Marvel and *Star Wars*," said Ann Austen. "*Power Rangers* has this reputation for being cheesy, even though we tried very hard not to make it cheesy and succeeded to some extent. But some of the cheese is part of the fun too, y'know? But the execs at Disney—some of whom probably never even watched the show, to be honest—just felt they could never get it into the Disney brand. It *was* successful. The toys sold well under the Disney era. But they were looking for something else, and it ended up being Marvel."

Saban—who in the intervening years had gobbled up international media broadcasters in Germany and Mexico and bolstered his (and Israel's) influence with the U.S. Democratic Party—personally reached out to Disney to start talks in late 2009.[2] He'd stayed away from kids media for a decade, but Disney, Saban said, "did not develop the property and exploit it in the way that it deserves."[3] He was a billionaire who vacationed with presidents, but Saban still had a soft spot for those heroes in spandex—and the money they could generate.

Power Rangers Samurai, an adaptation of *Samurai Sentai Shinkenger*, was rushed into development. Former producing extraordinaire Jonathan Tzachor got called out of the bullpen. Ilan Rosenberg, cinematographer for the show's first 10 seasons, was among several former Saban Entertainment stalwarts who joined him in New Zealand to ensure a smooth transition from Disney. Iris Hampton came back as casting director. To add throwback humor to the mix, Paul Schrier returned as Bulk, now the bumbling godfather of his best friend's son, Spike (Felix Ryan).

Tzachor brought on Amira Lopez, a Japanese American who'd watched *Super Sentai* while growing up in Tokyo, initially as a translator to expedite production of scripts for a scheduled fall shoot in New Zealand. *Power Rangers'* new network home—cable leader Nickelodeon—planned to air 22 episodes beginning in February 2011. From there, they'd deliver 22 more for February 2012 but use the same cast and source footage. Effectively, a 44-episode season was divided into two TV scheduling years, distinguished only by a one-word modifier: super.

Samurai and *Super Samurai* were heavily flavored by the source material, itself steeped in Japanese culture and iconography far more than any series before it. On a surface level, this works to great benefit: the suits, topped with helmets sporting kanji-shaped visors representing different elements of nature, are gorgeous, and the origami-inspired Zords are some of the most imaginative in show history. Viewed through the eyes of anyone beyond the target audience, it quickly borders on problematic. *Power Rangers*, by its very nature, is an act of cultural appropriation, but giving the surname "Shiba" to a blonde-haired, blue-eyed white man (Jayden, the series' primary Red Ranger, played by Alex Heartman) with no hint of or allusion to Japanese ancestry is hard to gloss over.

But Saban Brands—the entertainment-focused subsidiary under which the Saban Capital Group produced the show—didn't crave the same audience Disney chased. *Samurai* and *Super Samurai* were unapologetically made for children, and they were Megazord-sized hits. New episodes averaged more than 2 million viewers apiece, numbers not seen since before the sale to Disney, and toy sales increased in each season's debut year, doubling from $40 million to $80 million by the end of 2012.[4] *Power Rangers* was resuscitated by those who allowed it to flourish in 1993.

"Saban wanted to reboot the show for audiences that loved *MMPR*, and not the ones who were now 25 years old, but those who were 5, 6, 7 and 8," said James Bates, a Fox Kids and children's TV veteran initially brought on to touch up scripts during the development of *Samurai*. Saban Brands retained him as story editor. "My mission was to get the show back to being the best chicken nuggets that kids could ask for. If you give a kid a soufflé made by the greatest chef in the world, they're gonna say, 'What the F is this?'"

The company still cared about longtime fans and intended to cater to their tastes and sensibilities through other means—primarily premium, collector-oriented products but also a feature-length film already in predevelopment. Saban Brands also hoped to deliver a pair of anniversary seasons in 2013 and 2014 that would honor the franchise's 20-year history with winks, nods, and a battle promised to be "legendary."

The cast for those seasons, *Megaforce* and *Super Megaforce*, was revealed with help from Schrier at Power Morphicon 2012, the third edition of the annual grassroots fan convention and the first officially sponsored by the show's owners, as part of a torch-passing by the *Samurai* team. "This is not an end today," Schrier said. "This is a new beginning."

Amit Bhaumik, the story editor on *Wild Force*, was among the past *Power Rangers* scribes who returned as a consultant. Before production began, he'd written a rough outline for *Samurai* that sought to further the show from its source footage and align it closer to the work the show achieved in the late 1990s. His version was also set in Stone Canyon, a harmless nod to continuity for existing fans. Despite discouragement with *Samurai*'s direction after that experience, he returned to consult on the next adaptation. He quickly regretted it and left the show for good.

"[Jonathan] was very different to work with after our days in Valencia when we made *Wild Force*. It was very sad," Bhaumik said. "I always thought of him as a guy who cared about the show. He was there for the good seasons, and with him back there's potential to really make the show great." Instead, *Megaforce* and *Super Megaforce* became "bastardizations" of the *two* shows from which they were adapted.

Therein lies the core issue many adult fans have with those seasons: 101 episodes from across two *Super Sentai* series, *Tensou Sentai Goseiger* and *Kaizoku Sentai Gokaiger*, were blended into a 44-episode mishmash. The resulting seasons of *Power Rangers* seemingly were an experiment in just how little original footage could be produced. *Megaforce* has the distinction of being the *only* season in the show's history to, on average, use more *Sentai* footage in its episodes than original footage, while *Super Megaforce* comes up second with a 50-50 split.[5]

Goseiger thematically was constructed around literal guardian angels—a red flag for American executives who wanted to avoid any religious imagery and thought the show's motif might not be "toyetic" enough to survive two years at U.S. retail. The subsequent season, *Gokaiger*, aired in Japan as *Samurai*, premiered in the United States and was an attractive gateway series for many longtime *Power Rangers* fans who'd never dabbled in the underworld of tokusatsu fansubbing. It followed a group of alien pirates who accessed, via counterfeited "Ranger Keys," the powers and resources of all 34 previous *Super Sentai* teams and also featured cameos from across the series' history. It seemed ripe to exploit for the twentieth anniversary of *Power Rangers*, except "the *Gokaiger* season had a few issues," said Brian Casentini, Saban Brands' senior vice president of development and production. "First, many episodes featured Rangers from *Super Sentai* seasons that we had never adapted or didn't have the rights to; second, a lot of the footage featured very close gun fighting which was problematic from a broadcast network standards and practices perspective; third, *Gokaiger*'s pirate theme had become problematic politically due to recent Somali pirate attacks in the news; and fourth, pirate merchandise had not sold very well with other successful franchises like *Pirates of the Caribbean*. Therefore, we had to find a workaround."

The workaround: take footage from both seasons to construct a story and use the pirate-themed *Gokaiger* suits as an activatable upgrade for the base *Goseiger* suits without ever acknowledging the pirate motif. Functionally, it achieves the intended goals, but among fans who'd hoped for and anticipated a more honorific tribute to the show's legacy, it pushed the level of acceptability.

"I've never gone back and watched *Super Megaforce*, it's too painful," said Bates. He wrote the season premiere and a two-parter, "Vrak Is Back," which wrapped up a storyline carried over from *Megaforce*, but resigned as story editor five episodes into production of *Super Megaforce*. "Those are characters I developed, that I was spending 70 hours a week writing and working to make work while trying to make 11 different masters happy. . . . Almost everything we ended up doing was my second choice of how to do it."

Bates's original vision fleshed out character arcs, personality traits, and guiding motives for all the Rangers, who in the show end up more closely echoing the same archetypes delivered 20 years earlier in *MMPR*: jock, nerd, Valley girl, and so on. He imagined a role for David Yost to return as the heroes' teacher and mentor, which didn't materialize. "If you watch those first core episodes of *Megaforce*, you'll see the footprints of the show it was supposed to be," said Bates, who wrote the premiere, "Mega Mission," as a straight-up homage to "Day of the Dumpster." It introduces all the major players, including an overzealous CGI robot, Tensou, and a wall-mounted mentor, Gosei, whose names reference *Goseiger*. The team's Red Ranger, Troy (Andrew Gray), experiences a vision of a massive battle in the first scene, a recurring disturbance for his character that's never really expounded. It was a remnant of a version of *Megaforce* in which Troy was a "chosen one" with an inherent connection to the Morphin Grid. "We all had tons of ideas," Bates said. "But when it came down to the show, we ended up using more footage than I wanted it to."

More footage meant more toys. An inherent issue of wedding large amounts of footage from any two different seasons of *Super Sentai*, regardless of motif, is the sheer amount of stuff—suits, weapons, morphers, and Zords—that eats up screen time. The 44 episodes, unfortunately, had a hard time cohering into a sensible TV show due to the deluge. Of course, that's looking at it from the perspective of someone who was in college when it premiered. The seasons lagged *Samurai* and *Super Samurai* in viewership, but each averaged more than 1.5 million viewers per episode on Nick. Highlight packages and full episodes from the season rank among the most watched on the official Power Rangers

Power Rangers Megaforce, the show's twentieth season, echoes the original *Mighty Morphin Power Rangers* in many respects. From left to right: Ciara Hanna (Gia the Yellow Ranger), John Mark Loudermilk (Noah the Blue Ranger), Andrew Gray (Troy the Red Ranger), Azim Rizk (Jake the Black Ranger), and Christina Masterson (Emma the Pink Ranger). © Nickelodeon

YouTube channel. Clearly, there was an audience that found joy from the sugar rush.

Super Megaforce concludes with "Legendary Battle," which brings together every past team to fend off an armada of bad guys. Eleven former *Power Rangers* actors, all from Tzachor-produced seasons, returned for the episode, later reedited as a lengthier special using extra footage and scenes from the preceding episode, "The Wrath." (Several other actors were invited. Some declined for unspecified or union reasons. Others accepted Saban Brands' offer but were later disinvited because of budget concerns.) Each returnee gets a sliver of screen time, another tough pill to swallow for fans who'd stuck it out hoping for a big celebration. But as a finale? It's a solid send-off for the current team of Power

Rangers, whom youngest millennials and oldest Generation Alphas are likely to pine for in their twenties. The title fight features more than 100 suit actors, representing almost every Power Ranger who starred in the show's first 20 years, who emerge team by team in the only appropriate venue for such a *Power Rangers* showdown: a quarry.

"It legitimately felt like—and [*Avengers*] *Endgame* wasn't even around yet—but it felt like that," said John Mark Loudermilk, who played Noah, *Megaforce*'s Blue Ranger. "When I was watching *Endgame*, I got the same exact chills that I got when we were filming on set."

CHAPTER 18

Edge of Extinction

While *Power Rangers* in the 2010s leaned into making new fans from those freshly out of diapers, Saban Brands rolled out a litany of products and projects for fans who'd followed since the heyday.

In August 2012 came a monumental DVD release of the show's first seven seasons, collected together in two separate box sets and, initially, sold exclusively through the website of defunct nostalgia storefront Time Life. Those "Mega Sets," stuffed with special features by fan-centered producer Shout! Factory, were soon followed by two similar editions housing seasons 8 (*Lightspeed Rescue*) through 17 (*RPM*). By the start of 2014, all of that was repackaged alongside discs for *Samurai*, *Super Samurai*, and *Megaforce* to form "Power Rangers: Legacy," a 98-DVD set encompassing the show's first 767 episodes. Metal tins modeled after Power Coins contain the discs and come housed in an oversized (non-wearable) *MMPR* Red Ranger helmet, along with a 100-page episode guidebook. It's not the largest official TV-on-DVD set by disc count—the complete series release of Australian soap opera *Prisoner: Cell Block H* in 2007 required 179 discs— but it dwarfs that of any DVD project created for a kids show.

Shout! Factory's Brian Ward made efforts to interview every starring and recurring actor over the show's first 20 seasons, along with other key creatives, and Saban Brands went to great lengths to gather archival footage to supplement new extra features. One of the sets' only content blips: episodes from *Time Force* use broadcast masters aired *after* the September 11 terrorist attacks on the World Trade Center. Both Fox Kids and Disney made substantial edits to dialogue and footage deemed insensitive following those events. Several fans provided Ward with VHS and hard-drive copies of the original broadcasts, but most were unusable.

"I cut all these different versions together and none of them looked good,"[1] Ward said. "It came down to the decision that the hardcore fans that knew about the 9/11 edits weren't going to be the only people watching these shows, so it became a matter of quality over being able to fulfill the desires of those diehard fans." Ward was able to rectify the most glaring edit: in "Ransik Lives," a scene where *Time Force* antagonist Ransik delivers a terroristic speech that was dubbed over with an instrumental of the theme song for rebroadcasts. "The first master we got for that was the one that had the song over the whole thing, and after [the edits] were brought to my attention, I was like, 'Oh this is the wrong one, so at the very worst I'm going to take the audio from some fan's version and put it on.' But I didn't have to, we ended up finding the version of it that had the speech intact." Their bonus materials—six full discs—are stuffed with reflective sit-downs with cast and crew, videos highlighting longtime fans, and decades-old direct-to-VHS features produced throughout the 1990s. Included is footage from an extremely rare VHS release of the *Mighty Morphin Power Rangers* live show that toured around the United States and select international cities from 1994 to 1996. Led by famed concert promoters Marcel Avram and Danny O'Donovan, the tour cost more than $13 million to produce and travel. In some cities, demand was so high that it prompted two-a-day showings during a weeklong stay. "Would Rod [Stewart] be satisfied with this show if he were a Power Ranger?" said O'Donovan. "We're used to sending out Rod Stewart[2] and Morrissey on tour, and we wanted to give the Power Rangers the same kind of production quality that those stars would be happy with."

Shout! Factory collected the first 20 seasons of *Power Rangers* in a 98-disc set, limited to 2,000 editions, in 2014. Courtesy Kenn Glenn

Bandai, starting in 2013, churned out prop replicas befitting rock stars under its "Legacy Collection" banner, which also included reimagined, fan-targeted versions of various Megazords and action figures. But role-play items were the crème de la crème, especially the Power Morpher. Twenty years since its last time on store shelves, the device and its coins were cast in die-cast metal, featured lights and sounds, and came packaged with a belt holster. It's undeniably one of the best *Power Rangers* toys ever released and represented the detail and quality that Saban Brands felt its oldest fans deserved. It also got released in various repaints, including, for the first time ever, a Green/White Ranger edition.

Beyond DVDs, toys, and other tangible goods from licensees eyeing adults who'd grown up with *Power Rangers*, the company guided several content initiatives aimed at their affection.

The most ambitious was *Power Rangers HyperForce*, a live-streamed role-playing game produced by HyperRPG. The brainchild of Melissa Flores, Saban Brands' director of development and production, and Jason Bischoff, the company's director of consumer products, *HyperForce* is a very loosely scripted series framed around a group of Power Rangers in training at the Time Force Academy. For 26 episodes, they traveled across time and space, often teaming with past *Power Rangers* actors. Unshackled by the confines of budgets and rehearsals, the story goes a lot of places, physically and emotionally, that the TV show never could. Brian Casentini approved the general story arc but largely encouraged Flores and the HyperRPG cast and crew—which included a self-described superfan in YouTuber Andre "Black Nerd" Meadows as well as *Power Rangers* actors Paul Schrier (as Yellow Ranger Jack) and Peter Sudarso (Red Ranger Marvin)—to let their imaginations run wild.

Throughout the 1990s, Hamilton Comics, then Marvel, then Image, and finally Acclaim Comics all published kid-centric *Power Rangers* comic books. The Power Rangers' first comic appearance came in a 16-page mini-sized Hamilton book packaged with Fruit of the Loom underwear in June 1994. That book's so rare that Certified Guaranty Company has only ever graded seven copies, and only one has received a 9.8 rating. When Saban Brands reacquired the property, it inked a deal with Papercutz to create new graphic novels based on *Samurai*, *Megaforce*, and *MMPR*. These books, printed from 2012 to 2014, were again aimed at children, who weren't buying them.

With the comics license back up for grabs in 2015, a managing editor from Boom! Studios, Bryce Carlson, won out with a pitch centered on making books for nostalgic fans. And Carlson already had an ideal writer in mind—Kyle Higgins, an acquaintance with whom he'd frequently had conversations about the show and its on-page potential. Higgins, a rising star who'd spent the first half of the 2010s writing *Batman Beyond* and

Nightwing for DC Comics, grew up with *Power Rangers,* falling out of its orbit around *Turbo.* Tommy Oliver's return during *Dino Thunder* renewed his interest while in college. "I would be up until 3 a.m. on a random night watching interviews from Power Morphicon and things like that," Higgins said. "Because you're curious—anything that lasts that long and has that lineage and legacy, there's inherently a communal component to it."

It took several rounds of pitching for Higgins's vision to align with that of Saban Brands. "I remember telling them, look, I'll do one more round but at this point, if this doesn't work I'm not gonna do more," Higgins said. "The thing that some people might not realize is that type of work isn't paid, so at a certain point as a creator you really have to weigh the opportunity cost versus really seeing something through. Fortunately, it was a take that everyone responded to."

Higgins's story is planted in the *MMPR* era, playing on the intended audience's familiarity with the characters, but given room to stand on its own. It starts, at Higgins's insistence, not with an origin but rather with the moment in time when Tommy joined the team following the "Green With Evil" miniseries. "Watching those episodes as an adult and realizing they just fully integrate him immediately, that's where the writer brain kicks in and goes, 'Oh, I know exactly what to do here,'" Higgins said. "If *Power Rangers* is about the power of friendship and teamwork, then I knew I wanted to explore those ideas through a slightly different lens, which was 'What is it like to join a team but also having spent all this time trying to kill the Power Rangers?' There's a really interesting kind of moral dilemma there to explore for a character." Higgins likens Tommy's struggle to the one LeBron James faced during his first season with the Miami Heat in 2010. "It took at least half the season for them to figure out how to play together."

Notably, *Mighty Morphin Power Rangers (2016)* is set in modern times. Higgins had no desire to write a book that was "filling in" stories in the existing show. "I felt like if we were doing a book set in 1993, it would have become a pastiche very quickly because you're competing with material in such a direct way that is pretty legendary, has been around for many years and influenced and shaped a generation." However, the books flew off shelves and became so forward-facing that Saban Brands became more scrutinous. "It needed to find a way to kind of have its cake and eat it too. I started looking at it and referring to it as not a reboot, but a remix. If you squint, everything kind of fits, but if you're looking at it through the true letter of the law, of course it doesn't work with the show. None of us wanted to invalidate anything from the series.

"I've been a comic book reader and fan my whole life. As much as we all love continuity, it is also an incredibly limiting factor for telling stories. It can be additive, but the longer I've done this the more I've come around

The comic-book stories from Boom! Studios are highly regarded by existing *Power Rangers* **fans and newcomers.** Author's collection

to the idea that continuity should be used when it's additive but not subscribed to at all costs."

The series launched by Higgins and Indonesian artist Hendry Prasetya concluded in 2024 with Flores at the helm. Higgins's contributions ended with two books in 2018: the graphic novel *Soul of the Dragon*, a sort of "Old Man Tommy" story firmly set within the show's continuity and on which Jason David Frank consulted, and a one-shot special, *Shattered Grid* #1, which wrapped up the first sprawling event miniseries tied to

MMPR (2016). It centers on a multiverse variant of Tommy Oliver, who, we learn, is the only Tommy Oliver in any universe who never eventually becomes good. This Tommy, "Lord Drakkon," has conquered the world and killed several would-be teammates, using their Power Coins to empower armies of Ranger-like "Sentries." This "coinless" world and Lord Drakkon feature early in Higgins's run before emerging as the catalysts for an event that elicited two crossover episodes with the *HyperForce* RPG show, multiple action figures, and a live-action teaser trailer watched by millions. Frank, who played Lord Drakkon in the trailer as well as *HyperForce*, fronted the expense for most of its production along with Ramon Palermo, Higgins's friend and a visual effects guru. Saban Brands took care of costumes, props, and archival footage. Ron Wasserman scored the two-and-a-half-minute spot.

"We all did it for the love of the game," said Higgins, who directed the short. "You feel everything not only about this character's trepidation, but resilience about what he has to do, even if he doesn't necessarily want to do it. Those levels of subtext and subtlety, I hadn't seen Jason do very much."

"I would never, ever, put words in Jason's mouth, but all I can say is that at the time that we made that, it was something he and I were both very proud of and we were very much looking forward to continue working together in different ways. . . . Jason used to say, 'It's 10 shots, it's two minutes long and there's no action, and it's doing the numbers it's doing and having the impression it's having.' It all comes down to the acting."

Despite two flops in the 1990s, well before a full-fledged superhero boom at multiplexes, Saban was eager to go back to the movies.

Development started almost immediately after the purchase from Disney and initially revolved around the concept of a *Mighty Morphin Power Rangers* animated film to coexist alongside the ongoing TV show. That project got far along enough to have gone through multiple concept designs and a since-leaked teaser trailer that indicates it would have leaned comedic in tone. But in 2012, Lionsgate president Eric Feig and producer Allison Shearmur convinced Saban Brands to instead throw its weight behind a live-action film for teenagers and young adults. Lionsgate already had a writer too: Max Landis, a self-described fan of the show whose first produced feature script, found-footage superhero flick *Chronicle*, received kind reviews and grossed $126 million on a $15 million budget.

All parties were of the mind that the movie should morph the original teens into full-fledged characters with modern problems. "Sadly, Max's script did not fully live up to that vision and we worked with a number of other writers to achieve our goal," Casentini said. Through a sea of changes across multiple writers—*X-Men: First Class* and *Thor* scribes Ashley Miller and Zack Stentz were attached for a time too—the story ultimately was credited to the writing foursome of Michele Mulroney, Kiernan Mulroney, Matt Sazama, and Burk Sharpless. Further adjustments were made at the behest of director Dean Israelite, and the final screenplay is credited to just one writer, Academy Award nominee John Gatins. Nearly a decade later, figuring out who's responsible for which ideas is a fool's errand. (Every credited writer or their agent was contacted for this book; none responded. Dean Israelite politely declined an interview.)

Before he was hired, Israelite was well aware of Saban Brands' lofty franchise ambitions. "The Saban team, even before I came on, had a document that laid out six movies,"[3] said Israelite. "I love the franchise and what we've done with this movie and with these characters. I would love to keep going on this journey."

Despite a strong first weekend—$40.3 million—after opening on March 24, 2017, *Power Rangers* petered out domestically and elsewhere, legging out to just $85.4 million in North America while managing $57 million internationally. Formed on a projected $105 million budget, with at least the same amount in marketing (including a gaudy tie-in with Krispy Kreme, whose establishment figures into the film's climax), confidence in a sequel sagged in spite of a strong home-media showing and even stronger toy sales. Despite an "A" CinemaScore and generally warm feelings among fans, *Power Rangers (2017)*, just like its predecessors, was a flop. Its release window did it no favors.

"We didn't realize what a box-office behemoth *Beauty and the Beast* would be and that everyone from age 1 to 101 would go see that film," Casentini said. Disney's live-action remake of the incredibly popular 1991 animated feature, starring Emma Watson, grossed $1.2 billion worldwide and opened the week before. "That film and *The Boss Baby* [$528 million globally] took so much of the family audience that we sadly didn't achieve the box-office numbers that we were all hoping for."

Power Rangers (2017) fared much better than its 20-plus-year-old cousins among the critic class, but that was a low bar. Many, already fatigued by the onslaught of superhero cinema before the sentiment caught up to general audiences in the 2020s, painted the film as a harbinger of Hollywood's doom, a proverbial scraping of the IP barrel's bottom. Some foresaw complaints from fans who showed up expecting an action-adventure movie and received a coming-of-age drama. David Ehrlich, in his "C-minus" review for *IndieWire*, wrote, "The film is a blast during the few brief moments when it embraces the cartoon craziness[4] that's made the television show into such a cultural fixture." Scott Mendelson, writing for *Forbes*, admired the film's ability to peacefully coexist with the TV franchise he "hated" as a teen but grew to appreciate when his kids fell in love with it in the 2010s. "This is an interesting attempt to craft a grounded and character-driven adaptation, one that successfully blends genre with larger-than-life superhero spectacle," Mendelson wrote. "It's from a time when getting a darker, more serious big-budget feature based on your favorite kid-friendly property, one that felt like a real film, was a rare and splendid thing."[5]

Five up-and-coming talents made up the core cast: Ronald "RJ" Cyler (Billy), Rebecca "Becky G" Gomez (Trini), Ludi Lin (Zack), Dacre Montgomery (Jason), and Naomi Scott (Kimberly). Aside from Jason—Montgomery is from Australia but still white—all four characters are race swapped from their original versions and sport vastly reimagined personalities. Jason is a reckless jock whose off-the-field mistakes caught up to him; Billy, who's proudly on the autism spectrum, is more curious about the world than a book-smart geek speaker; Trini is an army brat questioning her sexuality, among other things about her place in the world; Zack is a thrill seeker whose emotional subplot (his mother is deathly ill) was weathered by the script-revision process; and Kimberly, in a villainous twist, distributed revenge porn and has a hard time reconciling her pettiness.

This ain't your parents' *Mighty Morphin Power Rangers*, and on whatever level it works for a viewer, it's attributable largely to the collection of young actors who've all continued to star in major projects or, in Becky G's case, churn out popular music; the award-winning Latin American musician, who rose to prominence by way of YouTube, was a bona fide star before signing on to the film. Their chemistry is infectious and integral to a film committed to the belief that becoming the best version of yourself—to become a Power Ranger—requires more than a Power Coin. You need other people. You need friends, the kind who will drag your lifeless body out of a harbor and walk it miles away to a buried spaceship, hoping that the galactic being trapped in its computer system can do something to help.

**Marketing for *Power Rangers* (2017) often used the tagline "Together We Are More."
It became a rallying cry for fans of the franchise.** © 2016 Lionsgate Entertainment Inc.

Zordon here is portrayed by Bryan Cranston, now far more famous than when he voiced Snizzard for $50. His Zordon, motivated by the failure to keep his team's Green Ranger—Rita Repulsa—from killing the others in prehistoric times, grows discontent with the new team's efforts to coalesce. He intends to revive himself to lead the fight while Rita slowly returns to power. It's only when they come to him, Billy's corpse in tow, that Zordon, cued by a portal to the Morphin Grid, knows the group is ready to fight for one another. "That was your only chance," declares Alpha 5, voiced by actor/comedian Bill Hader. "I know," says Zordon. "But only one can come back." Billy starts coughing up water, as do the eyes of everyone on- and off-screen.

Even the film's toughest critics lauded Elizabeth Banks's over-the-top performance as Rita Repulsa, a scene-devouring cartoon character in a film that largely discards its colorful origins. "I loved the Rita Repulsa in *Mighty Morphin Power Rangers* cause she's so larger-than-life and she's sort of insane, and she's got this crazy laugh,"[6] said Banks, "and I wanted to preserve some of that energy in the character."

Nearly a decade removed from its debut, *Power Rangers* (2017) remains a unique product of a time in Hollywood when superheroes definitively ruled. It came and went amid a slew of much more successful fare from Disney and Warner Bros. but continues to be a topic of conversation in online spaces—within but also frequently outside of the *Power Rangers* fandom. As Marvel's well-oiled machine started to grind its gears and "cinematic universes" started to lose steam among filmgoers, *Power Rangers'* failure to launch one oddly worked in its favor. A film with a nine-digit budget based on an iconic brand that's generated billions in revenue is increasingly regarded as a cult classic.

"What stands out about the film—and what consistently saves it, even when the direction is at its cruddiest—is its sincerity,"[7] critic Matt Zoller Seitz wrote. "It never had much artistic integrity to lose, so the fact that this film actually has some is amazing. This big-budget teen fantasy is essentially an unauthorized 'Transformers' movie that has a moral code and is suitable for kids, in stark contrast to the actual 'Transformers' franchise, which has prided itself on being snide, leering, and hateful. 'Power Rangers' is earnest, and it has a good heart. There should be more movies like it, only better-made."

CHAPTER 19

The End

Power Rangers' so-called Neo-Saban Era was a speedrun emulating the brand's first 17 years. There was an incredibly successful launch supported by fast-and-furious marketing initiatives. Toys galore. Stories told across a variety of media. A movie that failed to gain traction. Consistently declining TV ratings. And, finally, a sale to another company.

After 25 years as their only holder, Bandai America in February 2018 lost the master toy rights for *Power Rangers* to a juggernaut rival: Hasbro. Part of their agreement was a clause that allowed Hasbro to buy the entire property, if desired. Three months and $522 million later, Hasbro owned *Power Rangers*. "Shortly after entering into our licensing arrangement, it became clear that now was the time to begin investing in unlocking Power Rangers' full potential,"[1] Hasbro CEO Brian Goldner said then. Goldner, who got acquainted with[2] Haim Saban while working in the 1990s as a media buyer and then president for Bandai America, is credited by many as a silent force behind *Power Rangers'* staying power.

"One time, he and I had dinner in Valencia, and afterward we were in the parking lot chatting about toys and the show and the upcoming theme," said Chip Lynn. "He said to me, 'It's all about aspiration. If you can get kids to want to be the characters, they will buy the toy. You don't have to be a toy commercial, you have to be a great story with a great purpose so that kids will aspire to take part in that story, to become those characters, to befriend those Rangers. If you do that, then they're gonna buy the toy.'"

Following *Super Megaforce*, Lynn—who'd been working with Saban Brands to develop another *Power Rangers*–esque show that didn't bear fruit—was brought back to shepherd TV production in lieu of Jonathan Tzachor. "I'd been in charge of the show before, but it was never under calm circumstances," said Lynn, who didn't exactly avoid turmoil in his first at bat for Saban Brands. He spent a great deal of development time to adapt *Tokumei Sentai Go-Busters*, which was quite a departure, aesthetically, from most series due to its leatherlike suits. But Saban stepped in late to nix that after learning the next *Super Sentai* series, *Zyuden Sentai Kyoryuger*, was based on a theme that would play better with kids. "Haim and all his marketing people wisely decided, 'Nope, let's go with dinosaurs.'"

Lynn, still determined to spearhead story and scripts for *Power Rangers Dino Charge*, shouldered some of the load with Stateside friends and writers from across *Power Rangers'* then 21-year history: Ann Austen, James Bates, Mark Litton, and Jeffrey Newman, to name a few. Early on, though, it became clear to him that hands and brains were needed in New Zealand. It was as pragmatic as it was an act of self-preservation. The country had given the show so many crew, cast, and locations—why not welcome its voice?

Becca Barnes, a small-town South Islander who in college studied under legendary New Zealand filmmaker Geoff Murphy,[3] arrived first. She and classmate Alwyn Dale formed a tight bond and later worked together as copywriters for a daily-deal company akin to Groupon, "which basically meant writing ads full of terrible puns all day—good *Power Rangers* training, although I didn't know it," Barnes said. In 2014, she answered an ad for a nine-month internship with the writing department of a TV show produced in Auckland. "You know how sometimes in life, you see an opportunity come up that just makes your blood rush? This was that. I dropped everything I was meant to be doing that afternoon, found a screenwriting sample, and sent off an excitement-filled application." She hopped on a call with Lynn and Newman, *Dino Charge*'s coproducer, and made a quick impression on the pair. "She said that she loves kids television and quirky, strange stories," Lynn said, "and that most everything she writes or reads ends up with a tentacle in it. It became a running joke for the next 10 years that she got the job because of that. We thought, 'There's so many tentacles in *Power Rangers*, that's perfect.'"

Barnes initially took on *Power Rangers'* equivalent of grunt work: logging the usable Japanese footage. Other tasks ranged from inventing corporate and parent-friendly names for weapons to liaising with the art department, then led by Tracey Collins. Barnes spent weeks at home in her free time memorizing the names of Zords and familiarizing and re-familiarizing herself with *Super Sentai* footage. She became the go-to intern, and her input was so valued that while soliciting for a new intern, Lynn and Newman trusted her when she suggested Dale. By the time production began on the following season, *Dino Super Charge*, they spent ample time together writing episodes of *Power Rangers* in a

West Auckland McDonald's. "Nine months turned into nine years," said Barnes, who by the end of her time on *Power Rangers* in 2023 was, along with Dale, a coproducer and head writer. Their progression through the TV ranks echoed that of Lynn and Jackie Marchand and happened at a time when few American TV productions—for kids or adults—offered upward mobility. Many shows at the time were fortunate to even have a dedicated writers room.

After *Dino Charge*, Barnes and Dale brought another friend, Steve McCleary, into the fold, and the trio collectively worked under Lynn on four additional seasons: *Ninja Steel*, *Super Ninja Steel*, and two seasons of *Beast Morphers*, the long-stewing adaptation of *Go-Busters*. Episodes full of dinosaurs and ninjas pulled in seven-figure viewership on Nickelodeon, but by its second season in 2020, *Beast Morphers* averaged fewer than 400,000 viewers per episode. That was a far cry from *Samurai*'s 2.7 million and 60 percent fewer than *Super Ninja Steel* just two years earlier.[4] It was less a reflection of the show itself and more the changing landscape of TV. Premieres of *SpongeBob SquarePants*, Nick's flagship show, weren't faring much better than the seasoned superheroes with which he shared the airwaves. Cable was out, streaming was in.

The next season of *Power Rangers*—a planned adaptation of the newest dinosaur-themed show, *Kishiryu Sentai Ryusoulger*—was the last produced for Nickelodeon. They'd had a good run, but after 11 years, the *Power Rangers* again needed a new full-time home. Tudum.

Kelson Henderson, a veteran *Power Rangers* actor who across more than 200 episodes has played more than a dozen unique characters, portrays Mick Kanic in *Ninja Steel*, *Super Ninja Steel*, *Dino Fury*, and *Cosmic Fury*. Screenshot, Author's Collection

Power Rangers came under the purview of Entertainment One, a Toronto production company Hasbro acquired for $4 billion in August 2019. The company, colloquially referred to as eOne, was to usher in a new era of content expansion for Hasbro's deep franchise catalog; less than five years later, Hasbro sold it to Lionsgate for one-eighth of its purchase price.[5] It was partly a victim of terrible timing—Wall Street attitudes toward streaming and entertainment soured after the height of the COVID-19 pandemic—and a tragic personnel development. Goldner, a champion for Hasbro's TV and film initiatives and *Power Rangers*' biggest cheerleader, died on October 12, 2021. The 58-year-old CEO[6] had quietly battled prostate cancer for seven years.

"He was very personable, a wonderful guy, and *so* damn smart," Lynn said. "When I eventually worked with him again at Hasbro, I hadn't seen the guy in almost 20 years, and he came up and gave me a hug. He was a fantastic leader. It's so sad that he isn't with us anymore."

It was amid those circumstances that the final seasons of *Power Rangers* were formed.

From the outset, *Power Rangers Dino Fury* was supposed to be a single 22-episode season. When Hasbro and eOne elected for a two-season order, two-thirds of the season had already been written, necessitating a host of rewrites. The upside, though: the new primary network for season 2, Netflix, freed the creative team to tell a more serialized narrative than had been allowed while Saban Brands and Nickelodeon were calling the shots.

Lynn returned to the United States amid the pandemic but stayed a consultant during development of *Dino Fury*'s first season. In his stead came Simon Bennett, a seasoned Kiwi who'd directed dozens of episodes over the previous four seasons and, before that, spent 20 years directing and producing *Shortland Street*, a long-running New Zealand soap opera, in addition to stage productions, his true passion. He was delighted to work on a sci-fi action program like those he loved as a child—*Star Trek*, *The Tomorrow People*, and *Thunderbirds*—and brought with him a fresh and inquisitive perspective. Bennett's thoughts and observations about the show frequently challenged long-held beliefs about what it could and should be—and often riled up fans who didn't vibe with his frankness.

"I think the machinery that goes into making a show like *Power Rangers* is intrinsically fascinating," Bennett said. "I love it. I'm interested in sharing what I can about it, and that's always been the case with my work. And that's because I'm an enthusiast not necessarily of the product but of the process of making the show. . . . Whatever choice or decision

I might make, there are going to be five people who would have done it differently. And that's inevitable with any kind of creative role. Everyone has their own taste and their own sense of what it is they want to see."

Bennett and a robust stable of writers—Maya Thompson and Guy Langford joined the Barnes–Dale–McCleary triumvirate—crafted a two-season story that weaved together beats of planetary genocide, lost families, and all the patented action necessary to drive toy sales. Some of it even involved a famous past villain, Lord Zedd. *Dino Fury* won a GLAAD Media Award—the show's first marquee recognition since a Daytime Emmy nomination for sound editing way back in *Time Force*—for its portrayal of Izzy (Tessa Rao), the show's Green Ranger and *Power Rangers*' first explicitly queer character in the TV series. In "The Matchmaker," her stepbrother Javi (Chance Perez) attempts to set her up on a date with a male student on whom he mistakenly believes she has a crush. By episode's end, he realizes it was a female student—her well-established athletic rival, Fern (Jacqueline Joe)—that Izzy has the hots for.

"I think that there's still an important place in the world for stories that are about the hardships which LGBTQI+ folk experience because the world is still frankly a bit shit when it comes to global rights," said Barnes. "But when breaking this story, we were also keenly aware that the bulk of *Power Rangers* viewers are very young. If this was the first time seeing a gay crush on-screen, then we wanted it to come across as something totally normal that they themselves might encounter in their lives, their community, or their school."

Moments of situational irony and clever wordplay ramped up compared to years prior. Working under Hasbro and eOne was a much-needed breath of fresh air for the writers. Four years earlier, Saban Brands mandated them to stuff *Ninja Steel* full of fart jokes and dialogue that, when translated to screen, unfortunately made its teenage protagonists sound like toddlers. Attempts at meaningful serialization were for naught.

"We would try and show them kids shows of today, to sort of say, 'Look at how the storytelling is very different from what it was back in the old days,' but that would always fall on deaf ears," McCleary said. "There was very much a push of, 'No, this is what kids can understand. They won't remember things from a previous episode.' There were even times where it was like, 'Oh it doesn't actually matter if we contradict something from a previous episode.' . . . With the exception of, I guess Haim Saban, there was no one person ever making those decisions. There were multiple executives deciding to pay more and more attention."

"Dimensions in Danger," a twenty-fifth-anniversary celebration midway through *Super Ninja Steel*, functions as a mea culpa for "Legendary Battle." It brings back 10 former actors, this time from across every "era" of the show, and somewhat mirrors "Legacy of Power" by revolving its story around the brief kidnapping of Tommy Oliver. In his final appearance on the show, Jason David Frank also gets to play an evil android model of himself. Android Tommy helps an imminent threat, Lord Draven, build an army of android Rangers whose powers are modeled after other kidnapped Rangers, whom real Tommy frees from captivity with the help of his Master Morpher—an incredibly cool device that allows him to cycle through all five of his past powers.

In October 2017, while *Power Rangers Ninja Steel* was airing, writers were putting the final touches on the following season, *Super Ninja Steel*, set to debut in January 2018. They were also planning a future season, *Beast Morphers*, which in the early going called for the return of an iconic villain—Rita's monster maker, Finster. Courtesy Becca Barnes

All the past Rangers are better served here than in "Legendary Battle," and "Dimensions in Danger" ultimately is more impactful on the series' canon despite its more intimate nature. It firmly establishes that some seasons exist within their own timelines and that Tommy and Katherine end up marrying one another and have a child, J.J. (Katherine, the Master Morpher, and J.J. all feature prominently in Kyle Higgins's *Soul of the Dragon*. In that book, J.J. is a son but in the episode is explicitly not gender-specific. "We wanted to leave it as open as possible," Dale said. "That's sort of one of our mantras in terms of working on the franchise that we kind of appropriated from Russell T Davies, the showrunner of

Doctor Who who's now back on the job. 'Leave things open-ended, leave loose threads.'")

Its plot, while inherently simpler, bears a resemblance to that of the comics' "Shattered Grid" storyline, which concluded close to the prime-time premiere date of "Dimensions in Danger"—August 28, 2018. The TV and comic-book teams were siloed from one another and on different development timelines, though, so any similarities are coincidental. And they could have been more so: the first pitch for what became "Dimensions in Danger" involved a multiverse version of Tommy who stayed on Rita Repulsa's team. Saban Brands shot it down. "We all loved 'Shattered Grid' when we read it," McCleary said. "We knew that when our special came out that people would probably question it. We didn't crib from Kyle Higgins, and he did not take anything from us. I mean, if you think about it, evil Tommy is not a hard concept to come up with. The disappointing stuff on our end was that we came up with something that was very similar, we weren't allowed to use it, and then—because no one communicated with us—we didn't get to do any synergy with 'Shattered Grid.' Our show could have been part of 'Shattered Grid.' It would have been good to have a shot at attempting it."

In his final appearance on *Power Rangers,* Jason David Frank's Tommy Oliver wields a "Master Morpher," allowing him to access all his past Ranger forms. Screenshot, Author's Collection

Dino Fury closes on something of a cliffhanger: the Red Ranger, Zayto (Russell Curry), sacrifices himself during their final battle but, in the last scene, returns and informs the team that Lord Zedd, who fled following their last encounter earlier in the season, is up to no good off-world and must be stopped. The Rangers suit up, and the credits roll. "We were like, if that's the last thing people ever see of those characters or of *Power Rangers* in general, that'll be cool," McCleary said. "You can imagine they've gone off and fought Lord Zedd."

After filming for *Dino Fury*'s second season wrapped in May 2021, Bennett and Co. lobbied Hasbro, via eOne development vice president Kari Rosenberg, to continue the *Dino Fury* team's story for a third season. Research conducted by Saban Brands while *Ninja Steel* was airing had revealed that one of the show's core weaknesses was its revolving door of characters. "That was a disadvantage in terms of building audiences beyond the toddlers who watch for a couple years, grow out of it, and then a new generation of toddlers come in for the next season," Bennett said. "If *Power Rangers* wanted audiences to not grow out of the show as quickly, one way of achieving that was to have continuity of cast." It turns out that the faces *under* the helmets do matter to children.

Hasbro initially didn't bite. In the interim, the team planned out a 22-episode third season—one that, for the first time, would attempt to use no footage from *Super Sentai*. Ideally, it also would honor the show's thirtieth anniversary and make amends for one of its greatest sins by bringing back former *MMPR* star David Yost. "There's a sort of symbolic nature to bringing Billy back, it might feel like closing a circle, in some ways," Dale said. "The show left him in a really weird place, shipping him off to Aquitar, the aging. It was so bizarre, and I don't know if anybody was happy with that. Some stories don't feel like they're over, and it felt right." Yost was interested, but as 2021 wound down, there was no planned production. "Things looked a bit bleak," Bennett said, but come early 2022, the tide turned thanks to Netflix. They were game for a new season—and something else.

While the New Zealand team pitched season 30, Yost independently tried to sell Hasbro and eOne on the idea of an *MMPR* reunion miniseries based on spec scripts he wrote and aimed for a young-adult audience. He described it as "*Riverdale* meets *Star Trek* meet *Power Rangers*" and was confident he could get all the surviving members of the cast on board. "There wasn't a place for an eight-part adult *Power Rangers* series in terms of what Netflix were looking for and just the various ins and outs of the politics of the situation," said Bennett. "But the notion that the original *MMPR* team could be brought back together, which is something that had never happened in the past, struck a chord with the brand people and Kari, and they came up with the idea of doing a one-off special."

Barnes, Bennett, and Dale began developing and writing that special in February 2022 in addition to condensing down their 22-episode season to 10; Netflix wanted more, but Hasbro didn't have the appetite. The first draft for *Mighty Morphin Power Rangers: Once & Always*—a reference to a long-standing motto, "Once a Ranger, always a Ranger"—was tossed aside quickly. They had been asked to write a kid-centered special but executives' minds changed by the time it was delivered. From there, no fewer than 10 drafts took shape, each of them changing as the availability of former cast members ebbed and flowed. During preproduction, series veteran Jackie Marchand was brought in to shore up the work. One of eOne's producers, Hillary Zwick Turner, happened to be married to someone, former Disney exec Jermaine Turner, who'd enjoyed working with Marchand on *Power Rangers* and thought her knowledge would be valuable. She offered feedback and even cowrote a full draft of the script, but little of her vision made it to the screen. "They gave me a story consultant credit, which was fine, because my input was very minimal," Marchand says. "I liked it."

The special was limited to 55 minutes because of various factors involving feature-film rights. Saban Brands and Lionsgate, it turns out, were pleased enough by the overall performance of *Power Rangers* (2017) to continue development of a sequel. However, when Saban Brands sold the brand to Hasbro, which had an existing development deal with Paramount Pictures for its properties, things got messy. The net result affected *Once & Always*: at the time of its production, Paramount Pictures held *Power Rangers* film-development rights, and Lionsgate maintained certain rights to the property—including story, cast, and character elements contained within its film. "I consulted on a version of the sequel movie that wasn't really a sequel but was going to be a new iteration of live-action *Power Rangers* just after Hasbro acquired the brand," said writer Kyle Higgins. "Without getting into any big details or anything, it's not a version that they ultimately ended up doing, but it was a pretty wild meeting. It was originally supposed to be four execs and a few of us who had done the comics having a round table discussion with the director. And by the time we had the meeting, it was like 15 executives from Hasbro sitting around a boardroom. Very quickly, my perception was they have no idea what they just bought."

Once & Always ultimately featured only two of the five surviving cast members from the first season of *Mighty Morphin Power Rangers* in Yost, back for the first time since his unfulfilling departure in 1996's *Power Rangers Zeo*, and Walter Jones, returning as Zack for the first time. (But it was not Jones's first time back: he provided the voice of a Machine Empire general in *Wild Force*'s "Forever Red" in 2002.)

Austin St. John, who'd returned for a cameo in *Beast Morphers* just a couple years earlier, was unable to travel to New Zealand after he became embroiled in a federal lawsuit charging him and coconspirators with government pandemic loan fraud in May 2022; he agreed to a plea bargain in 2024. Jason David Frank and Amy Jo Johnson didn't participate for undisclosed reasons. The latter, in the lead-up to the premiere, indicated via social media that she "never said no"[7] but rather "didn't say yes to what was offered." The former—according to multiple people interviewed for this book—was on board and accounted for in the script, almost all the way up until filming began in September 2022.

In March of that year, Frank expressed discontent over Hasbro's handling of the franchise, alleging that all it cared about was selling toys. He also seemed fine letting Tommy Oliver rest and focusing on his own projects, including a self-produced feature film, *Legend of the White Dragon*, clearly influenced by *Power Rangers*. "I've done every reunion you can possibly think of," said Frank. "I love the brand. I love being me, but I'm 49, and I've been six different Rangers. It's hard to cover my tattoos up and go back to a softer Tommy." Hasbro also left a bad taste in his mouth due to its unwillingness to continue a promising project that started development under Saban Brands. Sparked by the great response to the *Shattered Grid* short, Frank and Higgins received the green light to work on an adult-targeted *Power Rangers* series set within the World of the Coinless, which sought to bring back former actors under a "new media" SAG agreement—meaning the series would have been intended for initial exhibition via an internet or mobile platform. "We were talking to some places that would have been a really great distribution partner for it, and building a big over-the-top series, that would have been something pretty neat," Higgins said. "Everyone was very, very supportive and kind towards what we were doing in the books but also what we were trying to do for this live-action project. But Hasbro acquired the brand and everything basically got put on hold and then ultimately didn't end up going anywhere, which is a bummer."

In lieu of Johnson and St. John, Steve Cardenas (Rocky) and Catherine Sutherland (Kat) filled their spandex. Both appeared in "Dimensions in Danger" and enjoyed their first time on set together in 20 years but were in something of a holding pattern for *Once & Always* until the original actors' situations were clear. It's likely, had they not been part of the main cast, they would have been offered minor supporting roles in the special, akin to those written for Aisha (Karan Ashley) and Adam (Johnny Yong Bosch) in the version that made it to air. Cardenas put pen to paper in early June 2022 while flying to Atlanta for Rangerstop & Pop, a *Power Rangers* convention cofounded by Ashley and fellow Yellow Ranger Nakia Burrise.

David Yost (left) and Walter Jones (center) returned to their spandex for the first time in decades as part of the Netflix special *Mighty Morphin Power Rangers: Once & Always*. Charlie Kersh debuts as Mihn, the daughter of Trini. © Hasbro/eOne

"I had all this joy inside, and I couldn't say a word to anyone," Cardenas said. "Then Power Morphicon happened a couple months later, and I still couldn't say anything then either. . . . Fans come out every week and show me support and love, so if there's anything I can ever do to give back to them, besides just the experience of meeting face-to-face, I'll always return. After I left the first time, I said I'd never let that be an issue for me again. I get to make money doing all the traveling and everything that I do now. *Power Rangers* and the fan base has been very good to me, so I'm very happy to give back."

Once & Always makes a bold narrative choice from the jump by framing its events around a battle that concludes with the on-screen death of Trini, the Yellow Ranger. She gets vaporized by a robotic Rita Repulsa, whose evil essence Billy accidentally culls from the Morphin Grid. "It wasn't a hard idea to have, but it was a hard idea to come to terms with having to deliver," said Dale. "This is big, this is going to mean a lot. We have to do it right and treat it with respect." In the writers' first conversation about the special, Barnes said that "the idea of Trini's daughter being a featured character and stepping into the Yellow Ranger boots came up."

While the veteran Rangers put butts in seats, the special's story revolves around Trini's daughter, Mihn, and her attempt to take on her mother's mantle and avenge her death. An extensive audition process left Iris Hampton frustrated. "Iris calls me in a panic, 'We can't find a girl, it's been several months,'" said Michael Chaturantabut, a renowned martial artist, trainer, and Hollywood stunt guru whom Hampton cast as Chad, the Blue Ranger, in *Lightspeed Rescue* more than two decades earlier. Since her return in 2010, she on several occasions leaned on Chaturantabut to find and train would-be Rangers. "'I need a girl who's Vietnamese or Vietnamese mix, she has to look this way, we need this age range, have amazing martial skills,' all that stuff. And I'm like, 'Yea, I've got the girl.'" Chaturantabut delivered Charlie Kersh, whose only immediate disqualifier was age; she was 15, and Hampton didn't want an underage actor. "They loved her so much that they figured it out," Chaturantabut said. "And that was it, she was off." Kersh, a Vietnamese adoptee and world champion in Xtreme Martial Arts, was an ideal fit to round out a team of actors who'd been assembled 30 years prior. "I guess you could say that all the stars[8] lined up right," Kersh said.

Filming of the final fight sequence in *Power Rangers Cosmic Fury*—a battle of wits, not brawn. Courtesy Simon Bennett

The special also establishes a motivation for Billy that carries over into the thirtieth season, *Cosmic Fury*. He joins the *Dino Fury* team on Planet Zordnia—a deep-cut reference to the home of season 3's Shogunzords—to fend off an invasion led by Lord Zedd and a pair of original mother–daughter villains, Bajillia and Squillia Naire, modeled after squids. ("Who did that?!" said Barnes.) Billy and Mick Kanic—the *Ninja Steel* team's mentor and one of 18 unique *Power Rangers* characters portrayed by savant Kelson Henderson since the show's move to New Zealand—were searching for signs of Zordon, whose essence Billy believes is still tethered to reality via the Morphin Grid. That belief gets confirmed by season's end when Gold Ranger Aiyon (Jordon Fite, another Chaturantabut trainee) meets a physical manifestation of Zordon—as Zayto, his dead best friend—within the Grid. "There's something I used to say in times such as these," surrogate Zordon says. "May the power protect you."

Together, *MMPR: Once & Always* and *Cosmic Fury* form an entertaining package soaked in quality fan service. (The latter also mostly achieves its goal of using no *Super Sentai* footage; on average, 96 percent of each episode is original footage, with only minimal Zord footage lifted from *Uchu Sentai Kyuranger*.) But that they both came together amid chaos and uncertainty was their most fitting tribute to the show's legacy. And *Cosmic Fury*'s final battle, won not with swords or Zords but with wits, showed that, even after 30 years, long-held tenets still have some sway.

"Y'know," Bennett said, "Power Rangers are not supposed to escalate things."

CHAPTER 20

Lightning Strikes

On June 28, 2023, confirmation came of a development that had been speculated about for months: production of *Power Rangers* in New Zealand was over. Almost overnight, a show that for 20 years jump-started and prolonged careers for hundreds in the local entertainment industry left its shores.

Hasbro didn't just cease production. Through 2022 and into 2023, almost every person in the company assigned to the development or marketing of anything related to *Power Rangers* was reassigned or let go as part of a drastic series of cost-saving measures amid sagging stock prices. In 2023 alone, the company laid off nearly 2,000 employees, or 29 percent of its total workforce. Chris Cocks, named CEO in January 2022, skewered Brian Goldner's vision of Hasbro as an entertainment juggernaut, opting instead to lean into its highest-margin products—board games like *Magic: The Gathering*, *Dungeons & Dragons*, and *Monopoly* but increasingly video games based on its popular brands—and decades-old toy brands of which it had a firm understanding, like *Transformers* and Mr. Potato Head. *Power Rangers* was designated as an "emerging brand" when it entered Hasbro's portfolio; six years into its ownership, a superhero property with instant name recognition, highly visible iconography, and sizable viewership still hadn't moved up the food chain.

After 30 straight years of continuously broadcasting or streaming new episodes, that part of *Power Rangers* was officially on hiatus. Fans who'd had a spandex IV drip hooked into their eyes for three decades suddenly were without their fix. They'd been conditioned to speculate annually about which *Super Sentai* elements would be adapted for the next season, to dig up behind-the-scenes information that might reveal cast members so they could excitedly throw their support behind the newest people

233

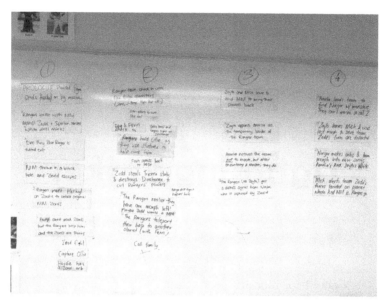

An early look at the writers board in August 2021 for a hypothetical third season of *Power Rangers Dino Fury*, **which at that point wasn't green-lit.** Courtesy Alwyn Dale

to join a small fraternity of superheroes, to wonder and justify how or if the latest season might bring back one of their favorite characters, to preorder new action figures of the latest team to display on their shelf, and to overly praise or criticize creatives who aimed to give longtime fans something to enjoy in the context of a TV show that, from day one to the last, prioritized kids in elementary school.

There were still stories to enjoy by way of Boom! Studios. In 2024, Melissa Flores's final issues of the yearlong event "Darkest Hour" ended the mainline series started by Kyle Higgins in 2016. Flores remained the writer for its successor, *Power Rangers Prime*, which kicked off in November 2024. While she didn't participate in the reunion special, Amy Jo Johnson, along with partner Matt Hotson, authored *The Return*, a four-issue limited comic series set in an alternate universe where the original six Power Rangers never separated. *Ranger Academy*, another limited series from young-adult author Maria Ingrande Mora, further explored the hows, whys, and whos behind those who morph. These efforts and more continued to push *Power Rangers* storytelling to new and adventurous heights.

There were still products to buy and experiences in which to take part. Although Hasbro suspended development of in-house *Power Rangers* toys—a decision that halted the fan-favorite "Lightning Collection" line, which in just five years churned out nearly 200 unique products, including highly articulated action figures, weapon replicas, and wearable helmets—several third-party licensees continued catering to the collectors' market and new audiences. Dedicated tabletop, deck-building, and mobile games received regular content updates. During 2024's Summer Game Fest,[1] the reveal of *Mighty Morphin Power Rangers: Rita's Rewind*—a retro-inspired side-scrolling action game developed by Digital Eclipse —received some of the loudest applause during the event and largest fanfare online afterward. *Power Rangers: Legacy Wars*—a freemium fighting game from nWay released as a tie-in for the 2017 film—was still churning out new updates eight years later. *Power Rangers Mighty Force*, an idle-battle game developed by East Side Games and Mighty Kingdom, launched in 2024 and delighted fans with its bite-sized narrative inserts.

But none of those touchpoints were the show—the thing that gave it all life, the thing that inspired millions of people to believe in the power of a collective and finding one's place within it.

"You get people of different backgrounds coming together in *Power Rangers* to create this thing that is *so much* more than the sum of its individual parts," said PockySquirrel, cohost of the podcast *Toku Ladies*. "You can be the kid who's too smart for his own good and that nobody understands and still be a part of this. You can be the token Jewish kid and still be a part of this. You can be the only person in your school of a particular race and still be part of this. No matter who you are, no matter what your strengths and weaknesses are, there are people out there for you. And you can find those people, come together with them, and also create something that is more than the sum of its parts. Those are the feelings that made me ugly cry when I met David Yost for the first time because I saw Billy find his people, and I believed I could have that. That's what *Power Rangers* means to me."

It isn't bright colors, campy vibes, low-budget effects, or the often-preached moral lessons that most separate *Power Rangers* from its caped peers. It's inclusion.

"That's the modus operandi of *Power Rangers*: I'm a leg and you're an arm, and we don't have a Megazord without each other," said George Hansen, a gay fan and former content creator. "We're all different pieces, but we can come together. I'm 6-foot-3; if I got to crouch to talk to some people and get on their level, I will. That's what *Power Rangers* is all about."

When they assembled in 2012's billion-dollar *The Avengers*, four-fifths of the title heroes were male, and none were people of color. After buying Marvel in 2010, it took Disney eight years to put a Black person at the forefront of its superhero industrial complex and nine for a woman. From day zero, *Power Rangers* showed that everyone could wear the spandex. "In the '90s, especially, that was something that stood out to me even as a kid," Higgins said. "I think that's part of why it resonates to this day. The message is universal and morally inspiring."

Sure, there have been missteps. Having a stereotype-laden Black man wear the black spandex out of the gate is tough to reconcile. But it's not hard to find fans who hold up Walter Jones's Zack Taylor as someone who blazed trails and continue to cherish him. "I liked the fact that he loved hip-hop and danced while he fought and everything," said Jinsakuu, a social media influencer. "It was cool and funny to see as a kid, but I can see where other Black folks might tune in and say, '*What is this?*' Accidental racism is what I call it." Jinsakuu noted that there have been Black characters who've worn every one of the show's prominent colors. (Jack, *S.P.D.*'s Red Ranger played by Brandon Jay McClaren, is his favorite: "A Black guy with dreads was nice to see.") *Dino Fury* and *Cosmic Fury* for the first time featured two Black characters on the same team. "Black people, we've had a Ranger in every season except for like two or three. If you're Indian? Hispanic? Arab? That's not always the case. *Power Rangers* can do better when it comes to diversity, but we've been catered to the most. I'm happy for us, but I would like for them to do more for others."

The show took 30 years to install a woman as the team's full-fledged leader when Amelia (Hunter Deno) assumes the reins in *Cosmic Fury*. That sparked controversy because of an uncomfortable perception: a Black man was forced out of his post for a white woman. It's a development that makes sense within *Cosmic Fury*'s story—wherein Zayto, the former Red Ranger and fulcrum around which much of *Dino Fury*'s story operates, is separated from the team and undertakes a sort of spiritual journey ending with his ascension to becoming a God-like figure—but without context is rough.

Some notable actors who've been Power Rangers in the past, from top left going clockwise: Rose McIver (Summer, *RPM*), Brandon Jay McClaren (Jack, *S.P.D.*), Cerina Vincent (Maya, *Lost Galaxy*), and Camille Hyde (Shelby, *Dino Charge/Dino Super Charge*).
Screenshots, Author's Collection

In *Cosmic Fury*, Javi loses his arm amid an act of heroism and gains a slick prosthetic arm, which—quite cleverly—remains intact when he morphs. The portrayal of the first disabled Power Ranger was heavily consulted on, ensuring for better or worse that the severity of the severed arm wasn't played up beyond medical shock. An incredibly scarring event isn't glossed over, but it also wasn't afforded a lot of room for exploration. For a show whose diversity exists largely in the form of skin color rather than anything else, it was momentous, but far more can be done. "Why couldn't we have a Ranger in a wheelchair whose wheelchair also morphs into some kind of amazing, powered-up mobility device?" said Bennett. "There's so much potential there."

Thirty seasons, three movies, and a made-for-TV special into the franchise, there have been no openly gay men wear a morpher (*Once & Always* does feature a gay civilian couple). Every Power Ranger who's appeared on-screen was of incredible physique, and almost all of them look like they walked off an Abercrombie & Fitch poster; where are the zit-riddled teens with potbellies? "There's an argument that says television should always be aspirational and that superheroes should be perfect, and we have encountered them in the past," Bennett said. "But it's very hard writing stories for perfect characters because interesting stories arise from character flaws rather than character perfection."

The 2017 movie's Billy was, rightfully, celebrated as the first major superhero with autism, but no other Power Ranger has been written with a neurodivergent condition despite about one in five people[2] living with one. There is no on-screen Power Ranger who openly struggled with their gender identity, though *Cosmic Fury* made a point to include a touching piece of trans-supporting dialogue. Says Zayto to an enemy-turned-ally who was transformed into a human and is uncomfortable with it, "Nobody should have to feel like they don't belong in their body."

"I've been harangued by a number of people on various online avenues for pursuing a supposed woke agenda, whatever that means," Bennett said. "My response to that is always: the world is full of different and diverse people in all their splendor. Why shouldn't television and communities on TV also reflect that? That's about normalizing people. People are people, and people are fascinating, and people are all different."

In a climate where regressive attitudes are warmly embraced by political leaders and influencers and hateful language is bandied about without any consideration for the people to whom it might prompt legitimate harm, *Power Rangers* from day one to the very end went out of its way to make marginalized people feel valued. If you subscribe to the belief that superhero media, above all, should inspire people to be their best and make humanity better, you'll have a hard time finding one that rose to that challenge as frequently, sincerely, and passionately as *Power Rangers*.

"I don't think storytellers should ever be bowing to prejudices or ideas that diminish other people or relegate them to being inferior subsets," Bennett said. "All people are equal, and I think *Power Rangers* is the perfect forum to carry that idea and celebrate it. I think we achieved that with both *Dino Fury* and *Cosmic Fury*. We could have gone much further, and I hope the show continues to do that."

That fans are even able to point out shortcomings is a testament to *Power Rangers'* ability to weather three decades of evolution in TV.

When *Mighty Morphin Power Rangers* premiered in 1993, television in the United States was dominated by three broadcast networks and an emergent fourth, which it helped buoy. By 2011, it had aired on at least one network owned by the companies behind three of those four networks; NBC Universal is the only dominant feather missing from the helmets. An anchor for Fox's trendsetting daily kids block was treated as an also-ran when it joined ABC's dying Saturday window. One day it was a vessel around which an ambitious but ill-timed Disney cable block was built, and the next it was a top-rated program on Nickelodeon; its most recent seasons premiered on a platform that started as a DVD rental company founded five months after *Turbo: A Power Rangers Movie* premiered in theaters.

Netflix was to be the home of whatever film and TV projects emerged from the collaboration of Jonathan Entwistle and Jenny Klein, who were tasked with developing a reimagined *Power Rangers* "universe" across multiple media. "We'll bring the spirit of analog into the future, harnessing the action and storytelling that made this brand a success," said Entwistle, whose breakout drama series *The End of the F***ing World* won a British Academy Television Award for Best Drama Series and a Peabody Award, when his attachment was announced in October 2020. The involvement of Klein—co-executive producer for the Emmy-nominated limited series *Daisy Jones & The Six*—was first reported in July 2022. The duo seemingly is no longer attached: *TVLine*[3] reported in June 2024 that Hasbro Entertainment was seeking "a new creative direction for the series" along with a new distribution partner. That same month, Jinsakuu reported that Hasbro was seeking to sublicense the show's entertainment rights, but as of March 2025 there were no reported developments.

It's easy to point to the 2017 movie as a proof of concept as to why *Power Rangers* inherently can't get buy-in from general audiences, at least not to the degree where it's sensible to pour hundreds of millions of dollars into its budget. Regardless of whether "superhero fatigue" or "poor quality" is to blame, a steady trend of box-office flops and streaming whimpers post–*Avengers: Endgame* makes it fair to wonder if *Power Rangers* missed its window to cause a stir unseen since its heyday.

It also raises the question: Why does it need to? The most cynical answer is "to prop up toy sales," which faced steep declines following the *Ninja Steel* seasons and 2017 movie. *Power Rangers* isn't the only action property facing a harsh reality—as video games and other screens are introduced earlier, kids toss aside action figures faster—but it arguably had the most to lose in a world where parents are comfortable with their three-year-olds operating an iPad.

"We knew where our bread was buttered," said Jermaine Turner, the Disney programming executive. "Of all the major franchises in the history of entertainment, most of them—*Star Wars, Harry Potter*, Marvel—20 percent of the fan base accounted for 80 percent of the consumer product sales. For the most part, I found it was usually the hard-core people like you or me who were dropping most of the money. . . . With *Power Rangers*, it's kind of the opposite. It's the kids—the parents of the kids—who drive that franchise."

As "kidults"[4]—older teens and adults who buy toys for themselves—increasingly account for a larger share of the market for action figures and collectibles, it stands to reason that *Power Rangers* might benefit from serving them more experiences that align better with their sensibilities rather than a kids show that, lately, failed to deliver in the toy aisle. From 2015 to 2021, Brand Finance ranked *Power Rangers* among its top 20 toy brands internationally, including twice in the top 10. It didn't make the top 25 from 2021 to 2023. Perhaps that played a role in Hasbro's decision, announced in late April 2024, to sublicense *Power Rangers*' master toy rights to rival Playmates Toys,[5] a Chinese company most noted for another line of kids toys still kicking well past their heyday: *Teenage Mutant Ninja Turtles*.

The paradox: people still watch *Power Rangers*. The show has never been more accessible. Most of its back catalog is available via one of the brand's two dedicated YouTube pages, one clearly for kids and the other more general. Across both, many episodes tout view counts in the tens of millions. Many series as of early 2025 were also available through multiple advertising-based video on demand platforms like The Roku Channel, Tubi, and Pluto TV, whose "Forever Kids" streaming channel started as a hodgepodge of nostalgic content but by early 2024 had morphed into a dedicated *Power Rangers* channel. As of 2024, each of the first 17 seasons were still widely purchasable on DVD via individual sets from Shout! Factory. All three seasons of *MMPR* and several newer seasons of the show were available on Netflix. The seven most recent seasons for which data were available—those encompassing *Ninja Steel*,

Beast Morphers, Dino Fury, and *Cosmic Fury*—garnered billions of minutes in watch time and millions of views per episode on Netflix in the first six months of 2023 alone.[6] Few legacy children's properties perform as well as *Power Rangers* on the platform; it's just difficult to know what, if anything, that means to the parties paying to create and host it—or the aging millennials who grew up with the "real" Power Rangers.

"It'll always be just one thing and six characters to millions of people," Hansen said. "There is kind of a stigma around this brand. It's either seen as 'kiddie' or retro or something that doesn't exist anymore. But it's been going strong for over 30 years."

Simon Bennett (left), Becca Barnes (center), and Alwyn Dale managed to avoid getting bitten by a prop Scuttleworm, a memorable villain from *Power Rangers Cosmic Fury*. Courtesy Becca Barnes

While Netflix and YouTube are primed to remain the most dominant streamers of TV and TV-like entertainment in the 2020s, short-form content increasingly sucks up eyeballs in the attention economy. Given the stratospheric usage of platforms like TikTok—especially by young users—there's a nonzero chance that *Power Rangers* someday exists not as a 22-minute show for kids or an hour-long young-adult series but as a daily two- to three-minute narrative blast of dopamine served up by an algorithm. Other emergent and advancing technologies, like generative artificial intelligence and virtual reality headsets, are certain to be tapped in support of *Power Rangers* "content" at some point.

"It's easy to sit your kids down in front of *Power Rangers* and have them sucked into it," said xtremeninja3, a young TikTok creator with nearly 180,000 followers and 10 million likes on his channel, which largely traffics in clips inspired by or about *Power Rangers*. "Now of course there are some kids out there that *Power Rangers* isn't going to be their thing, and that's cool, but I feel like as long as people keep having kids, kids are still going to watch *Power Rangers*."

An Egyptian Jew flees to Israel, joins the army, and becomes a music promoter. A bad turn takes him to France, where he parlays international rights to TV theme songs into a small Hollywood studio. While on a business trip in Japan, he stumbles on a local children's TV show that enraptures his own childlike imagination and entrepreneurial spirit. For nearly a decade, he's laughed out of television pitch rooms until happenstance puts him in front of a woman who'd been laughed at for trying to sell the same thing. A slapdash pilot made for a song begets a 40-episode order. A show scheduled in a doomed time slot becomes the No. 1 kids program in America—for four straight years. That show opens a path to political influence and one of the largest cash transactions involving a single person in U.S. history. When America's leading entertainment company struggled with it, the Egyptian Jew returns and reinvigorates the show. Eight years later, he flips it for half a billion dollars. That script's getting laughed out of a room faster than the *Bio-Man* pilot.

If there was anyone who thought *Power Rangers* would still be generating millions of dollars and memories more than 30 years after its premiere, it was Haim Saban. But even then, he charted only a 10-year plan. Saban likely never would have guessed it would be the mechanism through which he'd become a multibillionaire. There's only so much a person can dream.

"It's beyond anyone's expectations,"[7] Haim Saban said. That was in November 1993. In 2024, his reported net worth was north of $3 billion—a sliver of Disney's market cap (~$200 billion) but not too far from that of Hasbro (~$7 billion). That his companies have been the only ones to make *Power Rangers* thrive is curious only if you equate market valuations with affection; producers from every era cared about making a show that made a difference in the lives of those who watched it, but only one of its owners embraced it feverishly, admiring and appreciating all the quirky elements that made it sing.

"For seven years, he went around pitching it, and everybody thought he was crazy," said Jeff Pryor, Saban Entertainment's first publicist. "Nobody wanted to touch it. Most people would have given up after twice, maybe three times. But Haim never gave up on *Power Rangers*. He was the only one who really thought he had something."

The unknown is scary. As it became apparent that production of the show would end following *Cosmic Fury*, many fans took it on themselves to participate as pallbearers for a seemingly "dead" brand. Mike Eden, owner of the fan site PwrRngr, pointed out the celebratory thirtieth-anniversary logo's peculiar resemblance to a tombstone. Jane Perry, purveyor of the popular YouTube channel Toku Topics, created T-shirts honoring a series of widespread quality-control concerns in action figures as well as an incredibly poorly timed typo. On 2023's National Power Rangers Day—a recognized fan holiday celebrated every August 28 since 2018—an official Hasbro channel shared social media posts with the hashtag #PowermorRangers.[8] Such "own goals" were blood in the water for a fan base trying to heal emotional wounds through humor.

The unknown is full of opportunity too, though—to seek out content creators you might have missed before or those who emerge from closeted to open fandom, a rite of passage for many who love entertainment made for kids; to dive back in and explore seasons through a different lens, discovering new or different favorites along the way; to go down eBay rabbit holes and scrounge up great deals on toys you never thought you'd care about (guilty); to get into silly arguments about the show on social media (also guilty); or to create your own things that reflect and celebrate the show's impact on you and millions of others around the world (y'know, like a book).

"A friend of mine was working in a school for orphans in Cambodia and sent me videos of the kids lining up to do morph poses for the camera," Becca Barnes said. "These were kids who, prior to coming to the school, had been picking through a garbage dump to find things to sell for food. It's just amazing that they too saw *Power Rangers* and found fun in it despite their impossibly hard circumstances."

Capitalism exists, so it's foolish to think *Power Rangers* is or ever will be truly finished on TV. Still, let's look at some "final" counting stats for the show:

973 episodes: More than any other noneducational live-action kids show in America and the most of any sci-fi or fantasy show in TV history. *Doctor Who* and *Star Trek*, each of which originated in the 1960s, are its nearest challengers. (This number *doesn't* include the 2010 re-version or account for *Mighty Morphin Power Rangers: Once & Always*.)

545: The total number of episodes for which Jonathan Tzachor functioned as an executive producer, the most of any showrunner.

343 episodes: Paul Schrier's total number of credits on the show, more than any other actor.

207 unique guests: Those people directly related to *Power Rangers* who, as of 2024, have attended at least one Power Morphicon, the show's first and largest dedicated convention.

177 lead actors: The number of individuals who've appeared in the opening credits of at least one season. Several, including McClaren, Rose McIver (Summer/*RPM* Yellow Ranger), and Camille Hyde (Shelby/*Dino Charge* Pink Ranger), have become regulars on major-network programs.

Six: The number of cats who are, canonically, Power Rangers. (The six costumes worn by the *Mighty Morphin Meower Rangers*, feline stars of a short-lived YouTube parody series produced by Saban Brands, sold at auction for $3,750 in late 2024.)

Five: The most sets of powers wielded by a single Power Ranger—Tommy Oliver, the series' most popular character.

Four: The number of times *Power Rangers* appeared on a *TV Guide* cover, second only to *Sesame Street* among all kids programming.

Three: The number of movies spawned by the program.

Two: The number of times Haim Saban sold and the number of times he purchased the rights to *Power Rangers*.

One: Tyler Rinker. The Make-A-Wish Foundation and *Power Rangers* have teamed up to grant wishes for thousands of critically ill children. In 2019, Rinker was granted the wish of becoming an original Ranger, the *Beast Morphers* Orange Ranger, complete with his own comic-book cover.

That doesn't begin to cover the scope of *Power Rangers'* impact.

"None of us thought it was going to work to the extent that it did," Margaret Loesch said. "It blew our minds. . . . It's so refreshing, and honestly validating, when people come up to me and say how much they enjoyed the show and how much it and Fox Kids meant to them. That they couldn't wait to get home and watch. That we helped make their childhood. That is so, so much the antithesis of what I was hearing and being clobbered about back then."

Using brightly colored spandex, rubber suits, and otherworldly choreography, *Power Rangers* has told hundreds of stories that will excite and inspire well beyond their authors' lives. For more than 30 years, it has taught kids and reminded those who were once in their shoes that teamwork is key to so much more than getting the job done; that doing what's right, while often harder than doing what's easy, is always best; that you shouldn't judge a book by its cover; that getting hit in the face with a pie might not be the worst thing in the world; that there's more to life than power; and that you don't need to be a superhero to be a superhero.

Maybe *Power Rangers* isn't the best-directed, best-written, or best-acted show ever; or maybe it's all those things, just for an audience centuries away, whose tastes have evolved to a state of true refinement. Maybe it overstayed its welcome. Maybe those who believe that need to reunite with their inner child. Maybe it was too violent. Maybe it wasn't violent enough. Maybe it's for babies. Maybe it's for adult babies. Maybe it really is *just* a toy commercial, sprung by a cartoon schlepper who sharply learned from his father. Maybe it was once mighty and never will be again.

Or, maybe, no one will ever take the Power Rangers down.

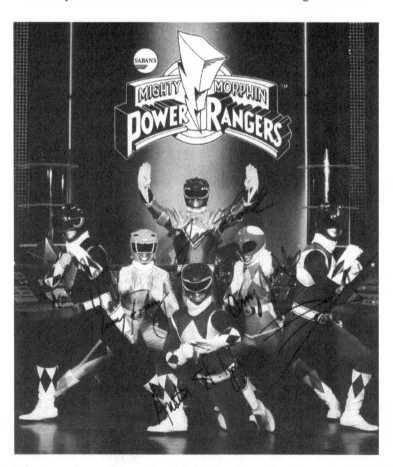

A Morphenomenal press image, signed by Walter Jones, Thuy Trang, Austin St. John, Jason David Frank, Amy Jo Johnson, and David Yost. Courtesy The Morphin Museum/ © Saban Entertainment

Acknowledgments

I don't know if writing a book is harder than fighting Rita Repulsa, but it certainly takes more time to defeat. Watching every single episode of *Power Rangers* requires more than 320 hours of free time. I spent one-third of that just *interviewing* people for this book, so it's safe to say I could have binged the entire show at least a couple times over in the time it took to get *Morphenomenal* to readers.

That wouldn't have been possible without so many people, first and foremost my wife, Stephanie. She was my fiancée when I started to devote myself to *Morphenomenal* and was the mother of our incredible two-year-old son by the time it published. A lot happened in three years. She is the strongest person I know, and I'm lucky to be on her team. This book is as much hers as it is mine. I promise I'll wait a little while to write the next one.

Mark Falkin saw something in *Morphenomenal* that hundreds of other literary agents didn't. Likewise for Chris Chappell, my gracious editor at Applause Books, and others on the Applause team, including Emily Burr, Barbara Claire, Ashleigh Cooke, Sally Rinehart, and Bruce Owens. Their buy-in and belief in this project are unrivaled. If you are able to work with any of them, do it.

This book would have been far less rich without the input of all those interviewed. Not everyone is quoted, nor is everyone's voice reflected in a way that is illustrative of the ample time they gave. But know that I'm forever grateful to all of you for carving out some space to talk about *Power Rangers* with me.

The same goes for the archives of so many content creators in the *Power Rangers* fandom, most of whom were creating content well before the phrase was a staple in our lexicon. There isn't a children's show on the planet with a fan base more dedicated to preserving its history and learning about those who've made it. I'm forever in debt, especially, to John Green, whose site is as quintessential to *Power Rangers* as anyone who's worn spandex; Steve Repsher, who's chronicled *Power Rangers'* ratings since before I could read and is the best Power Morphicon roommate a person could have; and Shamus Kelley and Tyler Waldman, who afforded me access to discreet archives of their respective podcasts.

Thanks to Jennifer K. Armstrong, Daniel Dockery, Claire McNear, Jeff Pearlman, and Kimberly Potts, whose pop-culture writing and book-writing advice (most of it procured through incredibly helpful podcasts and third-party interviews) empowered me to feel like I wasn't completely insane for thinking I could write a book about *Power Rangers*.

A smattering of applause to Justin Cox, Doug Fink, Derek Gayle, Curtis Goble, Jessalyn Matthews, Josh Sullivan, Bailey Vandiver, Dennis Varney, Waldman, and Emily Wilson. Without their eyes, this book would have been much harder to read. They're also just fantastic people.

Thanks also to Kelli Adanick and Jason Britt, who were incredibly supportive throughout and enabled this book to get across the finish line. To Rhett Lindsey, Kirk Norasak, Daniel "Slate" Slattery, Ryan Will, and Heath Wilson, who kept me laughing. To all my homies at the KHSAA Sweet 16 who made me stay up drinking until 3 a.m. the week before my manuscript was due. And to Kenn Glenn, my brother in Bowling Green, who encouraged me to still do this when I started second-guessing myself.

I can't thank enough all the folks with whom I've been lucky to work at the *Lexington Herald-Leader*, especially Mat Graf. No one has ever made me feel more confident and empowered as a journalist. A book like this might have existed without him and the *Herald-Leader*, but it wouldn't have been mine. Thank you to Mickey McCoy, Lee Mueller, and Dan Preece, who set me on the path to Lexington, Kentucky, and journalism. Thanks to all the other teachers who gave me the tools and confidence to write.

Thank you to my sisters, Brittany and Krystle, for playing *Power Rangers* with me even when you didn't want to. And finally to Mommy— for waiting to leave the house until *Power Rangers* went off and never making me feel like I had to turn it off.

Interviews

Quotes throughout the book are from these interviews unless cited in the endnotes.

By phone/video call

Barron Abramovitch, music engineer
Yuda Acco, art/set design
Greg Aronowitz, producer/visual effects
Ann Austen, writer/producer
James Bates, writer
Simon Bennett, producer/director
Eric Berry, fan
Erik Betts, stunt actor
Amit Bhaumik, writer/fan
John Blizek, director/editor
David Blyth, director
Alonzo Bodden, grip/comedian
Brett Born, accountant
Gregg Bullock, actor
Chris Boyatzis, psychologist
Jason Michael Bray, fan
Bryan Cahill, boom operator
Steve Cardenas, actor
Neil Cervin, cinematographer
Michael Chaturantabut, actor/martial artist
Betsy Chasse, production coordinator (*VR Troopers*)
Mark Cooper, fan/musician
Jim Cushinery, music
Alwyn Dale, writer

Julian Do, fan
Julie Dobrow, psychologist
Kevin Duhaney, actor
Adi Ell-Ad, editor
Dan Evans, producer
Elisabeth Fies, stunt actor
Isaac Florentine, director
Jason David Frank, actor
GreenNinja, RangerBoard user
Strathford Hamilton, director
George Hansen, fan
Christopher Hayden, fan/cofounder of Power Morphicon
Kyle Higgins, writer
Mark Hoffmeier, writer
Jinsakuu, fan/content creator
Bruce Kalish, producer
Worth Keeter, director
Shamus Kelley, journalist/fan
Ron Kenan, executive
Joseph Kuhr, writer
George Leon, marketing/licensing
Ellen Levy-Sarnoff, producer
Margaret Loesch, executive
Judd "Chip" Lynn, writer/producer
Annebritt Makebakken, ADR
Jackie Marchand, writer/producer
David McDermott, executive
Peter Mochrie, actor
Jason Narvy, actor

Scott Neitlich, toy-industry analyst
Hien Nguyen, stunt actor
Mike Nilsen, fan
Jane Perry, fan/content creator
Jeff Pryor, publicist
Robert Radler, director
Steve Repsher, fan
Mark Richardson, props
Simon Riera, cinematographer
Lance Robbins, executive
Paul Rosenthal, producer
Rick Schick, visual effects
Matt Sernaker, journalist/fan
Andrew Somers, rerecording mixer
Stewart St. John, writer
Eric Thomsen, marketing/licensing
The Toku Ladies (Danielle, Mara, Margot, PockySquirrel, and TerrierLee)
Jermaine Turner, executive
Ilia Volok, actor
Tyler Waldman, fan
Frank Ward, executive
Terence Winkless, director
Xtremeninja 3, fan/content creator
By e-mail/text
Becca Barnes, writer/producer
Sally Campbell, producer

Brian Casentini, executive
Decade, RangerBoard administrator
Bruno Friedland, fan/content creator
John Green, fan/historian
Lewis "Linkara" Lovhaug, fan/content creator
Sean McLin, cinematographer
Cameron Samurai, RangerBoard user
Chris Schoon, writer
Catherine Sutherland, actor
Jeremy Sweet, music
Titanium321, RangerBoard moderator
Brian Ward, DVD producer
By press conference (RangerStop & Pop 2023)
Karan Ashley, actor
Jasmeet Baduwalia, actor
Dwayne Cameron, actor
Hector David Jr., actor
Barbara Goodson, actor
Ciara Hanna, actor
John Mark Loudermilk, actor
Christina Masterson, actor
Abraham Rodriguez, actor
Daniel Southworth, actor
Catherine Sutherland, actor
Rorrie D. Travis, actor
David Yost, actor

Notes

PREFACE

1. **38 minutes:** "Shattered Grid Live Reading Panel | Power Morphicon 2018," Justin Naranjo, November 9, 2018 (recorded August 18, 2018), https://www.youtube.com/watch?v=4V1c_Vd0DQk&list=PLkCk1Dql2CVXQRZmLqvwQFjfwE4Jf3nyH&index=10&t=2406s.

2. **"superhero fatigue":** Darren Mooney, "All This Flying Is Making Me Tired: Superhero Fatigue," *the m0vie blog*, May 23, 2011.

3. **let $17.95:** "Mighty Morphin Power Rangers Fan Club Commercial (1994)," *thevideorewind*, October 13, 2015. $18.90 California, $21.95 Canada.

4. **"saddled with":** Collins, K. Austin, "The Hot Gods of 'Eternals' Will Bore You to Death with Their Feelings," *Rolling Stone*, October 26, 2021.

CHAPTER 1

1. **"toy store":** Malina Saval, "Haim Saban's Rise from Poor Kid in the Middle East to 'Power Rangers' Godfather," *Variety*, March 22, 2017.

2. Lisa Gubernick, "No More Harpists," *Forbes*, May 27, 1991.

3. *Welcome Back, Kotter:* Will Straus, "The Evolution of the TV Theme Tune," https://us.audionetwork.com, 2013. The only other TV themes to chart are Jan Hammer's theme for *Miami Vice* and "How Do You Talk to an Angel," which made a greater impression than *The Heights*, a short-lived Fox drama for which it was created.

4. **"significant library":** Lisa Gubernick, "No More Harpists," *Forbes*, May 27, 1991.

5. **"he is deadly":** Connie Bruck, "The Influencer," *The New Yorker*, May 3, 2010.

6. *RoboCop:* Stephen Harber, "Pryde of the X-Men: The Animated Series We Almost Got," *Den of Geek*, May 31, 2019.

7. **Shinsha:** Now TMS Entertainment.

8. **episodes on CBS:** Joan Hanauer, "TV's Worst Season Slowly Nearing an End," United Press International, May 15, 1978.

9. **Battle Fever J:** It was initially conceived as a *Captain America* adaptation but became a *Super Sentai* show with a United Nations theme.

10. **Pelc wrote:** Gene Pelc, editorial, *Comics Interview*, May 1983.

CHAPTER 2

1. **"I worked for the man":** "Tony Oliver PT2—Voice of Bang and Obscurio—Mighty Morphin Power Rangers Creator EP 145," *VO Buzz Weekly*, December 14, 2014.

2. **open casting call sheet from 1992:** David Yost (@David_Yost), "Original Casting Call Sheet for #MMPR . . . Then Called Dino-Rangers! Kimberly Blonde & Trini a Pessimist . . . HA!," X/Twitter, image of an open casting call sheet seeking lead actors for a nonunion TV series, March 3, 2015, 9:24 p.m., https://x.com/David_Yost/status/572945601773494272?s=20.

3. **"zero karate":** "Audri Dubois Reflects on Her Time with the Mighty Morphin Power Rangers," dante luna, May 10, 2018.

4. **"scare the hell":** "Audri Dubois Reflects on Her Time with the Mighty Morphin Power Rangers," dante luna, May 10, 2018.

5. **"everybody was laughing":** "Interview with David Yost Part 1," *No Pink Spandex* (podcast), August 23, 2010, https://www.youtube.com/watch?v=KelRKIMRDzA.

6. **"cast in another":** Brian Ward, host, "Katy Wallin Cast the Mighty Morphin Power Rangers," *Shout!Takes: A Shout! Factory Podcast*, August 3, 2018.

7. **stage fright:** "Interview with Amy Jo Johnson," *No Pink Spandex* (podcast), September 17, 2012, https://www.youtube.com/watch?v=4Qu_4yEqR0Q.

8. **"I could fly":** Amy Jo Johnson, "This Is My Friend Walter. I Met Him Almost 30 Years Ago," Facebook, January 2, 2021, https://www.facebook.com/photo?fbid=237446564414277&set=p.237446564414277.

9. **Partial scholarship:** Anne Valdespino, "Just Who Are These Rangers, Anyway?," *Orange County Register*, November 18, 1994.

10. **"I started a kata":** "[WALTER E JONES]—Learn Exactly How I Created HIP HOP KIDO | from The Original Black Ranger," *Fanward*, December 24, 2022, https://www.youtube.com/watch?v=Wy4_OAQY314.

11. **adopted a stage name:** "Pat O'Brien's Biggest Success Stories." https://web.archive.org/web/20130921182206/http://www.patobrientalentmanagement.com/www.patobrientalentmanagement.com/Biggest_Success_Stories.html.

12. **"I lost 20 bucks":** "How I Got the Role!! of the Red Power Ranger! (Jason Lee Scott)—Austin St. John: The Red Ranger," *Fanward*, July 19, 2018, https://www.youtube.com/watch?v=uo52IEcZEtI.

13. **"kill me with his pinky":** Ibid.

14. **"he made it look so pretty":** Ibid.

15. **inaugural Power Morphicon:** "Power Morphicon 2007—Tony Oliver's Documentary/Closing 1of6," JDMofGameFAQs Michael, July 12, 2007, https://www.youtube.com/watch?v=J8tGfxyX-qU&list=PL9525893DF3249D40&index=1.

16. **according to Shien Ueno:** *The Toys That Made Us*, season 3, episode 10: "Power Rangers" (Netflix, 2019).

17. **"quite literally":** "Tony Oliver's Creator/Producer Story on the Mighty Morphin Power Rangers Show," Carnell Holley, November 15, 2022, https://www.youtube.com/watch?v=SoX0QtOYTsw&t=202s.

18. **a fan translation:** "Nendoramachine's MONSTER Thread," *RangerBoard* (page 12, post no. 300), September 27, 2015, https://www.rangerboard.com/index.php?threads/172609/page-12#post-5025278.

19. **said Goodson:** "Barbara Goodson | Talking Voices (Part 1)," *Verite Entertainment*, December 27, 2016, https://www.youtube.com/watch?v=jUnV_uX0g4g.

20. **about four hours:** "Exclusive: David Fielding," Morphin Legacy, n.d., https://morphinlegacy.com/legacy-database/interviews/ii-interviews-allies-villains/exclusive-david-fielding.

21. **Recording dialogue:** Lynzee Loveridge, "Zordon Actor David J. Fielding Made Less Than $1000 on Power Rangers," *Anime News Network*, July 14, 2023.

22. **Fielding said:** "Exclusive Interview with David Fielding," Morphin Legacy, n.d., https://morphinlegacy.com/legacy-database/interviews/ii-interviews-allies-villains/exclusive-david-fielding.

23. **"mega ouch":** "'Aye-yi-yi-yi-yi!' That Time Romy J. Sharf, Alpha 5 on Power Rangers, Talked to a Puppet," *The Nerd Soapbox*, February 13, 2023, https://www.youtube.com/watch?v=cz7v9izVmu8. Sandi Sellner succeeded Sharf in the Alpha costume midway through production of season 2. Sellner filmed 45 episodes before Donene Kistler, a production assistant, took over in-suit duties for the remainder of the robot's appearances in the show through *Lost Galaxy*.

24. **"one night":** "Richard Horvitz (Alpha 5) POWER RANGERS Interview - Power Morphicon 2014," *HyperdrivePics*, June 30, 2015.

25. **"the contract was the contract":** dante luna, https://www.youtube.com/watch?v=Xwx1Sn05ouk.

26. **in 1986:** James Bates, "Kidd Stuff: A Crop of New Shows Sprouts from Saban Firm's TV Success," *Los Angeles Times*, August 12, 1986.

CHAPTER 3

1. **"desperate situations":** "Family Fun: Power Rangers Invade Hampton," *Daily Press* (Newport News, VA), October 13, 1994, https://www.dailypress.com/1994/10/13/family-fun-power-rangers-invade-hampton.

2. **Lynda Carter:** Neave Casey and Mary-Ellen Szalai, "Thuy Trang Interview," *Power Rangers Unlimited*, December 24, 1994, https://myriahac.tripod.com/id8.html.

3. **"peace on Earth":** "Scientology—'Trust,'" JeanneBa, January 11, 2007, https://www.youtube.com/watch?v=EtEaZoy1kg0.

4. **"the screen test":** Brian Ward, host, "Katy Wallin Cast the Mighty Morphin Power Rangers," *Shout! Takes: A Shout! Factory Podcast*, August 3, 2018.

5. **"Tony doesn't like to fight":** "Bulk and Skull Panel Part 01 of 02," kim-wil01w, October 29, 2011 (recorded August 27, 2010), https://www.youtube.com /watch?v=rVKLYYYe23w&t=1056s.

6. **"standing nearby quietly":** "Power Rangers 20th Anniversary (2014) Bulk and Skull Fondly Reminsce HD," *Shout! Studios*, August 28, 2013, https://www .youtube.com/watch?v=ejJh1opn6jY.

7. **"attracted to the camera":** Derek Diamond, host, "#132: Jason David Frank," *The Derek Diamond Experience* (podcast), January 31, 2017.

8. **An actor of Asian descent:** "Live with Regis & Kathy Lee—Jason David Frank," Juan Pablo Hurtado Valencia, January 15, 2011, https://www.youtube .com/watch?v=xVUQfGaCk2k&t=205s.

9. **"I was so nervous":** Lisa J, host, "Episode 103: Interview with Jason David Frank," *No Pink Spandex* (podcast), February 28, 2010, https://ia801607.us .archive.org/20/items/LisaJNoPinkSpandex-Episode103_InterviewwithJasonD avidFrank/NPS103.mp3.

10. **"perfect for this role":** Brian Ward, host, "Katy Wallin Cast the Mighty Morphin Power Rangers," *Shout!Takes: A Shout! Factory Podcast*, August 3, 2018.

11. **"And then Thuy":** Brian Ward, host, "Jason David Frank Morphs into Power Rangers," *Shout!Takes: A Shout! Factory Podcast*, August 10, 2018.

12. **"I love guitar":** "2021 Interview with Ron Wasserman! (Power Rangers Composer)," Jack Lucas Caffrey, January 22, 2021, https://www.youtube.com/ watch?v=81iw0MZpwh8&t=2197s.

13. **"so many fucking hi-hats":** "Ron Wasserman Extended Interview X-Men: The Animated Series Theme Song | RKVC," RKvc, September 13, 2018, https:// www.youtube.com/watch?v=nyK-LQMRKFE. Hi-hats, for the unaware like me, are the cymbal-like fixtures on drum sets.

14. **"I'm crazy flat":** "Ron Wasserman Extended Interview Power Rangers Theme Song | RKVC," RKvc, April 17, 2020, https://www.youtube.com/watch ?v=6o9DHV_C3a8.

15. **"I have no idea":** David Robb and Alex Ben Block, "Composers Say They're Paupers in Royalty Game," *The Hollywood Reporter*, September 18–20, 1998.

16. **Lucie Salhany:** Calvin Sims, "Profile: Lucie Salhany; In a Career of Hits, a Rare Swing and a Miss," *New York Times*, November 14, 1993.

CHAPTER 4

1. **$600,000:** Mike Freeman, "Fox Kids Net Calls On Power Rangers," *Broadcasting & Cable*, August 16, 1993.

2. **"most expensive":** Steve Coe, "Networks Make Big Play for Little Viewers," *Broadcasting & Cable*, August 31, 1992, 42–43. Some episodes of *B:TAS* cost $600,000, equivalent to about $1.2 million in 2023 U.S. dollars. The entire order in 1992 money exceeded $30 million.

3. **the 1992–1993 season:** "Monthly Rainfall by Season, Burbank, California (Hollywood Burbank Airport) 1939–2024," Los Angeles Almanac, https://www .laalmanac.com/weather/we11aa.php.

4. **"semi-retired"**: "Tony Oliver Power Ranger Panel Part 2," Marpolo1991, uploaded May 25, 2011.

5. **"her disciples"**: GrnRngr.com, https://www.grnrngr.com/zyu1.5/agreement.

6. **"walks of life"**: *Night Flight (Dynaman, Episode 01)*.

7. **"urban wilderness"**: "A Vision for Griffith Park," City of Los Angeles Department of Recreation and Parks, https://www.laparks.org/griffithpark/pdf/agenda/visionPk.pdf.

8. **In recollections**: "Bryan Cranston Is the Red Power Ranger," *The Late Show with Stephen Colbert*, March 21, 2017, https://www.youtube.com/watch?v=_aimea_GEaE.

9. **"you could lie your way"**: "Power Rangers Director Scott Page-Pagter Guest Stars," PowerRangersPlayback, January 20, 2021, https://www.youtube.com/watch?v=q3JuXJsozHo&t=47s.

10. **"be silly"**: "Mighty Morphin Power Rangers Anniversary Panel | Power Morphicon 2018," Justin Naranjo, October 9, 2018, https://www.youtube.com/watch?v=ctVp-oAR8Sw&t=921s.

CHAPTER 5

1. **"'a disaster'"**: Lawrie Mifflin, "Fox's Powerful Role in Children's TV," *New York Times*, July 3, 1995.

2. **Chicago Tribune**: "TV Teens Tackle a Way Wicked Foe," *Chicago Tribune*, May 4, 1993.

3. **Author Mike Freeman**: Mike Freeman, "Fox Kids Net Calls On Power Rangers," *Broadcasting & Cable*, August 16, 1993, 22.

4. **"Quite frankly"**: Ibid.

5. **original contract with Toei**: "Distribution Agreement," https://www.secinfo.com/dSq2u.759.15.htm#1wd9t.

6. **founder Naoharu Yamashina**: Andrew Pollack, "Naoharu Yamashina, Toy Maker, Dies at 79," *New York Times*, October 31, 1997.

7. **toy sales**: Advertisement for *Kamen Rider* merchandise, *Honolulu Advertiser*, December 13, 1974.

8. **spoopy**: Slang referencing cute or funny takes on stuff that's traditionally scary.

9. **like Tiger**: Much better known for its electronic handheld games, Tiger, in the early 1990s, dabbled in articulated plastic with toy lines dedicated to *Inspector Gadget* and *Captain Planet and the Planeteers*.

10. **in heavy rotation**: "Mighty Morphin Power Rangers on Fox Kids 1993 Promo Compilation," RetroCCN, uploaded to YouTube on November 29, 2022, https://www.youtube.com/watch?v=hHJQAlau7h0&t.

11. **8.2 rating**: "In Brief," *Broadcasting & Cable*, September 6, 1993.

12. **It got crazier**: Mike Freeman, "'Power Rangers' Powers Its Way to Top," *Broadcasting & Cable*, October 11, 1993.

CHAPTER 6

1. **said Robert Hughes:** Shamus Kelley, "Episode 245: Interview with Robert Hughes," Dan's Toku Rants, accessed via Google Drive.

CHAPTER 7

1. **Bill Sondheim:** Richard T. Ryan, "Power Rangers Toys Scarce, but the Videos Aren't." *Chicago Sun-Times*, December 22, 1993.
2. **"eighth-grade media project":** Ginny Holbert, "'Rangers' Strikes below the Belt," *Chicago Sun-Times*, October 14, 1993.
3. **"'Melrose Place'":** Kinney Littlefield, "Whole Family Can Enjoy 'Morphin,'" *Orange County Register*, November 26, 1993.
4. **Paul Valentine:** Jeffrey Hiday, "To Find Power Rangers at This Point One Would Need to Be a Superhero," *Providence Journal*, syndicated by *Daily Evening Item* (Lynn, MA), December 23, 1993.
5. **"secondary companies":** Ibid.
6. **"mixed at best":** Ibid.
7. **"Sneering clerks":** Anna Quindlen, "Public & Private; Mom Quixote," *New York Times*, December 5, 1993.
8. **"phenomenal":** "Santa Claus Poor Second to a TV Hero," Associated Press, accessed via *Modesto Bee*, December 21, 1993.
9. **Presidents' Day 1994:** Stephen Lynch, "Morphin Mania Shows Its Might," *Orange County Register*, February 22, 1994.
10. **"horrible nightmares":** "Interview with Amy Jo Johnson," *No Pink Spandex* (podcast), September 17, 2012, https://www.youtube.com/watch?v=4Qu_4yEqR0Q.
11. **"mobs of people":** Agustin Gurza, "Fans Try Mightily for Few Minutes with Power Rangers," *Orange County Register*, March 13, 1994.
12. **bring leis:** Wayne Harada, "Power Patrol," *Honolulu Advertiser*, September 2, 1994.
13. **"lei'd to death":** "Interview with Amy Jo Johnson," *No Pink Spandex* (podcast), September 17, 2012, https://www.youtube.com/watch?v=4Qu_4yEqR0Q.
14. **"That's our goal":** Mike Freeman, "Haim Saban: The 'Power' Is His," *Broadcasting & Cable*, December 20, 1993.
15. **unedited "Zyu2" footage:** ZYU 2 for YOU! (*No Sound)," Jeff Pruitt, February 17, 2014, https://www.youtube.com/watch?v=91BoKNRb2uY.

CHAPTER 8

1. **"toward disaster":** Pat Riley, *Showtime: Inside the Lakers' Breakthrough Season* (New York: Warner Books, 1988).

2. **$60,000 a year:** Weeks, Janet. "Would-Be Heroes Arrive in Force for Studio Call," *Orange County Register*, July 27, 1994.

3. **"window at McDonald's":** Todd Van Luling, "11 Behind The Scenes Stories You've Never Heard Before from the Original Power Rangers," *Huffington Post*, April 11, 2014, https://www.huffingtonpost.co.uk/entry/power-rangers-interview_n_6004472.

4. **"woke them up":** Oliver-James Campbell, 'I Could Have Made the Same Money at McDonald's': The Power Rangers on Fame, Regrets and Their Shock Reunion," *The Guardian*, April 14, 2023, https://www.theguardian.com/tv-and-radio/2023/apr/14/power-rangers-reunion-mighty-morphin-netflix.

5. **Pruitt said:** Lisa J, host, "Episode 269: Interview with Jeff Pruitt," *No Pink Spandex* (podcast), July 26, 2018, https://awwman.com/nps/main/2018/07/episode-269-interview-with-jeff-pruitt.

6. **Elie Dekel:** Janet Weeks, "Would-Be Heroes Arrive in Force for Studio Call," *Orange County Register*, July 27, 1994.

7. **Before bolting:** "Walter E. Jones on Leaving Mighty Morphin Power Rangers," Primo Radical, February 20, 2017, https://www.youtube.com/watch?v=LedERXOVXOk&list=PL6-nV5srBuu_lXlUI8y9LXWTStCoxSIDc&index=8.

8. **"being the protector":** "True 90's NickSclusive: Walter Jones, Paul Boretski, and Anik Matern," Alex Nantz, August 24, 2021 (recorded from an Instagram Live), https://www.youtube.com/watch?v=T_ZORTs5CMo&t=2740s.

9. **Simu Liu:** Joseph Deckelmeier (joedeckelmeier), "Happy National Power Rangers Day. Simu Liu Talks about the Greatest Crossover in History, FOREVER RED, and Why He Loves of the Franchise," TikTok, August 28, 2023, https://www.tiktok.com/@joedeckelmeier/video/7272527304797228334.

10. **"seemed stand-offish":** "A Morphenomenal Cast: A Look at Becoming a Power Ranger," *Mighty Morphin Power Rangers: The Complete Series* (Los Angeles: Shout! Factory, 2012), DVD special feature.

11. **"were here":** Ibid.

12. **"catering table":** "Uncensored Talk—Episode 1: Austin St John," The Bop, June 11, 2014, https://www.youtube.com/watch?v=FRuSjW6_LOQ&t=898s.

13. **"expected so much":** Jessica Saggio, "Q&A with Original Red Power Ranger Austin St. John," *Central Florida Future*, November 7, 2014, https://web.archive.org/web/20191006215907/http:/www.centralfloridafuture.com/story/entertainment/2014/11/07/red-ranger-comes-to-orlando/18657023.

14. **"proper exit":** "Exclusive Interview with Ryan Parrott Writer for Power Rangers Comics," The Illuminerdi, February 7, 2022, https://www.youtube.com/watch?v=zvTJXEEyE6Y.

15. **"Marlboro-laden voice":** Brett Homenick, "LORD ZEDD SPEAKS! Voice Actor Robert Axelrod on 'Mighty Morphin Power Rangers'!," Vantage Point Interviews, September 29, 2016, https://vantagepointinterviews.com/2016/09/29/lord-zedd-speaks-voice-actor-robert-axelrod-on-mighty-morphin-power-rangers.

16. **"similar to Darth Vader":** Ibid.

17. **"too rapidly":** Ibid.

18. **forty-ninth overall:** "Ratings Week," *Broadcasting & Cable*, August 1, 1994.

19. **Part 2:** "Ratings Week," *Broadcasting & Cable*, August 8, 1994.

20. **The finale:** "Ratings Week," *Broadcasting & Cable*, August 15, 1994.

CHAPTER 9

1. **"For *most* children":** Wilbur Schramm, Jack Lyle, and Edwin B. Parker, *Television in the Lives of Our Children* (Redwood City, CA: Stanford University Press, 1965).

2. **"sufficient data":** Linda Charlton, "Surgeon General Wants TV to Curb Violence for Children," *New York Times*, March 22, 1972.

3. **"30-minute commercial":** Karen Heller, "Morphin Mania," Knight-Ridder Newspapers, November 1, 1994.

4. **Roy Markowitz:** "Power Rangers 20-20," william232, July 5, 2008 (originally broadcast by *20/20* on ABC, reporting by John Stossel), https://www.youtube.com/watch?v=3DcVYaQ9ze4.

5. **"Ninja Turtles":** "Norway Pulls the Plug on Power Rangers," Associated Press, October 20, 1994. In 2021, the Norwegian Broadcasting Company produced extensive written and televised reports reexamining and questioning authorities' handling of this case.

6. **"the violence":** Teresa Walker, "Power Struggle," *Orange County Register*, May 19, 1994.

7. **"crazy over it:"** Ibid.

8. **"yucky monsters":** Ibid.

9. **"mutilate":** Ibid.

10. **"plots are stupid":** Ibid.

11. **"worse problems":** Ibid.

12. **"drug dealer":** Ibid.

13. **"real issues":** David Zurawik, "For Fox, Cartoon Violence No More Than Child's Play," *Baltimore Sun*, July 14, 1993.

14. **Robert Schumann:** Teresa Walker, "Power Struggle," *Orange County Register*, May 19, 1994.

15. **"weird letters":** Henry Sheehan, "'Power' People," *Orange County Register*, June 28, 1995.

CHAPTER 10

1. **May 1994 sweeps period:** David Tobenkin, "May 1994 Sweeps Ratings for Kids Programs," *Broadcasting & Cable*, July 25, 1994.

2. **it ruled Saturday morning:** Steve Coe, "Saturdays and the Fox Factor," *Broadcasting & Cable*, July 25, 1994.

3. **Stefani Weiss:** Karen Heller, "Morphin Mania," Knight-Ridder Newspapers, November 1, 1994.

4. **Bandai Namco:** The Japanese toy giant joined forces with video game company Namco in 2005.

5. **"'here's your suit'"**: "Power Rangers Actor Panel—Awesome Con 2021," Fandom Spotlite, August 22, 2021, https://www.youtube.com/watch?v =VH3QhenxRKw.

CHAPTER 11

1. **end of 1993:** Michael Fleming, "Scott Huddles on Fox 'Overkill,'" *Variety*, December 15, 1993.

2. **By April 1994:** Michael Fleming, "Rangers Near Fox Pic Pact," *Variety*, April 11, 1994.

3. ***The Guyver:*** Dave Crowe, "An Interview with . . . Steve Wang," *Sentai: The Journal of Asian S/F and Fantasy*, July 3, 1994.

4. **on motorcycles:** "Steve Wang on Guyver, Drive, and Kamen Rider (Action Talks #21)," Eric Jacobus, August 10, 2023, https://www.youtube.com/watch?v =ZVxyJMH1uXM.

5. ***Guyver* sequel:** "Koichi Sakamoto / 坂本 浩一 on Alpha Stunts, Sentai, and Kurata (Action Talks #37)," Eric Jacobus," November 23, 2023, https://www .youtube.com/watch?v=3IYswTt-tGU.

6. **"major creative differences":** "Steve Wang on Guyver, Drive, and Kamen Rider (Action Talks #21)," Eric Jacobus, August 10, 2023, https://www.youtube .com/watch?v=ZVxyJMH1uXM.

7. **"on the same page":** Ibid.

8. **"don't even know":** Ibid.

9. **relished the opportunity:** Jody Revenson and Ramin Zahed, *Saban's Power Rangers: The Ultimate Visual History* (San Rafael, CA: Insight Editions, 2018).

10. **first unearthed:** Shamus Kelley, "The Mighty Morphin Power Rangers Movie We Almost Got," Den of Geek, August 15, 2020.

11. **"barely resembles":** Research notes provided by Shamus Kelley.

12. **K.R.U.S.H.:** Keep Reaching Up Some How.

13. **"wedding in Vegas":** "Live Interview with Karan Ashley | Mighty Morphin Power Rangers, Once & Always," The Legacy of Nerd, June 1, 2023.

14. **Fitzpatrick said:** "Interview with Gabrielle Fitzpatrick," *No Pink Spandex* (podcast), August 24, 2012.

15. **Hargitay told Seth Meyers:** "Mariska Hargitay Was Fired from a Power Rangers Movie," *Late Night with Seth Meyers*, October 19, 2019, https://www .youtube.com/watch?v=IP7g0FCHOAA.

16. **"wasn't quite right":** Jody Revenson and Ramin Zahed, *Saban's Power Rangers: The Ultimate Visual History* (San Rafael, CA: Insight Editions, 2018), 55.

17. **Spicer said:** Ibid., 48.

18. **"started out rough":** Eric Berry, host, "Extra Episode #93: Ranger Command at Anime Central 2023," *Ranger Command Power Hour* (podcast), August 20, 2023.

19. **briefly hospitalized:** "Peta-Marie Rixon Live Online Interview (Alpha 5 from Power Rangers The Movie)," Morphin' Network, March 8, 2019 (streamed November 21, 2018), https://www.youtube.com/watch?v=WbqHY-OZh-g.

20. **"'No, no, no, no, no'"**: Rob Burman Interview: Mighty Morphin Power Rangers The Movie Suit Creator:Special F/X :MakeUp Artist," The Legacy of Nerd, May 16, 2023, https://www.youtube.com/watch?v=r0GNaBQB9QI&list =PL6-nV5srBuu_lXlUI8y9LXWTStCoxSIDc&index=3&t=1144s.

21. **"45-pound layer of cellophane"**: Ibid.

22. **seven hours**: Jody Revenson and Ramin Zahed, *Saban's Power Rangers: The Ultimate Visual History* (San Rafael, CA: Insight Editions, 2018).

23. **"smoked oysters"**: "Interview: Paul Freeman, Star of Raiders and Power Rangers | Creative Continuity with Mr. Lobo," Bestow TV, November 23, 2018, https://www.youtube.com/watch?v=G0vuG9k5xwE&t=343s.

24. **"the last 100 years"**: David Gritten, "Oberon to Ooze," *Los Angeles Times*, June 28, 1995.

25. **David Jenkins**: David Jenkins, "When CGI Went Bad: Revisiting the Original Power Rangers Movie," *Little White Lites*, March 23, 2017.

26. **Roger Ebert**: Roger Ebert, "Mighty Morphin Power Rangers: The Movie," rogerebert.com, June 30, 1995, https://www.rogerebert.com/reviews/mighty -morphin-power-rangers-the-movie-1995.

27. **professional dispatch**: Henry Sheehan, "Rangers Power onto Big Screen," *Orange County Register*, June 30, 1995.

CHAPTER 12

1. **8.7 rating**: Lawrie Mifflin, "Fox to Morph 'Power Rangers' into 'Goose-bumps' Every Friday," *New York Times*, May 8, 1995.

2. **"good friends"**: "Interview with Amy Jo Johnson," *No Pink Spandex* (podcast), September 17, 2012, https://www.youtube.com/watch?v=4Qu_4yEqR0Q.

3. **"really unhappy"**: Brian Carter, "Seeing a Different Shade of Yellow with Karan Ashley," *Los Angeles Sentinel*, March 12, 2015.

4. **"my mistake"**: "Mighty Morphin Power Rangers Q&A | Pensacon 2022," The Kryptics, February 18, 2022, https://www.youtube.com/watch?v =QSYIkcOzodo.

5. **"as big a push"**: Steve Coe, "Saban Re-Powers 'Rangers,'" *Broadcasting & Cable*, April 22, 1996, 35–37.

6. **"equity elements"**: Ibid.

7. **"too many times"**: "Interview with David Yost Part 3," *No Pink Spandex* (podcast), August 25, 2010, https://www.youtube.com/watch?v=jfKzd_ItYi4 &t=20s.

8. **May 1996 sweeps**: David Tobenkin, "Tough Times for Kids Syndicators," *Broadcasting & Cable*, August 12, 1996, 31.

9. **Rugrats**: Rich Brown, "Nickelodeon on a Roll," *Broadcasting & Cable*, June 26, 1995, 30.

10. **a profit**: "In Brief," *Broadcasting & Cable*, June 26, 1995.

CHAPTER 13

1. **11-year-old actor**: Kim Lamb Gregory, "Just Kickin' It," *Thousand Oaks Star*, May 6, 1997.

2. **"feeling in my heart"**: "Behind the Scenes of Turbo: A Power Rangers Movie," Atta Boy Luther, April 8, 2017, https://www.youtube.com/watch?v=tl8vv-7MYt0&t=306s.

3. **"they were auditioning"**: "Power Rangers Playback: Why We LEFT Power Rangers | with Cat & Nakia," PowerRangersPlayback, December 9, 2020, https://www.youtube.com/watch?v=M1_mARsw9Zg&t=278s.

4. **"they denied it"**: Ibid.

5. **mild hit**: Joe Schlosser, "E Is for Entertainment," *Broadcasting & Cable*, July 28, 1997, 43. *Beetleborgs* posted a 4.0 rating in the May 1997 sweeps period, *Power Rangers: Turbo* drew a 5.2.

6. **launch in 1998**: Donna Petrozzello, "Fox, Cronin Ready for Fall Season," *Broadcasting & Cable*, July 13, 1998, 42–45.

7. **May 1997**: Joe Schlosser, "E Is for Entertainment," *Broadcasting & Cable*, July 28, 1997, 43.

8. **42 percent**: Lynette Rice, "Nets on Learning Curve with Kids," *Broadcasting & Cable*, October 13, 1997, 10–11.

9. **defend Angel Grove**: Joe Rovang, "Mega Rangers Element Breakdown," sirstack.livejournal.com, July 16, 2011, https://sirstack.livejournal.com/50847.html.

CHAPTER 14

1. **"Attila the Hun"**: Lynette Rice, "Saban Seeks Cable Family Ties," *Broadcasting & Cable*, December 1, 1997, 30–34.

2. **dwindling**: "Fox to Affils: Show Me the Money," *Broadcasting & Cable*, January 26, 1998, 26–27.

3. **Early 1997**: Joe Schlosser, "SAG Walks Out on Saban," *Broadcasting & Cable*, February 2, 1998, 11.

4. **"public education program"**: Nick Madigan, "Saban Disputes SAG Accusations," *Variety*, January 29, 1998.

5. **hopes and dreams**: Ibid.

6. **"is stupid"**: Joe Schlosser, "Fox Takes Over FCN," *Broadcasting & Cable*, February 23, 1998, 45–46.

7. **$120 million**: Kristine Lamm, "The Downside of the Upfront," *Broadcasting & Cable*, July 27, 1998, 24–26.

8. ***Toonsylvania***: "Fox Kids #1 February Sweeps," *Broadcasting & Cable* (paid advertisement), March 9, 1998, 2.

9. **80 percent**: Kim McAvoy, "One-Hit Wonder," *Broadcasting & Cable*, February 7, 2000, 32–36.

10. **"unique and shocking"**: "Rangerstop 2016—Valerie Vernon Interview," RVT Entertainment, December 5, 2016, https://www.youtube.com/watch?v=QYDo4LmiTeI. Originally, Patricia Ja Lee was brought back as Cassie to assume Kendrix's role on the team, but a dispute between Lee and the production led to Perkins's casting. Lee filmed at least one episode as a regular *Lost Galaxy* cast member; part of her face is briefly visible in the episode "Turn Up the Volume."

11. **400 percent**: Anthony DellaFlora, "Power Rangers Hope to Inflate Ranks of Fans," *Albuquerque Journal*, April 9, 1999.

12. **Fox Family viewership:** John Higgins, "In Haim's Way: Cronin Is gone," *Broadcasting & Cable*, May 29, 2000, 32.

13. **Technical default:** John Higgins, "Mighty Morphin Debt Collectors," *Broadcasting & Cable*, October 11, 1999, 17–18.

14. **$2.3 billion:** Luisa Beltran, "Viacom Pays $2.3B for BET," CNN Money, November 3, 2000, https://money.cnn.com/2000/11/03/deals/viacom. Viacom also assumed $600 million in BET debt.

15. **March 2001:** Bernard Weinraub, "A Cartoon Giant's Rich Reward," *New York Times*, March 4, 2001.

16. **"safety net":** Bill Carter, "Disney Discusses Strategy behind Buying Fox Family," *New York Times*, July 24, 2001.

CHAPTER 15

1. **$101.2 million:** Bloomberg News, "Fox Will Lease Its Saturday Morning Slot to 4Kids," *New York Times*, January 23, 2002.

2. **merchandising juggernaut:** "Power Rangers Celebrate 10th Anniversary as Top Selling Brand for the Past Decade," PRNewswire, October 3, 2002 (accessed via Power Rangers Usenet archive).

3. **mostly unchanged:** Douglas Sloan (Dino Dude), "A Message from Dino Dude," RangerBoard (page 1, post no. 1), August 28, 2004.

4. **'"let me do this"':** Tyler Waldman, host, "An Interview with Koichi Sakamoto," *Rangercast* (podcast), December 25, 2023.

5. **November 20, 2022:** Jackie Marchand (jackieyo), "Fighting Spirit Was a Not-So-Veiled Metaphor about Battling Your Inner Demons. I Hope Jason Is at Peace Now," X/Twitter, November 20, 2022, https://twitter.com/jackieyo/status/1594412241662590976.

CHAPTER 16

1. **"ain't always easy":** Douglas Sloan (Dino Dude). "What if Doug Sloan Returned for PR 2007?," RangerBoard, (page 5, post no. 119), January 29, 2006, https://www.rangerboard.com/index.php?threads/80529/page-5#post-1684290.

2. **worsened under Disney:** Steve Repsher (BurgundyRanger), "PR Ratings Tracker," Power Rangers On-Air Central, https://www.angelfire.com/scifi/prstuff/ratings.html.

3. **13 percent Japanese:** Julian Do (@Martian_Ranger), "Power Rangers RPM Original to Sentai Footage Chart," Twitter/X, December 13, 2016.

4. **Q&A:** Fury Diamond, "RangerCrew Q & A with Eddie Guzelian," RangerCrew (message board, defunct), February 26, 2009, https://web.archive.org/web/20120227104531/http://www.rangercrew.com/forum/showthread.php?7974-Eddie-Guzelian (accessed via Internet Archive).

CHAPTER 17

1. **Cynthia Littleton:** Cynthia Littleton, "Saban Re-Acquires Rights to 'Rangers,'" *Variety*, May 12, 2010.
2. **late 2009:** Ibid.
3. **"the way that it deserves":** Brian Stelter and Brooks Barnes, "Disney Sells a Franchise That Mothers Didn't Like," *New York Times*, May 12, 2010.
4. **end of 2012:** Victor Luckerson, "The Power Rangers Turn 20 and Morph Back into Relevance," *Time*, August 28, 2013.
5. **50-50 split:** Julian Do (@Martin_Ranger), "Power Rangers Megaforce/Super Megaforce US to Sentai Footage Chart," Twitter/X, December 11, 2016, https://twitter.com/Martian_Ranger/status/807830273882607616.

CHAPTER 18

1. **"looked good":** Lisa J, host, "Episode 174: Interview with Brian Ward," *No Pink Spandex* (podcast), April 2014, https://awwman.com/nps/main/2014/04/episode-174-interview-with-brian-ward-director-of-dvdblu-ray-production-at-shout-factory. Also absent from the set—explicit, backmasked audio aired in the original broadcast of "The End of Time, Part I." In the original broadcast, the Cyclobots, *Time Force*'s foot soldiers, say, "You are the size of a fucking condo" and "You bitch, that's too much money" when their audio is played in reverse. These were changed in future broadcasts.
2. **Rod Stewart:** Chuck Crisafulli, "Get the Rockzords a Backstage Pass," *Los Angeles Times*, December 4, 1994.
3. **"six movies":** Shirley Li, "Power Rangers Director Talks Franchise Future, Confirms Six-Film Plan," *Entertainment Weekly*, March 24, 2017.
4. **"cartoon craziness":** David Ehrlich, "'Power Rangers' Is a Mega-Budget Reboot That's Embarrassed of the TV Show It's Based On," *IndieWire*, March 19, 2017.
5. **"splendid thing":** Scott Mendelson, "'Power Rangers' Review: A 'Batman Begins'-Style Reboot That Works," *Forbes*, March 20, 2017.
6. **"crazy laugh":** "'Power Rangers': Elizabeth Banks on Playing Villain Rita Repulsa," *Access Hollywood*, March 23, 2017, https://www.youtube.com/watch?v=G6hLalDuOCk.
7. **"its sincerity":** Matt Zoller Seitz, "Power Rangers," RogerEbert.com, March 24, 2017, https://www.rogerebert.com/reviews/power-rangers-2017.

CHAPTER 19

1. **"full potential":** "Hasbro to Acquire Saban Brands' Power Rangers and Other Entertainment Assets," press release, Hasbro, May 1, 2018.

2. **acquainted with:** Paul Grimaldi, "In Charge at Hasbro," *Providence Journal*, May 18, 2008.

3. **Geoff Murphy:** A Kiwi legend who worked on Peter Jackson's *Lord of the Rings* trilogy.

4. **two years earlier:** Steve Repsher (BurgundyRanger), "PR Ratings Tracker," Power Rangers On-Air Central, https://www.angelfire.com/scifi/prstuff/ratings.html.

5. **one-eighth of its purchase price:** Etan Vlessing and Georg Szalai, "Hasbro to Sell Entertainment One Film, TV Unit to Lionsgate for $500M," *The Hollywood Reporter*, August 3, 2023.

6. **58-year-old CEO:** G. Wayne Miller, "Brian D. Goldner, CEO of Hasbro, Dies at 58," *Providence Journal*, October 12, 2021.

7. **"never said no":** Amy Jo Johnson (@_amyjojohnson), "For the Record I Never Said No. . . I Just Didn't Say Yes to What Was Offered. But Other Fun Stuff Is In-Store! Looking Forward to Watching My Friends Kick Ass! 😊#PowerRangers30." Twitter/X, January 18, 2023, https://twitter.com/_amyjojohnson/status/1615727965756596227?ref_src=twsrc%5Etfw%7Ctwcamp%5Etweetembed%7Ctwterm%5E1615727965756596227%7Ctwgr%5Efc1fe02918fa527fb13c56c0cfa1c444fa343d07%7Ctwcon%5Es1_&ref_url=https%3A%2F%2Fdeadline.com%2F2023%2F03%2Famy-jo-johnson-denies-claims-power-rangers-reunion-movie-money-netflix-1235310407%2F.

8. **"all the stars":** Meredith Harbman, "Vietnamese Adoptee Charlie Kersh Stars in Power Rangers!," Holt International, June 8, 2023, https://www.holtinternational.org/vietnamese-adoptee-charlie-kersh-stars-in-power-rangers.

CHAPTER 20

1. **Summer Game Fest:** "Mighty Morphin Power Rangers: Rita's Rewind," Digital Eclipse, June 7, 2024, https://www.youtube.com/watch?v=s7wSPJZPqas.

2. **one in five people:** DCEG Staff, "Neurodiversity," National Cancer Institute, April 25, 2022, https://dceg.cancer.gov/about/diversity-inclusion/inclusivity-minute/2022/neurodiversity#:~:text=Driven%20by%20both%20genetic%20and,exhibits%20some%20form%20of%20neurodivergence.&text=Neurodivergent%20conditions%2C%20including%20attention%20deficit,are%20overrepresented%20in%20STEM%20fields.

3. **TVLine:** Matt Webb Mitovitch, "Power Rangers Series No Longer Moving Forward at Netflix—Hasbro to Redevelop with New Partner," TVLine, June 11, 2024.

4. **"kidults":** Sarah Whitten, "Adults Are Buying Toys for Themselves, and It's the Biggest Source of Growth for the Industry," CNBC, December 19, 2022.

5. **Playmates Toys:** "Hasbro and Playmates Toys Enter Strategic Relationship to Produce and Distribute Power Rangers Product Globally Starting in 2025," press release, Hasbro, April 22, 2024.

6. **per episode:** Joshua Moore, "What Netflix's Data Dump Tells Us about Power Rangers," *Ranger Reader*, January 11, 2024.

7. **"beyond anyone's expectations":** Kinney Littlefield, "It's Morphin Time!," *Orange County Register*, November 26, 1993.

8. **#PowermorRangers:** Hasbro Pulse (@HasbroPulse), "Happy #PowerRangersDay! Join Us in Honoring the Legacy of #PowermorRangers!," August 28, 2023, https://twitter.com/HasbroPulse/status/1696177712480551113.

Bibliography

BOOKS

Fujimoto, Michi. *Mighty Morphin Power Rangers: The Ultimate Play Set*. Los Angeles: Troubadour Press, 1994.

Higgins, Kyle. *Mighty Morphin Power Rangers*. Los Angeles: Boom! Studios, 2016–2018.

International Directory of Company Histories. Vol. 24. Detroit: St. James Press, 1999.

Ishinomori, Shotaro. *Super Sentai Himitsu Sentai Gorenger*. Los Angeles: Seven Seas Entertainment, 2021.

Jones, Derek. *Censorship: A World Encyclopedia*. London: Routledge, 2001.

Parrott, Ryan. *Go Go Power Rangers*. Los Angeles: Boom! Studios, 2017–2020.

———. *Power Rangers*. Los Angeles: Boom! Studios, 2020–2022.

Phillips, Phil. *The Truth about Power Rangers*. Lancaster, PA: Starburst Publishers, 1995.

Revenson, Jody, and Ramin Zahed. *Saban's Power Rangers: The Ultimate Visual History*. San Rafael, CA: Insight Editions, 2018.

Riley, Pat. *Showtime: Inside the Lakers' Breakthrough Season*. New York: Warner Books, 1988.

Schramm, Wilbur, Jack Lyle, and Edwin B. Parker. *Television in the Lives of Our Children*. Redwood City, CA: Stanford University Press, 1965.

LAWS/FEDERAL DOCUMENTS

https://www.grnrngr.com/zyu1.5/agreement

"Children's Protection from Violent Programming Act." Report of the Committee on Commerce, Science, and Transportation on S.363 (1997). https://www.govinfo.gov/content/pkg/CRPT-105srpt89/html/CRPT-105srpt89.htm.

Children's Television Act of 1990. H.R. 1677, 101st Cong. § 1 (1990). https://www.congress.gov/bill/101st-congress/house-bill/1677/text.

"Distribution Agreement." https://www.secinfo.com/dSq2u.759.15.htm#1wd9t.

National Endowment for Children's Educational Television Act of 1990. H.R. 1677, 101st Cong. § 2 (1990).

Telecommunications Act of 1996. S. 652, 104th Cong. (1996).

"Television and Growing Up: The Impact of Televised Violence." Report to the Surgeon General United States Public Health Service from the General's Scientific Advisory Committee on Television and Social Behavior (1971). https://www.ojp.gov/ncjrs/virtual-library/abstracts/television-and-growing-impact-televised-violence.

ARTICLES

Advertisement for *Kamen Rider* merchandise. *Honolulu Advertiser*, December 13, 1974.

Andrews, Edmund. "'Flintstones' and Programs Like It Aren't Educational, F.C.C. Says." *New York Times*, March 4, 1993.

Bandura, Albert, Dorothea Ross, and Sheila Ross. "Transmission of Aggression through Imitation of Aggressive Models." *Journal of Abnormal and Social Psychology* 63 (1961): 575–82.

Bates, James. "Kidd Stuff: A Crop of New Shows Sprouts from Saban Firm's TV Success." *Los Angeles Times*, August 12, 1986. https://www.latimes.com/archives/la-xpm-1986-08-12-fi-18776-story.html.

Beltran, Luisa. "Viacom Pays $2.3B for BET." CNN Money, November 3, 2000. https://money.cnn.com/2000/11/03/deals/viacom.

Bloomberg News. "Fox Will Lease Its Saturday Morning Slot to 4Kids." *New York Times*, January 23, 2002.

Boyatzis, Chris J., Gina M. Matillo, and Kristen M. Nesbitt. "Effects of 'The Mighty Morphin Power Rangers' on Children's Aggression with Peers." *Child Study Journal* 25 (1995): 45–55.

Brown, Rich. "Nickelodeon on a Roll." *Broadcasting & Cable*, June 26, 1995, 30.

Bruck, Connie. "The Influencer." *The New Yorker*, May 3, 2010. https://www.newyorker.com/magazine/2010/05/10/the-influencer.

Campbell, Oliver-James. "'I Could Have Made the Same Money at McDonald's': The Power Rangers on Fame, Regrets and Their Shock Reunion." *The Guardian*, April 14, 2023. https://www.theguardian.com/tv-and-radio/2023/apr/14/power-rangers-reunion-mighty-morphin-netflix.

Carter, Bill. "Disney Discusses Strategy behind Buying Fox Family." *New York Times*, July 24, 2001.

Carter, Brian. "Seeing a Different Shade of Yellow with Karan Ashley." *Los Angeles Sentinel*, March 12, 2015. https://lasentinel.net/seeing-a-different-shade-of-yellow-with-karan-ashley.html.

Casey, Neave, and Mary-Ellen Szalai. "Thuy Trang Interview." *Power Rangers Unlimited*, December 24, 1994. https://myriahac.tripod.com/id8.html.

Charlton, Linda. "Surgeon General Wants TV to Curb Violence for Children." *New York Times*, March 22, 1972.

Coe, Steve. "Networks Make Big Play for Little Viewers." *Broadcasting & Cable*, August 31, 1992, 42–43.

———. "Saban Re-Powers 'Rangers.'" *Broadcasting & Cable*, April 22, 1996, 35–37.

———. "Saturdays and the Fox Factor." *Broadcasting & Cable*, July 25, 1994, 58–59.

Collins, K. Austin. "The Hot Gods of 'Eternals' Will Bore You to Death with Their Feelings." *Rolling Stone*, October 26, 2021.

Crisafulli, Chuck. "Get the Rockzords a Backstage Pass." *Log Angeles Times*, December 4, 1994.

Crowe, Dave. "An Interview with . . . Steve Wang." *Sentai: The Journal of Asian S/F and Fantasy*, July 3, 1994.

DCEG Staff. "Neurodiversity." National Cancer Institute, April 25, 2022. https:// dceg.cancer.gov/about/diversity-inclusion/inclusivity-minute/2022/neuro diversity#:~:text=Driven%20by%20both%20genetic%20and,exhibits%20some %20form%20of%20neurodivergence.&text=Neurodivergent%20conditions %2C%20including%20attention%20deficit,are%20overrepresented%20in %20STEM%20fields.

DellaFlora, Anthony. "Power Rangers Hope to Inflate Ranks of Fans." *Albuquerque Journal*, April 9, 1999.

Dolan, Kerry. "Beyond Power Rangers." *Forbes*, November 26, 2001.

Ehrlich, David. "'Power Rangers' Is a Mega-Budget Reboot That's Embarrassed of the TV Show It's Based On." *IndieWire*, March 19, 2017.

Eraker, Harald, Mari Allgot Lie, Inger Sunde, and Anne Linn Kumano-Ensby. "The Day When Children Became Perpetrators (Translated)." Norwegian Broadcasting Corporation, November 18, 2021.

"Family Fun: Power Rangers Invade Hampton." *Daily Press* (Newport News, VA), October 13, 1994. https://www.dailypress.com/1994/10/13/family-fun -power-rangers-invade-hampton.

Fleming, Michael. "Rangers Near Fox Pic Pact." *Variety*, April 11, 1994.

———. "Scott Huddles on Fox 'Overkill.'" *Variety*, December 15, 1993.

"Fox Kids #1 February Sweeps." Paid advertisement. *Broadcasting & Cable*, March 9, 1998, 2.

Freeman, Mike. "Fox Kids Net Calls On Power Rangers." *Broadcasting & Cable*, August 16, 1993, 22.

———. "'Power Rangers' Powers Its Way to Top." *Broadcasting & Cable*, October 11, 1993, 32–33.

Gould, Jack. "TV Violence Held Unharmful to Youth." *New York Times*, January 11, 1972.

Gregory, Kim Lamb. "Just Kickin' It." *Thousand Oaks Star*, May 6, 1997.

Grimaldi, Paul. "In Charge at Hasbro." *Providence Journal*, May 18, 2008.

Gritten, David. "Oberon to Ooze." *Los Angeles Times*, June 28, 1995.

Gubernick, Lisa. "No More Harpists." *Forbes*, May 27, 1991.

Gurza, Agustin. "Fans Try Mightily for Few Minutes with Power Rangers." *Orange County Register*, March 13, 1994.

Hanauer, Joan. "TV's Worst Season Slowly Nearing an End." United Press International, May 15, 1978.

Harada, Wayne. "Power Patrol." *Honolulu Advertiser*, September 2, 1994.

Harber, Stephen. "Pryde of the X-Men: The Animated Series We Almost Got." *Den of Geek*, May 31, 2019.

"Hasbro to Acquire Entertainment One Adding Brands and Expanding Storytelling through Global Entertainment." Press release, Hasbro, August 22, 2019.

"Hasbro to Acquire Saban Brands' Power Rangers and Other Entertainment Assets." Press release, Hasbro, May 1, 2018.

"Hasbro and Playmates Toys Enter Strategic Relationship to Produce and Distribute Power Rangers Product Globally Starting in 2025." Press release, Hasbro, April 22, 2024.

Hastings, Reed. "How I Did It: Reed Hastings, Netflix." *Inc.*, December 1, 2005. https://www.inc.com/magazine/20051201/qa-hastings.html.

Heller, Karen. "Morphin Mania." Knight-Ridder Newspapers, November 1, 1994.

Hiday, Jeffrey. "To Find Power Rangers at This Point One Would Need to Be a Superhero." *Providence Journal*, syndicated by *Daily Evening Item* (Lynn, MA), December 23, 1993.

Higgins, John. "In Haim's Way: Cronin Is Gone." *Broadcasting & Cable*, May 29, 2000, 32.

———. "Mighty Morphin Debt Collectors." *Broadcasting & Cable*, October 11, 1999, 17–18.

Holbert, Ginny. "'Rangers' Strikes below the Belt." *Chicago Sun-Times*, October 14, 1993.

Homenick, Brett. "Lord Zedd Speaks! Voice Actor Robert Axelrod on 'Mighty Morphin Power Rangers'!" Vantage Point Interviews, September 29, 2016. https://vantagepointinterviews.com/2016/09/29/lord-zedd-speaks-voice -actor-robert-axelrod-on-mighty-morphin-power-rangers.

"In Brief." *Broadcasting & Cable*, September 6, 1993, 81.

———. *Broadcasting & Cable*, June 26, 1995, 60.

James, Meg. "He Believed in 'Power Rangers' When Nobody Else Did, and It Turned Him into a Billionaire." *Los Angeles Times*, March 19, 2017.

Jenkins, David. "When CGI Went Bad: Revisiting the Original Power Rangers Movie." *Little White Lites*, March 23, 2017. https://lwlies.com/articles/mighty -morphin-power-rangers-the-movie-1995-cgi.

Kastor, Elizabeth. "Fuzzy Logic at the Toy Fair." *Washington Post*, February 8, 1993. https://www.washingtonpost.com/archive/lifestyle/1993/02/09/ fuzzy-logic-at-the-toy-fair/140b4a7d-04fe-4eb2-bbcd-653ca8b9bc96.

Kelley, Shamus. "The Mighty Morphin Power Rangers Movie We Almost Got." *Den of Geek*, August 15, 2020.

Lamm, Kristine. "The Downside of the Upfront." *Broadcasting & Cable*, July 27, 1998, 24–26.

Lawson, Carol. "Toys Will Be Toys: The Stereotypes Unravel." *New York Times*, February 11, 1993. https://www.nytimes.com/1993/02/11/garden/toys-will -be-toys-the-stereotypes-unravel.html/

Li, Shirley. "Power Rangers Director Talks Franchise Future, Confirms Six-Film Plan." *Entertainment Weekly*, March 24, 2017.

Littlefield, Kinney. "It's Morphin Time!" *Orange County Register*, November 26, 1993.

———. "Whole Family Can Enjoy 'Morphin.'" *Orange County Register*, November 26, 1993.

Littleton, Cynthia. "Saban Re-Acquires Rights to 'Rangers.'" *Variety*, May 12, 2010.

Loveridge, Lynzee. "Zordon Actor David J. Fielding Made Less Than $1000 on Power Rangers." *Anime News Network*, July 14, 2023.

Luckerson, Victor. "The Power Rangers Turn 20 and Morph Back into Relevance." *Time*, August 28, 2013.

Lynch, Stephen. "Morphin Mania Shows Its Might." *Orange County Register*, February 22, 1994.

Madigan, Nick. "Saban Disputes SAG Accusations." *Variety*, January 29, 1998.

Martin, Hugo. "Universal Studios Hollywood Breaks Attendance Record and Reaches Capacity for First Time." *Los Angeles Times*, January 3, 2017.

McAvoy, Kim. "One-Hit Wonder." *Broadcasting & Cable*, February 7, 2000, 32–36.

McClellan, Steve. "Fox to Affils: Show Me the Money." *Broadcasting & Cable*, January 26, 1998, 26–27.

———. "It's Not Just for Saturday Mornings Anymore." *Broadcasting & Cable*, July 26, 1993, 26.

Mendelson, Scott. "'Power Rangers' Review: A 'Batman Begins'-Style Reboot That Works," *Forbes*, March 20, 2017.

Mifflin, Lawrie. "Fox to Morph 'Power Rangers' into 'Goosebumps' Every Friday." *New York Times*, May 8, 1995.

———. "Fox's Powerful Role in Children's TV." *New York Times*, July 3, 1995.

Miller, G. Wayne. "Brian D. Goldner, CEO of Hasbro, Dies at 58." *Providence Journal*, October 12, 2021.

Mitovitch, Matt Webb. "Power Rangers Series No Longer Moving Forward at Netflix—Hasbro to Redevelop with New Partner." TVLine, June 11, 2024.

Mooney, Darren. "All This Flying Is Making Me Tired: Superhero Fatigue." *the m0vie blog*, May 23, 2011.

"Norway Pulls the Plug on Power Rangers." Associated Press, October 20, 1994.

Petrozzello, Donna. "Fox, Cronin Ready for Fall Season." *Broadcasting & Cable*, July 13, 1998, 42–45.

Pollack, Andrew. "Naoharu Yamashina, Toy Maker, Dies at 79." *New York Times*, October 31, 1997.

"Power Rangers Celebrate 10th Anniversary as Top Selling Brand for the Past Decade." Press release, Bandai, October 3, 2002. (Accessed via Power Rangers Usenet archive.)

Prasad, Isobel. "Huge Blow to Industry as Power Ranger Ending Production in NZ." *1News*, June 28, 2023. https://www.1news.co.nz/2023/06/28/huge-blow-to-industry-as-power-rangers-ending-production-in-nz.

Price, Jason. "It's Morphin' Time!—Walter E. Jones Looks Back on 25 Years of 'Power Rangers.'" *Icon Vs. Icon*, February 23, 2018. https://www.iconvsicon.com/2018/02/23/its-morphin-time-walter-e-jones-looks-back-on-25-years-of-power-rangers.

Quindlen, Anna. "Public & Private; Mom Quixote." *New York Times*, December 5, 1993.

"'Rangers' Producers Praise Show's Reinstatement Abroad." Associated Press, October 21, 1994.

"Rangerstop 2016—Valerie Vernon Interview." RVT Entertainment, December 5, 2016. https://www.youtube.com/watch?v=QYDo4LmiTeI.

"Ratings Week." *Broadcasting & Cable*, August 1, 1994, 31.

———. *Broadcasting & Cable*, August 8, 1994, 25.

———. *Broadcasting & Cable*, August 15, 1994, 20.

Rice, Lynette. "Nets on Learning Curve with Kids." *Broadcasting & Cable*, October 13, 1997, 10–11.

———. "Saban Seeks Cable Family Ties." *Broadcasting & Cable*, December 1, 1997, 30–34.

Robb, David, and Alex Ben Block. "Composers Say They're Paupers in Royalty Game." *The Hollywood Reporter*, September 18–20, 1998.

Ryan, Richard T. "Power Rangers Toys Scarce, but the Videos Aren't." *Chicago Sun-Times*, December 22, 1993.

Saggio, Jessica. "Q&A with Original Red Power Ranger Austin St. John." *Central Florida Future*, November 7, 2014. https://web.archive.org/web/20191006215907/http://www.centralfloridafuture.com/story/entertainment/2014/11/07/red-ranger-comes-to-orlando/18657023.

"Santa Claus Poor Second to a TV Hero." Associated Press (accessed via *Modesto Bee*), December 21, 1993.

Saval, Malina. "Haim Saban's Rise from Poor Kid in the Middle East to 'Power Rangers' Godfather." *Variety*, March 22, 2017.

Schlosser, Joe. "E Is for Entertainment." *Broadcasting & Cable*, July 28, 1997, 43.

———. "Fox Takes Over FCN." *Broadcasting & Cable*, February 23, 1998, 45–46.

———. "SAG Walks Out on Saban." *Broadcasting & Cable*, February 2, 1998, 11.

Seitz, Matt Zoller. "Power Rangers." RogerEbert.com, March 24, 2017. https://www.rogerebert.com/reviews/power-rangers-2017.

Sheehan, Henry. "'Power' People." *Orange County Register*, June 28, 1995.

———. "Rangers Power onto Big Screen." *Orange County Register*, June 30, 1995.

Sims, Calvin. "Profile: Lucie Salhany; In a Career of Hits, a Rare Swing and a Miss," *New York Times*, November 14, 1993.

Stelter, Brian, and Brooks Barnes. "Disney Sells a Franchise That Mothers Didn't Like." *New York Times*, May 12, 2010.

Tobenkin, David. "May 1994 Sweeps Ratings for Kids Programs." *Broadcasting & Cable*, July 25, 1994, 52.

———. "Tough Times for Kids Syndicators." *Broadcasting & Cable*, August 12, 1996, 31.

"TV Teens Tackle a Way Wicked Foe." *Chicago Tribune*, May 4, 1993.

Valdespino, Anne. "Just Who Are These Rangers, Anyway?" *Orange County Register*, November 18, 1994.

———. "Shifting Powers." *Orange County Register*, November 18, 1994.

Van Luling, Todd. "11 Behind the Scenes Stories You've Never Heard Before from the Original Power Rangers." *Huffington Post*, April 11, 2014. https://www.huffingtonpost.co.uk/entry/power-rangers-interview_n_6004472.

Vlessing, Etan, and Georg Szalai. "Hasbro to Sell Entertainment One Film, TV Unit to Lionsgate for $500M." *The Hollywood Reporter*, August 3, 2023.

Walker, Teresa. "Power Struggle." *Orange County Register*, May 19, 1994.

Wallace, Amy. "Haim Saban, Power Ranger." *Portfolio*, August 13, 2008. https://web.archive.org/web/20101112052403/http://www.portfolio.com/executives/features/2008/08/13/Profile-of-Fundraiser-Haim-Saban/index3.html.

Weeks, Janet. "Would-Be Heroes Arrive in Force for Studio Call." *Orange County Register*, July 27, 1994.

Weinraub, Bernard. "A Cartoon Giant's Rich Reward." *New York Times*, March 4, 2001.

Whitten, Sarah. "Adults Are Buying Toys for Themselves, and It's the Biggest Source of Growth for the Industry." *CNBC*, December 19, 2022. https://www.cnbc.com/2022/12/19/kidults-biggest-sales-driver-toy-industry.html.

Xeno, Rex. "A Brief History of Eiji Tsuburaya." *The Tokusatsu Network*, July 9, 2021.

Zurawik, David. "For Fox, Cartoon Violence No More Than Child's Play." *Baltimore Sun*, July 14, 1993.

WEBSITES

"Alumni Guests: Walter Jones." Indiana Comic Convention. https://indianacomicconvention.com/guest/walter-jones.

"Audri Dubois Reflects on Her Time with the Mighty Morphin Power Rangers." dante luna, May 10, 2018.

"'Aye-yi-yi-yi-yi!' That Time Romy J. Sharf, Alpha 5 on Power Rangers, Talked to a Puppet." *The Nerd Soapbox*, February 13, 2023. https://www.youtube.com/watch?v=cz7v9izVmu8.

"Behind the Scenes of Turbo: A Power Rangers Movie." Atta Boy Luther, April 8, 2017. https://www.youtube.com/watch?v=tl8vv-7MYt0&t=306s.

"Bryan Cranston." *Anime News Network Encyclopedia*. https://www.animenewsnetwork.com/encyclopedia/people.php?id=3037.

"Bryan Cranston Is the Red Power Ranger." *The Late Show with Stephen Colbert*, March 21, 2017. https://www.youtube.com/watch?v=_aimea_GEaE.

"Bulk and Skull Panel Part 01 of 02." kimwil01w, October 29, 2011 (recorded August 27, 2010). https://www.youtube.com/watch?v=rVKLYYYe23w&t=1056s.

"CGC Census." CGC Comics. https://www.cgccomics.com/census/grades_standard.asp?title=Mighty+Morphin+Power+Rangers&publisher=Hamilton+Comics&issue=1&year=1994&issuedate=1994.

David Yost (@David_Yost). "Original Casting Call Sheet for #MMPR . . . Then Called Dino Rangers! Kimberly Blonde & Trini a Pessimist . . . HA!." X/Twitter, image of an open casting call sheet seeking lead actors for a nonunion TV series, March 3, 2015, 9:24 p.m. https://x.com/David_Yost/status/572945601773494272?s=20.

Deckelmeier, Joseph (joedeckelmeier). "Happy National Power Rangers Day. Simu Liu Talks about the Greatest Crossover in History, FOREVER RED, and

Why He Loves of the Franchise." TikTok, August 28, 2023. https://www.tiktok
.com/@joedeckelmeier/video/7272527304797228334.

Do, Julian (@Martin_Ranger). "Power Rangers Megaforce/Super Megaforce US
to Sentai Footage Chart." Twitter/X, December 11, 2016. https://twitter.com/
Martian_Ranger/status/807830273882607616.

———. "Power Rangers RPM Original to Sentai Footage Chart." Twitter/X, December 13, 2016. https://x.com/Martian_Ranger/status/808742835537121280?s=20

Ebert, Roger. "Mighty Morphin Power Rangers: The Movie." RogerEbert.com,
June 30, 1995. https://www.rogerebert.com/reviews/mighty-morphin-power
-rangers-the-movie-1995.

"E-mu Proteus." *Vintage Synth Explorer*. https://www.vintagesynth.com/e-mu/
proteus.

"Exclusive Interview with David Fielding." Morphin Legacy, n.d. https://
morphinlegacy.com/legacy-database/interviews/ii-interviews-allies-villains/
exclusive-david-fielding.

"Exclusive Interview with Ryan Parrott Writer for Power Rangers Comics."
The Illuminerdi, February 7, 2022. https://www.youtube.com/watch?v
=zvTJXEEyE6Y.

"5 Questions with Paul Schrier." *PowerRangersPlayback*, May 18, 2022. https://
www.youtube.com/watch?v=_qgaCubv8Yc.

"Fox Family Worldwide, Inc. History." Funding Universe. https://www.fundin
guniverse.com/company-histories/fox-family-worldwide-inc-history.

Frank, Jason David (Jason David Frank—Official Fan Page). "Oh Lord My Mom
Saves Everything LOL." Facebook, July 19, 2017. https://www.facebook.com/
jasondfrank/photos/a.278616396686/10154866066356687/?type=3.

Fury Diamond. "RangerCrew Q & A with Eddie Guzelian." RangerCrew
(message board, defunct), February 26, 2009. https://web.archive.org/web
/20120227104531/http:/www.rangercrew.com/forum/showthread.php?7974
-Eddie-Guzelian. (Accessed via Internet Archive.)

GrnRngr.com (owner: John Green).

Harbman, Meredith. "Vietnamese Adoptee Charlie Kersh Stars in Power Rangers!" Holt International, June 8, 2023. https://www.holtinternational.org/
vietnamese-adoptee-charlie-kersh-stars-in-power-rangers.

"How I Got the Role!! of the Red Power Ranger! (Jason Lee Scott)—Austin St.
John: The Red Ranger." *Fanward*, July 19, 2018. https://www.youtube.com/
watch?v=uo52IEcZEtI.

"In Loving Memory of Thuy Trang." https://www.thuytrangtribute.com.

"Interview with Amy Jo Johnson." *No Pink Spandex* (podcast), September 17, 2012.
https://www.youtube.com/watch?v=4Qu_4yEqR0Q.

"Interview with David Yost Part 1." *No Pink Spandex* (podcast), August 23, 2010.
https://www.youtube.com/watch?v=KelRKIMRDzA.

"Interview with David Yost Part 3." *No Pink Spandex* (podcast), August 25, 2010.
https://www.youtube.com/watch?v=jfKzd_ItYi4&t=20s.

"Interview with Gabrielle Fitzpatrick," *No Pink Spandex* (podcast), August 24,
2012. https://www.youtube.com/watch?v=lT9WoGOeUM0.

"Interview: Paul Freeman, Star of Raiders and Power Rangers | Creative Continuity with Mr. Lobo." Bestow TV, November 23, 2018. https://www.youtube.com/watch?v=G0vuG9k5xwE&t=343s.

Johnson, Amy Jo (@_amyjojohnson). "For the Record I Never Said No . . . I Just Didn't Say Yes to What Was Offered. But Other Fun Stuff Is In-Store! Looking Forward to Watching My Friends Kick Ass! 😂 #PowerRangers30." Twitter/X, January 18, 2023. https://twitter.com/_amyjojohnson/status/1615727965756596227?ref_src=twsrc%5Etfw%7Ctwcamp%5Etweetembed%7Ctwterm%5E1615727965756596227%7Ctwgr%5Efc1fe02918fa527fb13c56c0cfa1c444fa343d07%7Ctwcon%5Es1_&ref_url=https%3A%2F%2Fdeadline.com%2F2023%2F03%2Famy-jo-johnson-denies-claims-power-rangers-reunion-movie-money-netflix-1235310407%2F.

———. "This Is My Friend Walter. I Met Him Almost 30 Years Ago." Facebook, January 2, 2021. https://www.facebook.com/photo?fbid=237446564414277&set=p.237446564414277.

"Koichi Sakamoto / 坂本 浩一 on Alpha Stunts, Sentai, and Kurata (Action Talks #37)." Eric Jacobus, November 23, 2023. https://www.youtube.com/watch?v=3IYswTt-tGU.

"Live Interview with Karan Ashley | Mighty Morphin Power Rangers, Once & Always." The Legacy of Nerd, June 1, 2023. https://www.youtube.com/watch?v=q9ugEMaujs8.

"Live with Regis & Kathy Lee—Jason David Frank." Juan Pablo Hurtado Valencia, January 15, 2011. https://www.youtube.com/watch?v=xVUQfGaCk2k&t=205s.

Marchand, Jackie (jackieyo). "Fighting Spirit Was a Not-So-Veiled Metaphor about Battling Your Inner Demons. I Hope Jason Is at Peace Now. Everyone Take Care of Yourselves and Reach Out to Others if You Need Help. 💜" X/Twitter, November 20, 2022. https://twitter.com/jackieyo/status/1594412241662590976.

"Mariska Hargitay Was Fired from a Power Rangers Movie." *Late Night with Seth Meyers*, October 19, 2019. https://www.youtube.com/watch?v=IP7g0FCHOAA.

"Mighty Morphin Power Rangers Anniversary Panel | Power Morphicon 2018." Justin Naranjo, October 9, 2018. https://www.youtube.com/watch?v=ctVp-oAR8Sw&t=921s.

"Mighty Morphin Power Rangers Fan Club Commercial (1994)." *thevideorewind*, October 13, 2015. www.youtube.com/watch?v=dJbqv_TWMmo.

"Mighty Morphin Power Rangers on Fox Kids 1993 Promo Compilation." RetroCCN, uploaded to YouTube on November 29, 2022. https://www.youtube.com/watch?v=hHJQAlau7h0&t.

"Mighty Morphin Power Rangers Q&A | Pensacon 2022." The Kryptics, February 18, 2022. https://www.youtube.com/watch?v=QSYIkcOzodo.

"Mighty Morphin Power Rangers: Rita's Rewind." Digital Eclipse, June 7, 2024. https://www.youtube.com/watch?v=s7wSPJZPqas.

"Monthly Rainfall by Season, Burbank, California (Hollywood Burbank Airport) 1939–2024." Los Angeles Almanac. https://www.laalmanac.com/weather/we11aa.php.

"Morphicon 3: Saban's Mega Power Panel." kimwil01w, September 12, 2012. https://www.youtube.com/watch?v=uEdQi9ctxe8.

"My Story." Richard Horvitz. https://www.richardhorvitz.com/blog/my-story.

"Nendoramachine's MONSTER Thread." RangerBoard (page 12, post no. 300), September 27, 2015. https://www.rangerboard.com/index.php?threads/172609/page-12#post-5025278.

"1993-08 | Fox Kids | Mighty Morphin | 'You Thought They Were Extinct' Premiere Promo." Power Rangers Ultraverse, August 27, 2023. https://www.youtube.com/watch?v=kSmeoDpAp0I&pp=ygUreW91IHRob3VnaHQgdGhleSB3ZXJlIGV4dGluY3QgcG93ZXIgcmFuZ2Vycw%3D%3D.

Pasternack, Alex. "How the 'X Files' Composer Made TV's Creepiest Theme Song, Partly by Accident." *Vice*, March 18, 2016. https://www.vice.com/en/article/wnxn8y/radio-motherboard-mark-snow-and-the-truth-of-the-x-files-music.

"Pat O'Brien's Biggest Success Stories." https://web.archive.org/web/20130921182206/http://www.patobrientalentmanagement.com/www.patobrientalentmanagement.com/Biggest_Success_Stories.html.

"Peta-Marie Rixon Live Online Interview (Alpha 5 from Power Rangers The Movie)." Morphin' Network, March 8, 2019 (streamed November 21, 2018). https://www.youtube.com/watch?v=WbqHY-OZh-g.

"Power Morphicon 2007—Tony Oliver's Documentary/Closing 1of6." JDMof-GameFAQs Michael, July 12, 2007. https://www.youtube.com/watch?v=J8tG-fxyX-qU&list=PL9525893DF3249D40&index=1.

"Power Rangers 20-20." william232, July 5, 2008 (originally broadcast by *20/20* on ABC, reporting by John Stossel). https://www.youtube.com/watch?v=3DcVYaQ9ze4.

"Power Rangers Actor Panel—Awesome Con 2021." Fandom Spotlite, August 22, 2021. https://www.youtube.com/watch?v=VH3QhenxRKw.

"Power Rangers Brand Profile." Brand Finance, accessed March 17, 2024. https://brandirectory.com/brands/power-rangers.

"'Power Rangers': Elizabeth Banks on Playing Villain Rita Repulsa." *Access Hollywood*, March 23, 2017. https://www.youtube.com/watch?v=G6hLalDuOCk.

"Power Rangers Director Scott Page-Pagter Guest Stars." *PowerRangersPlayback*, January 20, 2021. https://www.youtube.com/watch?v=q3JuXJsozHo&t=47s.

"Power Rangers Pilot (Uncut)." HistoryRanger, November 3, 2022. https://www.youtube.com/watch?v=bxpNrIc9XRw.

"Power Rangers Playback: Why We LEFT Power Rangers | with Cat & Nakia." PowerRangersPlayback, December 9, 2020. https://www.youtube.com/watch?v=M1_mARsw9Zg&t=278s.

"Power Rangers RPG | HyperForce: Welcome to Time Force Academy | Tabletop RPG (Premiere)." Hyper RPG, October 31, 2017. https://www.youtube.com/watch?v=4X0CxlxoagY&list=PLSw_XqD9Vt8P6m692FDGk-P3iSqQJbEFE.

"Power Rangers Shattered Grid Official Trailer (2018) Jason David Frank." Movie Trailers Source, March 24, 2018. https://www.youtube.com/watch?v=yT94jm8fXZA.

"Power Rangers Zeo—Ford Ranger Truckload of Toys Sweepstakes—Fox Kids (1996)." member berries, April 22, 2017. https://www.youtube.com/watch?v=nMewv--qVWA.

"Ranger Locations." https://rangerlocations.wixsite.com/uslocations.

Repsher, Steve (Burgundy Ranger). "PR Ratings Tracker." Power Rangers On-Air Central. https://www.angelfire.com/scifi/prstuff/ratings.html.

"Richard Horvitz (Alpha 5) Power Rangers Interview—Power Morphicon 2014." *HyperdrivePics*, June 30, 2015. https://www.youtube.com/watch?v=O5HYr-wVD4_A.

Rob Burman Interview: Mighty Morphin Power Rangers The Movie Suit Creator:Special F/X :MakeUp Artist." The Legacy of Nerd, May 16, 2023. https://www.youtube.com/watch?v=r0GNaBQB9QI&list=PL6-nV5srBuu_lXlUI8y9LXWTStCoxSIDc&index=3&t=1144s.

Rovang, Joe. "MMPR 107A "Yo Ho Ho and a Bottle of . . . Rangers?" Script (Scans)." sirstack.livejournal.com, December 3, 2008. https://sirstack.livejournal.com/12744.html.

"Scientology—'Trust.'" JeanneBa, January 11, 2007. https://www.youtube.com/watch?v=EtEaZoy1kg0.

"Shattered Grid Live Reading Panel | Power Morphicon 2018." Justin Naranjo, November 9, 2018 (recorded August 18, 2018). https://www.youtube.com/watch?v=4V1c_Vd0DQk&list=PLkCk1Dql2CVXQRZmLqvwQFjfwE4Jf3nyH&index=10&t=2406s.

Sloan, Douglas (Dino Dude). "A Message from Dino Dude." RangerBoard (page 1, post no. 1), August 28, 2004. https://www.rangerboard.com/index.php?threads/44413.

———. "What if Doug Sloan Returned for PR 2007?" RangerBoard (page 5, post no. 119), January 29, 2006. https://www.rangerboard.com/index.php?threads/80529/page-5#post-1684290.

"Steve Wang on Guyver, Drive, and Kamen Rider (Action Talks #21)." Eric Jacobus, August 10, 2023. https://www.youtube.com/watch?v=ZVxyJMH1uXM.

Television Academy Foundation. Interview with Margaret Loesch, The Interviews: An Oral History of Television website, 2019. https://interviews.televisionacademy.com/interviews/margaret-loesch.

Tony Oliver. https://www.tonyoliverentertainment.com.

"Tony Oliver Power Ranger Panel Part 2." Marpolo1991, uploaded May 25, 2011.

"Tony Oliver PT1—Producer of Mighty Morphin Power Rangers—Learn Voice Over EP 144." *VO Buzz Weekly*, December 7, 2014.

"Tony Oliver PT2—Voice of Bang and Obscurio—Mighty Morphin Power Rangers Creator EP 145." *VO Buzz Weekly*, December 14, 2014.

Train Me JDF. https://trainmejdf.com/staff.

"True 90's NickSclusive: Walter Jones, Paul Boretski, and Anik Matern." Alex Nantz, August 24, 2021 (recorded from an Instagram Live). https://www.youtube.com/watch?v=T_ZORTs5CMo&t=2740s.

"Turbo: A Power Rangers Movie." Box Office Mojo. https://www.boxofficemojo.com/release/rl1198228993/weekend.

"28 Minutes of Power Rangers PSA Promos 1993–2011 Mighty Morphin Power Rangers." The Fan Club, September 17, 2021. https://www.youtube.com/watch?v=M2RbY0gufjE&t=675s.

"2021 Interview with Ron Wasserman! (Power Rangers Composer)." Jack Lucas Caffrey, January 22, 2021. https://www.youtube.com/watch?v=81iw0MZpwh8&t=2197s.

"Uncensored Talk—Episode 1: Austin St John." *The Bop*, June 11, 2014. https://www.youtube.com/watch?v=FRuSjW6_LOQ&t=898s.

"A Vision for Griffith Park." City of Los Angeles Department of Recreation and Parks. https://www.laparks.org/griffithpark/pdf/agenda/visionPk.pdf.

"VR Troopers—Cybertron Pilot." Bryan Gibson, April 13, 2012. https://www.youtube.com/watch?v=qtsES2hCrAo.

"[Walter E Jones]—Learn Exactly How I Created HIP HOP KIDO | from The Original Black Ranger." *Fanward*, December 24, 2022. https://www.youtube.com/watch?v=Wy4_OAQY314.

"Walter E. Jones on Leaving Mighty Morphin Power Rangers." Primo Radical, February 20, 2017. https://www.youtube.com/watch?v=LedERXOVXOk&list=PL6-nV5srBuu_lXlUI8y9LXWTStCoxSIDc&index=8.

"ZYU 2 for YOU! (*No Sound)." Jeff Pruitt, February 17, 2014. https://www.youtube.com/watch?v=91BoKNRb2uY.

PODCASTS

Berry, Eric, host. "Extra Episode #93: Ranger Command at Anime Central 2023." *Ranger Command Power Hour* (podcast), August 20, 2023.

Diamond, Derek, host. "#132: Jason David Frank." *The Derek Diamond Experience* (podcast), January 31, 2017.

Ellison, Bill, host. "MSM 325 Ext. Ver.—Margaret Loesch—Smurfs, Transformers and More!" *Mississippi Moments* (podcast), August 30, 2012.

Lisa J, host. "Episode 103: Interview with Jason David Frank." *No Pink Spandex* (podcast). February 28, 2010. https://ia801607.us.archive.org/20/items/LisaJNoPinkSpandex-Episode103_InterviewwithJasonDavidFrank/NPS103.mp3.

———. "Episode 174: Interview with Brian Ward." *No Ink Spandex* (podcast), April 2014. https://awwman.com/nps/main/2014/04/episode-174-interview-with-brian-ward-director-of-dvdblu-ray-production-at-shout-factory.

———. "Episode 269: Interview with Jeff Pruitt." *No Pink Spandex* (podcast), July 26, 2018. https://awwman.com/nps/main/2018/07/episode-269-interview-with-jeff-pruitt.

Kelley, Shamus. "Episode 245: Interview with Robert Hughes." *Dan's Toku Rants*. Accessed via Google Drive.

Raz, Guy, host. "Power Rangers: Haim Saban." *How I Built This with Guy Raz* (podcast), March 26, 2017. https://wondery.com/shows/how-i-built-this/episode/10386-power-rangers-haim-saban.

Waldman, Tyler, host. "An Interview with Koichi Sakamoto." *Rangercast* (podcast), December 25, 2023.

Ward, Brian, host. "Jason David Frank Morphs into Power Rangers." *Shout!Takes: A Shout! Factory Podcast*, August 10, 2018.

———. "Katy Wallin Cast the Mighty Morphin Power Rangers." *Shout!Takes: A Shout! Factory Podcast*, August 3, 2018.

FILM/TV

"A Morphenomenal Cast: A Look at Becoming a Power Ranger." *Mighty Morphin Power Rangers: The Complete Series* (Los Angeles: Shout! Factory, 2012), DVD special feature.

Big Bad Beetleborgs (Saban Entertainment, 1996)
Season 1, episode 39: "Jo's Strange Change"

Mighty Morphin Power Rangers (Saban Entertainment)
Season 1, episode 1: "Day of the Dumpster" (1993)
Season 1, episode 2: "High Five" (1993)
Season 1, episode 3: "Teamwork" (1993)
Season 1, episode 6: "Food Fight" (1993)
Season 1, episode 7: "Big Sisters" (1993)
Season 1, episode 10: "Happy Birthday, Zack" (1993)
Season 1, episode 11: "No Clowning Around" (1993)
Season 1, episode 14: "Foul Play in the Sky" (1993)
Season 1, episode 17: "Green With Evil, Part I" (1993)
Season 1, episode 18: "Green With Evil, Part II" (1993)
Season 1, episode 19: "Green With Evil, Part III" (1993)
Season 1, episode 20: "Green With Evil, Part IV" (1993)
Season 1, episode 21: "Green With Evil, Part V" (1993)
Season 1, episode 22: "The Trouble with Shellshock" (1993)
Season 1, re-version episode 32: "A Star is Born" (2010)
Season 1, episode 34: "The Green Candle, Part I" (1993)
Season 1, episode 35: "The Green Candle, Part II" (1993)
Season 1, episode 38: "A Bad Reflection on You" (1993)
Season 1, episode 39: "Doomsday, Part I" (1993)
Season 1, episode 40: "Doomsday, Part II" (1993)
Season 1, episode 41: "A Pig Surprise"(1994)
Season 1, episode 42: "Something Fishy" (1994)
Season 1, episode 48: "Plague of the Mantis" (1993)
Season 1, episode 49: "Return of an Old Friend, Part I" (1994)
Season 1, episode 50: "Return of an Old Friend, Part II" (1994)
Season 2, episode 1 "The Mutiny, Part I" (1994)
Season 2, episode 2 "The Mutiny, Part II" (1994)
Season 2, episode 3 "The Mutiny, Part III" (1994)
Season 2, episode 17: "White Light, Part I" (1994)
Season 2, episode 18: "White Light, Part II" (1994)

Season 2, episode 22: "The Ninja Encounter, Part I" (1994)
Season 2, episode 23: "The Ninja Encounter, Part II" (1994)
Season 2, episode 24: "The Ninja Encounter, Part III" (1994)
Season 2, episode 27: "The Power Transfer, Part I" (1994)
Season 2, episode 28: "The Power Transfer, Part II" (1994)
Season 2, episode 39 "Rangers Back in Time, Part I" (1995)
Season 2, episode 40 "Rangers Back in Time, Part II" (1995)
Season 2, episode 41 "The Wedding, Part I" (1995)
Season 2, episode 42 "The Wedding, Part II" (1995)
Season 2, episode 43 "The Wedding, Part III" (1995)
Season 2, episode 44 "Return of the Green Ranger, Part I" (1995)
Season 2, episode 45 "Return of the Green Ranger, Part II" (1995)
Season 2, episode 46 "Return of the Green Ranger, Part III" (1995)
Season 2, episode 50: "Wild West Rangers, Part I" (1995)
Season 2, episode 51: "Wild West Rangers, Part II" (1995)
Season 3, episode 1: "A Friend in Need, Part I" (1995)
Season 3, episode 2: "A Friend in Need, Part II" (1995)
Season 3, episode 3: "A Friend in Need, Part III" (1995)
Season 3, episode 4: "Ninja Quest, Part I" (1995)
Season 3, episode 5: "Ninja Quest, Part II" (1995)
Season 3, episode 6: "Ninja Quest, Part III" (1995)
Season 3, episode 7: "Ninja Quest, Part IV" (1995)
Season 3, episode 16: "A Ranger Catastrophe, Part I" (1995)
Season 3, episode 20: "Changing of the Zords, Part III" (1995)
Season 3, episode 24: "A Different Shade of Pink, Part III" (1995)
Season 3, episode 29: "Master Vile and the Metallic Armor, Part I" (1995)
Season 3, episode 33: "Rangers in Reverse" (1995)
Season 3, episode 34 "Alien Rangers of Aquitar, Part I" (1996)
Season 3, episode 35 "Alien Rangers of Aquitar, Part II" (1996)
Season 3, episode 43 "Hogday Afternoon, Part II" (1996)
Mighty Morphin Power Rangers: Once & Always (Hasbro/Netflix, 2023)
Mighty Morphin Power Rangers: The Movie (20th Century Fox, 1995)
Power Rangers (Lionsgate, 2017)
Power Rangers Cosmic Fury (Hasbro/Netflix, 2023)
    Season 30, episode 1: "Lightning Strikes"
    Season 30, episode 8: "Changing Sides"
    Season 30, episode 10: "The End"
Power Rangers Dino Fury
    Season 28, episode 13: "The Matchmaker" (Hasbro, 2021)
    Season 29, episode 22: "The Nemesis" (Hasbro/Netflix, 2022)
Power Rangers Dino Thunder (Disney, 2004)
    Season 12, episode 4: "Legacy of Power"
    Season 12, episode 5: "Back in Black"
    Season 12, episode 27: "Fighting Spirit"
Power Rangers in Space (1998, Saban Entertainment)

Season 6, episode 1: "From Out of Nowhere, Part I"
Season 6, episode 2: "From Out of Nowhere, Part II"
Season 6, episode 26: "The Secret of the Locket"
Season 6, episode 27: "Astronema Thinks Twice"
Season 6, episode 28: "The Rangers' Leap of Faith"
Season 6, episode 29: "Dark Specter's Revenge, Part I"
Season 6, episode 30: "Dark Specter's Revenge, Part II"
Season 6, episode 43: "Countdown to Destruction, Part I"
Season 6, episode 44: "Countdown to Destruction, Part II"
Power Rangers Lightspeed Rescue
Season 8, episode 29: "Trakeena's Revenge, Part I"
Season 8, episode 30: "Trakeena's Revenge, Part II"
Power Rangers Lost Galaxy
Season 7, episode 1: "Quasar Quest, Part I"
Season 7, episode 31: "The Power of Pink"
Season 7, episode 32: "Protect the Quasar Saber"
Season 7, episode 34: "Turn Up the Volume"
Power Rangers Megaforce (Saban Brands, 2013)
Season 20, episode 1: "Mega Mission"
Power Rangers Operation Overdrive
Season 15, episode 20: "Once a Ranger"
Season 15, episode 21: "Once a Ranger II"
Power Rangers Samurai (Saban Brands, 2011)
Season 18, episode 3: "The Team Unites"
Power Rangers SPD (Disney, 2005)
Season 13, episode 1: "Beginnings, Part 1"
Season 13, episode 2: "Beginnings, Part 2"
Season 13, episode 4: "Walls"
Season 13, episode 37: "Endings, Part 1"
Season 13, episode 38: "Endings, Part 2"
Power Rangers Super Megaforce (Saban Brands, 2014)
Season 21, episode 16: "Vrak Is Back, Part I"
Season 21, episode 17: "Vrak Is Back, Part II"
Season 21, episode 19: "The Wrath"
Season 21, episode 20: "Legendary Battle"
Power Rangers Super Ninja Steel (Saban Brands, 2018)
Season 25, episode 10: "Dimensions in Danger"
Power Rangers Time Force (Saban Entertainment, 2001)
Season 9, episode 1: "Force from the Future, Part 1"
Season 9, episode 2: "Force from the Future, Part 2"
Season 9, episode 4: "Ransik Lives"
Season 9, episode 40: "The End of Time, Part 3"
Power Rangers Turbo (Saban Entertainment, 1997)
Season 5, episode 1: "Shift into Turbo, Part I"
Season 5, episode 16: "Honey, I Shrunk the Rangers, Part I"

Season 5, episode 17: "Honey, I Shrunk the Rangers, Part 2"
Season 5, episode 18: "Passing the Torch, Part I"
Season 5, episode 19: "Passing the Torch, Part II"
Season 5, episode 44: "Chase into Space, Part I"
Season 5, episode 45: "Chase into Space, Part II"
Power Rangers Wild Force (Disney, 2002)
Season 10, episode 24: "Reinforcements from the Future, Part I"
Season 10, episode 25: "Reinforcements from the Future, Part II"
Season 10, episode 26: "The Master's Last Stand"
Season 10, episode 27: "Unfinished Business"
Season 10, episode 33: "The Soul of Humanity"
Season 10, episode 34: "Forever Red"
Power Rangers Zeo (1996, Saban Entertainment)
Season 4, episode 1: "A Zeo Beginning, Part I"
Season 4, episode 2: "A Zeo Beginning, Part II"
Season 4, episode 3: "The Shooting Star"
Season 4, episode 6: "Rangers in the Outfield"
Season 4, episode 15: "There's No Business Like Snow Business, Part I"
Season 4, episode 23: "It Came from Angel Grove"
Season 4, episode 47: "Rangers of Two Worlds, Part I"
Season 4, episode 48: "Rangers of Two Worlds, Part II"
The Toys That Made Us (Netflix, 2019)
Season 3, episode 10: "Power Rangers"
Turbo: A Power Rangers Movie (Saban Entertainment, 1997)

Index

Page numbers in bold refer to illustrations. Fictional characters are listed alphabetically by first name.